5th Edition

The Essential Guide to
Family & Medical Leave

Lisa Guerin, J.D. & Attorney Deborah C. England

NOLO
LAW for ALL

FIFTH EDITION	JUNE 2018
Editor	SACHI BARREIRO
Cover Design	SUSAN PUTNEY
Book Design	TERRI HEARSH
Proofreading	SUSAN CARLSON GREENE
Index	RICHARD GENOVA
Printing	BANG PRINTING

Names: Guerin, Lisa, 1964- author. | England, Deborah C., 1959- author.
Title: The essential guide to family & medical leave / Lisa Guerin, J.D. &
   Attorney Deborah C. England.
Other titles: Essential guide to family and medical leave
Description: 5th edition. | Berkeley, CA : Nolo, 2018. | Includes index.
Identifiers: LCCN 2018010268 (print) | LCCN 2018010460 (ebook) | ISBN
   9781413325300 (ebook) | ISBN 9781413325294 (pbk.)
Subjects: LCSH: Leave of absence--Law and legislation--United States--Popular
   works. | Parental leave--Law and legislation--United States--Popular
   works. | Sick leave--Law and legislation--United States--Popular works. |
   United States. Family and Medical Leave Act of 1993--Popular works.
Classification: LCC KF3531 (ebook) | LCC KF3531 .G84 2018 (print) | DDC
   344.7301/25763--dc23

This book covers only United States law, unless it specifically states otherwise.

Please note

We believe accurate, plain-English legal information should help you solve many of your own legal problems. But this text is not a substitute for personalized advice from a knowledgeable lawyer. If you want the help of a trained professional—and we'll always point out situations in which we think that's a good idea—consult an attorney licensed to practice in your state.

Acknowledgments

The authors would like to thank all of the folks at Nolo who made this book possible, including:

Alayna Schroeder, for her thoughtful, clarifying, and extraordinarily quick editing on the first edition.

Sachi Barreiro, for her careful reading, helpful suggestions, and meticulous edits on subsequent editions.

Sigrid Metson and Kelly Perri, for their insights on managing FMLA leave and for their good cheer and hard work in marketing this project.

Janet Portman and Mary Randolph, for their sustained enthusiasm and support.

Terri Hearsh, for creating a beautiful book design.

Stan Jacobsen, for his research assistance.

The authors would also like to thank their friends, colleagues, and mentors in the field of employment law, including:

Michael Gaitley, senior staff attorney, the Legal Aid Society— Employment Law Center

Everyone at Rudy, Exelrod and Zieff

Patrice Goldman

The Honorable John True.

Dedication

To my father, Jim England, who could have used a leave law while raising four kids. And, to my mother, in loving memory.

Deborah C. England

About the Authors

Lisa Guerin is the author or coauthor of several Nolo books, including *The Manager's Legal Handbook*, *Dealing With Problem Employees*, *The Essential Guide to Federal Employment Laws*, *The Essential Guide to Workplace Investigations*, *Create Your Own Employee Handbook*, and *The Employee Performance Handbook*. Ms. Guerin has practiced employment law in government, public interest, and private practice, where she represented clients at all levels of state and federal courts and in agency proceedings. She is a graduate of Boalt Hall School of Law at the University of California at Berkeley.

Deborah C. England has practiced employment law in San Francisco for more than 20 years, representing clients in litigation in state and federal courts. Ms. England has published numerous articles and essays on employment and civil rights law and has spoken frequently on these topics before legal and HR professional organizations. She is also the author of *The Essential Guide to Handling Workplace Harassment & Discrimination* (Nolo).

Table of Contents

Appendixes

An Overview of Family and Medical Leave

The Family and Medical Leave Act (FMLA) is a law with an undeniably noble purpose: to help employees balance the demands of work with personal and family needs. Since the FMLA was enacted in 1993, millions of employees have relied on it to protect their jobs while taking time off to recover from a serious illness, to care for an ailing family member, or to bond with a new child. The FMLA has been amended several times since its enactment, most notably in 2008 to allow military family leave.

Surveys consistently show that the FMLA has not had a negative impact on business growth or profitability. In a 2013 survey by the federal Department of Labor, for example, more than 90% of responding employers said that complying with the FMLA had either a positive effect or no noticeable effect on their companies. This same survey also revealed that suspected employee abuse of the FMLA was rare (2.5% of responding employers) and actual proven abuse even more so (only 1.6% of responding employers).

At the same time, surveys also reveal that employers find it difficult to comply with some parts of the FMLA. In 2017, more than half of employers responding to the Littler Annual Employer Survey found it difficult to accommodate requests for unpredictable intermittent leave or requests to extend leave beyond the requirements of the FMLA. In a 2007 survey conducted by the Society for Human Resource Management, more than half of respondents said it was either "very difficult" or "somewhat difficult" to track intermittent leave, to determine whether a health condition qualifies for FMLA leave, and to manage the FMLA's notice, designation, and certification requirements.

Experience has shown that it can be difficult to apply the FMLA when dealing with employees in the real world. For example, do you know what to do in the following situations?

- An employee who needs leave is also covered by workers' compensation, a state family and medical leave law, and/or the Americans with Disabilities Act—and the requirements of those laws appear to conflict with the FMLA.
- An employee asks for time off but won't tell you why or is reluctant to reveal personal medical information that might entitle the employee to leave.

- An employee wants to take FMLA leave at your company's busiest time of year.
- An employee wants to take time off as needed for a chronic ailment, rather than all at once, and can't comply with your company's usual call-in procedures.
- An employee doesn't give exactly the right amount or type of notice, hands in a medical certification form late, or can't return to work as scheduled.
- An employee decides, after taking FMLA leave, not to come back to work.

These issues—and many more like them—come up every day, and managers have to figure out how to handle them legally and fairly, while protecting their companies interests. That's where this book comes in: It explains, in plain English, how the FMLA works. It can be tricky to figure out what to do in a particular situation, and this book's step-by-step approach will help you sort things out and meet your obligations.

This chapter will help you get started. It introduces the FMLA's basic requirements, with special emphasis on your responsibilities as a manager. It explains how other laws and company policies can affect your obligations under the FMLA when an employee needs time off for family or medical reasons. And it provides a roadmap to the rest of the book, so you'll be able to easily find the answers to all your FMLA questions.

What the FMLA Requires

In a nutshell, the FMLA requires larger companies to allow employees to take time off to fulfill certain caretaking responsibilities or to recuperate from serious health problems. If your company is covered by the law, an eligible employee is entitled to take up to 12 weeks of unpaid leave every 12 months to bond with a new child, recover from his or her own serious health condition, care for a close family member with a serious health condition, or handle qualifying exigencies arising from a family member's military duty.

The FMLA provides a separate entitlement for military caregiver leave. Employees may take up to 26 weeks of leave, in a single 12-month period, to care for a family member who incurs or aggravates a serious illness or injury in the line of duty while on active military duty. However, this provision doesn't renew every year like the 12-week leave provisions described above. Instead, it is available only once per servicemember, per injury. Employees who are entitled to this military caregiver leave may also take other types of FMLA leave, but they can take no more than 26 weeks off, total, in a single 12-month period for all types of FMLA leave.

FMLA leave is unpaid, although an employee may choose—or the company may require employees—to use up accrued paid leave, such as sick leave or vacation, during this time off. The employer must continue the employee's group health coverage during FMLA leave. When the employee's leave is over, the employee must be reinstated to the same position or an equivalent position, with the same benefits as the employee had before taking time off. Although there are a few exceptions to this requirement, they apply only in very limited circumstances.

> **CAUTION**
>
> **Special rules apply to public employers and schools.** The FMLA imposes slightly different obligations on government employers and schools, which we don't cover in this book. Similarly, in unionized workplaces, a collective bargaining agreement—the contract between the company and the union—might impose different family and medical leave obligations. Because every collective bargaining agreement is different, we can't cover them all here.

Your Obligations as a Manager

The moment an employee comes to your office and says, "My wife is having a baby," "My mother has to have surgery," "My son was injured in Afghanistan," or "I've been diagnosed with cancer," you'll have to figure out whether the FMLA applies, provide notices and meet other paperwork requirements, manage the employee's time off, and reinstate the employee according to strict rules and guidelines.

Ten Steps to FMLA Compliance

Whenever you're faced with a leave situation that might be covered by the FMLA, you should ask yourself the questions listed below. This checklist will help you make sure that you meet all your legal obligations and don't forget anything important. Each of these topics is covered in detail in this book.

Step 1: Is your company covered by the FMLA? The answer is yes if you've had at least 50 employees for at least 20 weeks in the current or previous year. If your company is covered, it must post a notice and may have to provide written notice to employees, even before an employee requests leave. Company coverage is explained in Chapter 2.

Step 2: Is the employee covered by the FMLA? An employee who has worked for at least 12 months, and has worked at least 1,250 hours during the year before taking leave, at a company facility that has at least 50 employees within a 75-mile radius, is covered. Chapter 3 explains how to make these calculations.

Step 3: Does the employee need leave for a reason covered by the FMLA? Leave is available for the employee's own serious health condition or to care for a family member with a serious health condition, as explained in Chapter 4. Leave is also available to bond with a new child, which is covered in Chapter 5. Military family leave—for a qualifying exigency related to a family member's military service or to care for a family member who suffers a service-related illness or injury—is also covered by the FMLA; we explain these rules in Chapter 6.

Step 4: How much leave is available to the employee? An employee is entitled to take a total of 12 workweeks of leave in a 12-month period, either all at once or intermittently, to bond with a new child, handle qualifying exigencies relating to a family member's military service, care for a family member with a serious health condition, or recuperate from a serious health condition. An employee who needs military caregiver leave is entitled to up to 26 weeks off in a single 12-month period. Chapter 7 will help you figure out how much leave an employee may take.

Step 5: Did you and the employee meet your notice and paperwork requirements?
The employee must give reasonable notice and provide certain information; you must designate FMLA leave and give the employee required notices, among other things. Chapter 8 provides the details.

Step 6: Did you request a certification (and if so, did the employee return it)?
You can—and should—ask an employee who needs leave for a serious health condition, a serious illness or injury to a servicemember, or a qualifying exigency related to a family member's military service, to complete a certification form. Chapter 9 explains how.

Step 7: Did you successfully manage the employee's leave? You must continue the employee's health benefits, manage and track intermittent leave, arrange for substitution of paid leave, and more. In addition, you have to make sure the work gets done while the employee is out, whether by distributing the employee's responsibilities to coworkers, hiring a temporary replacement, or outsourcing the job. Chapter 10 covers all of these issues.

Step 8: Did you follow the rules for reinstating an employee returning from leave? You must return the employee to the same or an equivalent position and restore the employee's seniority and benefits, unless an exception applies. Chapter 11 explains these rules, as well as what to do if the employee doesn't return from leave.

Step 9: Have you met your obligations under any other laws that apply?
Whether or not the FMLA applies, the employee may be protected by the Americans with Disabilities Act, workers' compensation statutes, state family and medical leave laws, and other laws. To find out about your obligations under these other laws, see Chapter 12.

Step 10: Have you met your record-keeping requirements? If your company is covered by the FMLA, you must keep certain payroll, benefits, leave, and other records, and you'll certainly want to keep proper documentation of your decisions and conversations, in case you need to rely on them later. These issues are covered in Chapter 13.

The Compassionate Manager

One of the challenges of implementing the FMLA is that you must meet your legal obligations within a context that can be emotional. After all, employees who qualify for FMLA leave are undergoing major life changes. On the positive side, the employee may be welcoming a new child, with all the joy and excitement that brings. On the more sobering side, perhaps the employee is losing a parent or spouse to a terminal illness, caring for a seriously ill or injured child, or suffering through a painful disease. Although you have to follow the law's requirements and make sure your company's needs are met, no one wants to be the hardhearted administrator who responds to an emotionally distraught employee by handing over a stack of forms to be completed in triplicate.

The FMLA recognizes that employees who need time off for pressing family or health concerns might not always be able to dot every "i" and cross every "t." The law provides guidance on what to do if, for example, an employee is too ill or injured to communicate with you, can't return to work on time because of continuing health problems, or doesn't complete forms properly. These rules will help you balance your legal obligations with the natural human desire to be compassionate during a difficult time.

And, as we'll remind you from time to time, you have little to gain from imposing strict deadlines and paperwork requirements on employees who are truly in dire straits. Judges and juries are people, too, and they can find ways to enforce the spirit of the law in favor of an employee who needed its protection, even if the employee failed to meet deadlines, give adequate notice, hand in forms on time, or provide required information.

Of course, people have different comfort levels when dealing with emotional subjects. Some can easily offer support and a shoulder to cry on; others would rather volunteer for a root canal. If you fall on the more stoic end of this spectrum, take heart: You don't need to become a therapist—or the employee's best friend—to show some understanding in a difficult situation. Just remember that a little kindness goes a long way. Acknowledge what your employees are dealing with, cut them some slack if necessary, and work with them to make the law serve its purpose.

Why You Need to Get It Right

Properly managing your FMLA obligations is a win-win situation. Employees win because they get time off when they really need it, with the assurance that their jobs will be waiting for them when they come back. You and your company win because helping employees balance work and family leads to greater employee loyalty to the company and all of the other benefits that flow from it, including better morale, stronger retention, and even improved productivity.

That's the carrot; here's the stick: Violating the FMLA can lead to serious trouble. And we don't just mean the morale problems and associated woes that can crop up if employees feel that their needs aren't important to the company. Mishandling family and medical leave issues can also give rise to lawsuits, not just against your company, but against you, individually, as the manager who made the flawed decision. Of course, this is the ultimate worst-case scenario, and chances are good that you'll never have to face it. If you're one of the unlucky few, however, your personal assets—such as your home, your car, and your bank accounts—could be on the line, not to mention your career and reputation.

> CAUTION
>
> **FMLA lawsuits are on the rise.** More employees are filing lawsuits alleging violations of the FMLA than ever before. For the year ending on March 31, 2017, there were more than 1,200 FMLA cases filed in the federal courts alone; this number has been increasing year over year. The upshot for employers is clear: Compliance with the FMLA—and proof of compliance, in the form of records and policies—is more important than ever.

How Other Laws and Company Policies Come Into Play

The FMLA isn't the only law you need to consider when employees need time off for family or medical reasons. Other federal and state laws might also come into play, depending on the circumstances. In addition, a company's own policies often affect family and medical leave by, for example, providing paid sick, vacation, or family leave; requiring employees to follow certain procedures before taking time off; or dictating how seniority, benefits, and other issues are handled when an employee is on leave.

Lessons from the *Real World*

Human resources manager can be sued, individually, for violating the FMLA.

Elaine Brewer worked for Jefferson-Pilot Standard Life Insurance Company for 29 years. In July 2002, she requested leave to have eye surgery, estimating she would be out for one to three weeks. While she was out, she gave status reports on her condition to her direct supervisor and to Felicia Cooper, Jefferson-Pilot's senior human resources manager. After three weeks of leave, Brewer's eyes had not yet healed sufficiently for her to return to work. At that point, for the first time, Jefferson-Pilot gave Brewer notice of her rights under the FMLA.

On July 31, 2002, Cooper spoke to Brewer by phone and asked for the names of her health care providers. Cooper then contacted the health care providers and asked them to submit medical certification forms documenting Brewer's condition. On August 2, 2002, before receiving the certification forms back from Brewer's doctors, Cooper accused Brewer of lying about her condition. Although Brewer said she would be able to return to work on August 5, Cooper fired Brewer for dishonesty and insubordination. On August 5, Brewer's doctor returned the certification form, indicating that Brewer had been receiving medical care during her entire leave.

Brewer sued Jefferson-Pilot and Cooper, individually, for violating the FMLA. Cooper argued that she could not be sued personally because she was not Brewer's employer. However, the court disagreed: Relying on the language of the FMLA and the regulations interpreting it, the court found that anyone who acts in the interest of the employer in relation to an employee could be sued as an employer. Because Brewer claimed that Cooper received her medical status reports, controlled the paperwork relating to her leave, contacted the doctors, and fired her for allegedly lying about her condition, Cooper was a proper defendant in the lawsuit.

Brewer v. Jefferson-Pilot Standard Life Insurance Company, 333 F.Supp.2d 433 (M.D. N.C. 2004).

This possibility of overlap means three very important things to managers:

- Whenever an employee requests time off pursuant to any law or company policy, you must ask yourself whether the FMLA applies.
- The employee isn't required to explicitly ask for "FMLA leave"; it's your responsibility to determine whether the employee's time off is FMLA qualified. An employee on workers' comp leave, temporary disability leave, parental leave, or even vacation might be protected by the FMLA, if the employee meets all of the criteria. And you will certainly want to count that time off as FMLA leave, not only to make sure the employee's rights are protected, but also to put some limit on the total amount of time an employee can take off in a year.
- When the FMLA and another law or policy both apply, you may have to provide more than the FMLA requires. If other laws or your company's policies give employees additional rights, you must honor them as well. The employee is entitled to every protection available, whether it is provided by the FMLA, another law, or your company's policies.

Overlapping Laws

The basic rule about what to do when the FMLA and another law overlap is easy to state: You must follow every applicable provision of every applicable law. In other words, you may not focus solely on the FMLA and ignore your company's obligations under other state or federal laws. If both laws apply to the same situation, you must give the employee the benefit of whichever law is more generous or provides greater rights.

Here are some of the other laws that might also apply to an employee who takes FMLA leave (Chapter 12 explains each in detail, and you can find information on each state's leave laws in Appendix A):

- **Antidiscrimination laws,** which prohibit discrimination based on certain protected characteristics. The Americans with Disabilities Act (ADA) and similar state laws might come into play if an employee's serious health condition is also a protected disability. Laws that prohibit gender and pregnancy discrimination might also overlap with the FMLA.
- **Workers' compensation statutes,** which require most employers to carry insurance that pays for medical treatment and partial wage

replacement for employees who suffer work-related injuries or illnesses. An employee who needs workers' compensation leave almost always has a serious health condition under the FMLA, as explained in Chapter 12.

- **State leave laws,** which require employers to give time off for specified reasons. Certain states may give employees the right to take pregnancy disability leave, parental leave, leave for a family member's military service, or other types of family and medical leave. If the employee takes leave for a reason that's covered by both state law and the FMLA, you can count that time off against the employee's allotment of FMLA hours. However, if state law provides leave that isn't covered by the FMLA, you can't count those types of leave against the employee's FMLA entitlement. This means that the employee might be legally entitled to take more time off than the FMLA allows. (See Appendix A for detailed information on state family and medical leave laws.)

- **State insurance programs,** which provide some wage replacement, usually funded by payroll deductions, for employees who are unable to work due to a temporary disability (including pregnancy and childbirth). A handful of states, including California, have paid family leave insurance programs, which provide similar benefits to employees who take time off to bond with a child or care for a family member. An employee on FMLA leave might be entitled to some compensation from this type of program.

Company Policies

Company policies interact with the FMLA in a slightly different way. For the most part, your company may give employees more rights than the FMLA provides, but it may not take FMLA rights away. For example, if your company has a family and medical leave policy that allows employees to take up to 16 weeks of parental leave, you cannot disregard that policy and give employees only the 12 weeks required by the FMLA. If your company's policies are less generous, however, the company must follow the FMLA: It must, for example, give employees a full 12 weeks of parental leave, even if the company's policies provide for only six.

The FMLA regulations make clear that employers may require employees to follow their usual company procedures when taking leave, as long as those rules don't violate the FMLA. For example, your company may enforce its usual notice rules—such as requiring two weeks notice to use paid vacation time—for employees who want to use paid leave during their FMLA leave. And, your company may generally require employees using FMLA leave to follow other leave requirements, such as calling a particular person to report an absence, as long as those rules don't require more notice than the FMLA. These rules are explained in Chapter 8.

In addition to these general rules, the FMLA also makes explicit reference to particular types of employer policies. For example, the FMLA says that you can fire an employee for substance abuse, even if the employee takes FMLA leave to go to rehab, but only if your company has a policy allowing it to do so.

Because this is a potentially confusing area, we've devoted Appendix B to company policies that can affect your FMLA obligations. This appendix identifies the most common areas in which company policy might come into play and provides some sample policy language that will help you maximize your company's rights. In addition, you'll find policy alert icons throughout the book. These icons let you know that your company's policy could determine your rights and obligations regarding that topic.

How to Use This Book

This book explains every aspect of the FMLA, from figuring out whether your company is covered by the law to reinstating an employee returning from FMLA leave. We cover these topics in the order in which they will generally come up as you administer an employee's leave. In addition, we provide helpful appendixes that explain how your state's laws and your company's policies could affect your company's FMLA rights and obligations.

We strongly advise you to read the whole book, even if you are already familiar with some aspects of the FMLA. Because the FMLA imposes fairly tight deadlines on employers—and because the way you handle initial issues can affect your company's rights down the road—you'll find it very helpful to understand the whole picture before you have to handle a leave request.

Also, there have been significant changes in the law and regulations in recent years, so you may need to learn some different requirements. Once you've reviewed every chapter, you can use the book as a reference, to quickly look up the information you need.

Lessons from the *Real World*

Employee may sue for FMLA entitlements promised in employee handbook, even though employee didn't meet FMLA eligibility requirements.

Steven Peters marketed pharmaceutical products to health care providers for Gilead Sciences, Incorporated. Peters was off work for shoulder surgery from December 5 to December 16, 2002; Gilead sent him a letter identifying his time off as FMLA leave. The letter tracked language in the company's employee handbook, including that employees were entitled to 12 weeks of leave, followed by reinstatement. The letter also described the eligibility requirements for FMLA leave, but didn't include the requirement that the company employ 50 employees within 75 miles. In fact, this requirement wasn't met.

On March 4, 2003, Peters began a second period of leave after he began using neurontin, a drug that can cause serious side effects. Gilead again sent him a letter identifying his time off as FMLA leave but Peters never got this letter. On April 16, Gilead received a letter from Peters's doctor, releasing him to return to work on May 5. On April 21, Gilead offered Peters's position to someone else, who accepted it and began work a week later. On April 25, Gilead sent Peters a letter indicating that it could not reinstate him because he held a "key" position (apparently an effort to use the "key employee" exception, covered in Chapter 11).

Peters sued, and Gilead claimed that he wasn't entitled to FMLA leave because he didn't meet the eligibility requirements. The Court of Appeals eventually found that, although Peters may not have had an actual FMLA claim, he could still sue Gilead for promissory estoppel. Because Gilead's handbook and letter promised that Peters was entitled to reinstatement after 12 weeks of leave, Gilead might be responsible for the damages Peters suffered because of his reliance on the promise in taking leave.

Peters v. Gilead Sciences, Inc., 533 F.3d 594 (7th Cir. 2008).

Each chapter includes features that will help you meet your obligations, including:

- **Chapter Highlights,** which summarize the basic rules covered in the chapter
- **Lessons From the Real World,** which show how courts have handled particular disputes between real employees and real employers
- **Examples,** which will help you understand how to apply the material to real-life situations
- **Sample Forms,** which allow you to request information from, and provide information to, employees about FMLA leave (you'll find blank copies of all forms on this book's companion page at Nolo's website; see Appendix C for details)
- **Managers' Checklists and Flowcharts,** which you can use to make sure you've considered every important factor when making decisions about key FMLA issues, and
- **Common Mistakes—And How to Avoid Them,** which will help you steer clear of legal trouble in applying the FMLA.

Complying with the FMLA can be a challenge, but the materials in this book will help you handle your responsibilities legally, fairly, and confidently. The first step is to figure out whether your company is covered by the law—and, if so, to give employees notice of their rights under the law—using the guidelines in Chapter 2. If you already know that your company is covered and has met its posting and policy obligations, move on to Chapter 3, which will help you figure out which employees are eligible for leave.

Get Updates, Forms, and More on Nolo.com

When there are important changes to the information in this book, we'll post updates online. (See Appendix C for a link to the dedicated online companion page for this book.) And if you notice a useful form in this book, including a letter, checklist, or government form, you'll have access to a digital version via the same companion page. You'll find other useful information on that page, too, such as blog posts on the latest employment law happenings.

Is Your Company Covered by the FMLA?

Chapter Highlights

☆ Your company is covered by the FMLA if it has employed 50 or more employees for 20 or more weeks in the current or preceding year.

☆ Employees who count toward the 50 or more minimum include:
- all full-time employees
- all part-time employees
- employees on leave if they are expected to return to work, and
- employees who work jointly for your company and another company.

☆ These workers don't count toward the 50-employee minimum:
- independent contractors
- employees working outside the United States or its territories
- employees hired or terminated during a calendar week (for that week only), and
- employees who are not expected to return from leave.

☆ For purposes of the FMLA's 20-week minimum, employees are employed by your company in any week in which they are on payroll.

☆ The 20 weeks of employing 50 or more employees don't have to be consecutive, as long as they occur in the current or preceding year.

☆ If your company is a joint employer, its responsibilities under the FMLA depend on whether it is a "primary" or "secondary" employer.

☆ If your company is a covered employer, you must:
- post general FMLA information at every worksite, and
- include information about the FMLA in your company's written policies or distribute it to new employees.

Before you get your first request for FMLA leave, you have to figure out whether the law applies to your company. Companies subject to the law are required to post notices about the FMLA and include FMLA information in employee handbooks or other company policies. You don't have the luxury of waiting for an employee to raise the issue; you are legally required to inform your employees of their FMLA rights and obligations. If your company doesn't provide this information, it can't deny FMLA leave to employees for failing to meet their obligations under the law (for example, to provide advance notice of the need for leave or a medical certification from a health care provider). Your company could even face a lawsuit for interfering with or denying the employee's FMLA rights.

This chapter will help you figure out whether the FMLA applies to your company. It covers:

- whether your company is directly covered by the FMLA
- whether your company is covered by the FMLA as a joint employer, and
- what actions you must take, right away, if your company is covered.

Calculating the Size of Your Company

Your company is covered by the FMLA if it employed 50 or more employees for each working day during 20 or more weeks in the current or preceding year. The purpose of this 50-employee rule is to exempt small businesses from the FMLA. Congress recognized that these businesses might not be able to afford to provide the leave and benefits—and bear the administrative burdens—mandated by the law.

Most companies won't be splitting hairs: Companies with well more than 50 employees know they are subject to the FMLA, and very small companies know they aren't. However, for companies that are close to that 50-employee dividing line, the details about which employees count toward the minimum become very important. For example, managers sometimes aren't sure whether part-time employees count toward the minimum, or whether to count temporary workers who are placed—and technically employed—by an outside agency. To evaluate whether the FMLA applies to your company, you'll need to know the rules for counting employees.

Step 1: Does Your Company Employ 50 or More People?

It seems like a simple question—anyone can count to 50, right? However, when you're making the calculation, you'll need to include each of these employees:

- every full-time employee
- every part-time employee
- employees on leave, whether paid or unpaid, including medical leave, FMLA leave, vacation, and disciplinary or workers' compensation leaves, as long as your company reasonably expects them to return to work, and
- employees, such as temps, who work jointly for your company and another company (called "joint employees," and discussed below).

SKIP AHEAD
If your company has fewer than 50 employees. If your company has not employed 50 people at any given time in the last two years, your company will not be directly subject to the FMLA. However, if you're a joint employer with a company that is subject to the FMLA, you will still have some legal responsibilities even if you don't have 50 employees on your own. (For more information, see "Joint Employers and the FMLA," below.)

If your company has employed at least 50 employees at any time in the last two years, or is a joint employer, keep reading.

Step 2: Did Your Company Employ 50 or More Employees for 20 or More Workweeks?

The FMLA applies only to companies that have employed 50 or more employees for each working day during 20 or more weeks of the current or preceding year. Employees whose names appear on your company's payroll at any time in a calendar week count as employed for each working day of the workweek. However, employees hired or terminated during a calendar week don't count for that week. Independent contractors and employees working outside the United States or its territories do not count towards the 50-employee minimum.

> **EXAMPLE:** You are the HR manager of Blue Lagoon Pool Maintenance and Repair Service in Scottsdale, Arizona, which has 34 year-round employees but hires extra part-time employees when pool season comes around. Blue Lagoon hires 25 part-time employees the first week of May. When calculating whether Blue Lagoon has enough employees to be subject to the FMLA, you don't count the new part-time employees for the first week of May, but you do count them for every week they work after that, even if they only work one day a week. As of the middle of October, all the part-time employees still work for Blue Lagoon, so you correctly determine that Blue Lagoon will have at least 50 employees for 20 or more weeks of the year. Blue Lagoon will be subject to the FMLA.

Remember though, that the 20 weeks don't have to be consecutive. For example, if your company is a seasonal employer and has more than 50 employees during all of spring and fall (six months of the year), but only ten employees during summer and winter, your company will be covered by the FMLA. And a company that has reduced its workforce from at least 50 employees to less than 50 employees within the last year is still covered by FMLA if it employed 50 or more employees for any 20 weeks in the preceding calendar year.

> **EXAMPLE:** Your company, Razberry Jam Productions, employs 62 field workers from March 15 to May 1 every year, and 53 seasonal cannery workers from June 1 to October 15. The rest of the year, your company maintains a bare-bones staff of 15 shipping and administrative employees. In April, Wendy, a shipping clerk, asks for leave to take care of her husband as he recovers from surgery. Her manager denies the leave, telling Wendy that he has counted back 20 calendar weeks and the cannery was closed for most of that period, so the FMLA doesn't apply to Razberry Jam Productions.
>
> Should you step in and reverse the manager's decision? Yes. The manager should have looked at the entire current and preceding year for the company. If he had done that, he would have seen that your company employed over 50 employees for more than 20 weeks in that period. Your company was covered by the FMLA.

If your company didn't employ 50 employees for at least 20 weeks in the current or preceding year, it isn't covered by the FMLA. But, if your company is a "secondary" joint employer (discussed in "Joint Employers and the FMLA," below), it may still have to comply with certain FMLA requirements.

Covered Companies May Not Have Eligible Employees

To be eligible for leave under the FMLA, it's not enough that employees work for a covered company; they must also meet certain individual eligibility requirements, as explained in Chapter 3. One of these requirements is that the employee must work within a 75-mile radius of 50 or more company employees.

As a result of this rule, a company that's covered by the FMLA might not have a single eligible employee. For example, a nationwide company might have outlets in a hundred major metropolitan areas, each employing 20 to 30 employees. Yet, if none of those outlets are with 75 miles of another, none of the company's employees would be eligible to take FMLA leave. In this situation, the company would still have to post notices and provide information on the FMLA (see "If Your Company Is Covered," below), but it wouldn't have to provide leave.

Joint Employers and the FMLA

Even if it doesn't meet the criteria described above, your company could still be subject to the FMLA if it is a "joint employer." A joint employer shares control with another company over the working conditions of the other company's employees. This happens when your company contracts with temporary agencies or shares employees with a contractor or subcontractor, for example. If, counting joint employees, your company meets the requirements described above, your company is subject to the FMLA. However, its FMLA responsibilities to the joint employees depend on whether it's a "primary" or a "secondary" employer, as we explain below.

Is Your Company a Joint Employer?

There are no hard and fast rules that determine whether your company is a joint employer. Instead, you must look at all the circumstances of the relationship between the two companies to determine whether your company acts like an employer. The main factors to consider are whether your company:

- has the power to hire and fire some employees of the other company
- has the power to set rates and methods of pay for employees of the other company
- has the right to supervise the work and work schedules of employees of the other company, and
- is responsible for maintaining employment records for employees of the other company.

These factors are hallmarks of a joint employer relationship, according to a majority of federal circuit courts. (A handful of courts apply a slightly different test.) No one factor or combination of factors automatically creates a joint employer relationship. But as a practical matter, if your company uses temps or employees supplied by another company, it is probably a joint employer. (Note that while the Department of Labor had issued additional guidance in 2016 on the joint employer test, that guidance has since been withdrawn.)

Lessons from the *Real World*

Even if your company is not covered by the FMLA, you might be obliged to grant FMLA leave as a joint employer.

Darren Cuff worked as a manager for Trans States Airlines, a regional airline. When Cuff requested FMLA leave, Trans States denied his request and terminated him, in part because the company had only 33 employees at the time. Cuff then filed an FMLA violation lawsuit, arguing that Trans States was a joint employer with another regional airline, GoJet, which had also used Cuff's services. GoJet had 343 employees at the time of Cuff's termination.

The court agreed that the two airlines were joint employers of Cuff, noting that Cuff represented both companies in negotiations and meetings with contractor airlines and area airports, the logos of both companies were on Cuff's business card, and internal company directories listed Cuff as the point person for operations questions for both companies. Cuff was therefore entitled to FMLA leave.

Cuff v. Trans States Holdings, Inc., 768 F.3d 605 (7th Cir. 2014).

Professional Employer Organizations

The FMLA regulations address the increasingly common arrangement by which one company retains another to handle payroll and administrative benefits for the first company's employees on an ongoing basis. The DOL calls the companies that are hired to do this work "professional employer organizations" (PEOs). Although the question of joint employment turns on the "economic realities" of the situation based on all of the facts and circumstances, the regulations make clear that a PEO and its client/employer typically are not joint employers as long as both of the following are true:

- The PEO simply performs administrative functions (such as those related to payroll, benefits, and updating employment policies).
- The client/employer doesn't have the right to hire, fire, assign, or direct and control the PEO's employees.

If, however, the PEO and the client/employer are joint employers, the client/employer usually will be the primary employer.

EXAMPLE: Your company, Internet Service Solutions (ISS), operates a customer call center to service the accounts of customers of an Internet service provider, Internet View. To find new customer service representatives, ISS hires temporary employees through a placement service, Techno Temps. ISS supervisors interview prospective Techno Temps candidates for their departments, choose which to hire, and decide how much to pay them. If the supervisor likes the Techno Temp employee's work, the employee might later be offered a job directly by ISS. If a Techno Temps placement doesn't work out, ISS can terminate employment. Currently, 20 of ISS's customer service representatives are Techno Temps employees.

In this situation, ISS is a joint employer with Techno Temps because ISS has the power to hire and fire Techno Temps employees working at ISS, sets their pay rates, and supervises them on a day-to-day basis. As a result, all joint employees have to be counted by both ISS and Techno Temps to determine whether the two companies are covered by the FMLA.

Depending on the circumstances, ISS might also be a joint employer with Internet View. For example, if ISS is a subsidiary of Internet View, and human resources operations like recruiting, payroll, and personnel files are all managed by Internet View, ISS and Internet View are probably joint employers.

Primary and Secondary Employers

Figuring out whether your company is a joint employer is just your first task; it tells you whether you have any obligations under the FMLA. To find out what those obligations are, you must figure out whether your company is the "primary" employer or the "secondary" employer.

Is Your Company a Primary or Secondary Employer?

If your company is a joint employer, use the criteria below to determine whether your company is a primary or secondary employer.

A primary employer has authority to:
- hire and fire the employee seeking leave
- place the employee in a particular position
- assign work to the employee
- make payroll, and
- provide employment benefits.

If your company is responsible for these tasks, your company is the primary employer. If not, your company is the secondary employer. Once again, these factors give guidance but are not hard and fast rules.

> **EXAMPLE:** Your company has 33 employees on its regular payroll. You also have 21 IT technicians working for you, who are directly employed by IS-2, a temporary agency. IS-2 hires and fires these technicians, issues their paychecks, and provides medical insurance coverage for them. One of the IT technicians, Aaron, needs to take time off for the birth of his child.
>
> Who is Aaron's primary employer? Because IS-2 handles all of the employment obligations for the IT technicians, IS-2 is Aaron's primary employer. Your company is the secondary employer because it uses Aaron's services but is not otherwise responsible for his employment.

TIP

When in doubt, act like the primary employer. If you aren't sure whether your company is a primary or secondary employer, the best practice is to assume that it is a primary employer and give employees the required notices, as discussed below. If a court is later asked to decide the issue, you'll have met your company's obligations either way.

Primary and Secondary Employers' Responsibilities

So what are the responsibilities of the primary and secondary employers? The primary employer's responsibilities are pretty much the same as those of any company subject to the FMLA. It must provide FMLA notices to joint employees, grant and administer their FMLA leaves, and restore them to their jobs when FMLA leave is over. The primary employer can't interfere with employees' FMLA rights or discriminate against employees for asserting those rights or helping other employees assert their rights. We'll discuss how to implement all of these requirements in later chapters.

The secondary employer's responsibilities are a little less onerous. As long as the secondary employer is still jointly employing anyone with the primary employer when the employee's leave ends, the secondary employer must let the employee return to the same position he or she held before the leave. Additionally, the secondary employer can't interfere with a joint employee's exercise of FMLA rights and can't retaliate or discriminate against the employee for asserting FMLA rights or for helping other employees assert their rights. Even a secondary employer that would not otherwise be covered by the FMLA (for example, because it employs fewer than 50 employees including joint employees) is bound by these obligations.

Figuring Out Your FMLA Responsibilities

If you're a joint employer, it can be confusing to figure out what your FMLA responsibilities are. You may be a primary employer with regard to some of your employees, but a secondary employer with regard to other employees.

Or, you may be a secondary employer only, or you may have no obligations under the FMLA at all. The following examples will help you determine which category you fall under. The key is to calculate joint employees in both your company's count and the other joint employer's count. Let's continue with the example from above.

EXAMPLE 1: Your company has 33 regular employees and 21 IT technicians placed by IS-2. Because you're a joint employer with IS-2, you must count the IT technicians in your total employee count. Your company has a total of 54 employees, which means it is covered by the FMLA. You're the primary employer of your 33 regular employees and the secondary employer of the 21 IT Technicians. This means that you will have different FMLA obligations depending on which employee requests FMLA leave.

EXAMPLE 2: Susan, one of your regular employees, needs time off to bond with her new child. Aaron, one of the IT technicians, needs time off for a serious health condition. What are your obligations?

Because you're the primary employer for Susan, you must follow all FMLA requirements, including providing Susan with the required notices, granting her request for FMLA leave (assuming she meets all eligibility requirements), and reinstating her to the same or an equivalent position at the end of her leave. When it comes to Aaron, you have the more limited obligations of a secondary employer. You don't have to provide notice or administer FMLA leave; those are the responsibilities of Aaron's primary employer, IS-2. But, if you still have any joint employees with IS-2 working for you at the time Aaron returns from leave, you must accept his placement at your company.

EXAMPLE 3: Now, suppose your company has only 10 regular employees and 21 IT technicians placed by IS-2. Because your total employee count is 31, you are not covered by the FMLA. However, IS-2 has 34 other employees, for a total of 55 employees. IS-2 is subject to the FMLA. As a result, you have the more limited obligations of a secondary employer when it comes to the 21 IT technicians. But, you won't have any FMLA obligations towards your regular employees.

Integrated Employers

A parent and subsidiary company or two or more affiliated companies (sometimes called "sister companies") must each count all of the other company's employees, even those who work only for one company, when calculating whether they meet the 50-employee test. These "integrated" companies are viewed under the FMLA as a single employer. Companies are "integrated employers" when there is:

- common management
- interrelation between operations
- centralized control of labor relations, and
- common ownership or financial control.

So, if your company is integrated with another company, it must include all of the other company's employees in the FMLA count—even if your company shares no staff with the other company and has entirely separate work facilities.

✓   **Managers' Checklist: Does the FMLA Apply to My Company?**

☐ My company had 50 or more employees on payroll during each of 20 workweeks in this year or the last calendar year.

    ☐ I included all employees on leave in this count.

    ☐ I included all part-time employees on payroll during any workweek.

    ☐ I did not include employees hired or fired during any workweek in the count for that workweek.

    ☐ I did not include employees working outside the United States or its territories in this count.

    ☐ I counted all employees jointly employed by my company and a joint employer, including temp agency employees.

    ☐ I counted all employees of my company and any other company that is integrated with it.

CAUTION

A successor in interest might have FMLA obligations to "inherited" employees. If your company bought or merged with another company, the company that's left after the merger or sale may be a "successor in interest." If so, the transferred employees will have the same FMLA rights they would have had if continuously employed by a single company. If your company is not covered by the FMLA and it buys another company that is, it must honor the FMLA rights of the employees of the other company who become its employees after the sale. If you think your company might be a successor in interest, you may want to consult with an attorney to determine your company's responsibilities under the FMLA.

If Your Company Is Covered

Once you determine that your company is covered by the FMLA, you must immediately provide information to employees about their rights and obligations under the law (unless your company is a secondary employer only). You'll have to post a notice explaining the FMLA and distribute written information on the law to employees.

Posting Requirements

Employees rely on you to provide them with information about the FMLA. Your obligation begins with the requirement to hang a poster explaining employees' FMLA rights. The poster must be in a "conspicuous" place where it can be readily seen by employees and job applicants, and it must be in writing that is large enough to read easily. The posting requirement applies even if your company doesn't have any FMLA-eligible employees on site: Currently ineligible employees may become eligible under the FMLA at a later date and will need to know their rights.

The FMLA regulations allow employers to post FMLA information electronically. However, you must make sure that it can readily be seen by employees and job applicants. An electronic posting on your company's intranet, for example, wouldn't satisfy the posting requirement unless it could be easily accessed by applicants as well.

FORM

Fortunately, you don't have to put together a poster from scratch. The U.S. Department of Labor (DOL) has an approved poster (WH-1420) that you can download and use. You can find English and Spanish versions of this poster at this book's online companion page; see Appendix C for more information.

If a "significant portion" of your company's workforce doesn't speak English, the poster must be in the language in which those employees are literate. The family leave laws of some states may also require a poster written in the language in which a specific number or percentage of your company's employees are literate. Additionally, some states have other posting requirements under their own family, medical, or pregnancy leave laws. For example, California requires employers covered by its family leave law to post a notice alerting employees to their rights under the FMLA, the state family leave law, and the state's pregnancy disability leave law. (Contact your state's department of labor to learn about your state's posting requirements; see Appendix A for contact information.)

TIP

Post the FMLA information in every language that your company's employees speak, including English. That way, you will not have to worry that some employees are not getting the required information.

If your company fails to post the general FMLA information discussed above, it can't deny leave to, discipline, or take any action against an employee because the employee has not complied with FMLA notice and procedural requirements. And, the DOL could penalize your company $169 for each violation of the posting requirement. If your company's failure to post the FMLA information interferes with an employee's FMLA rights, the employee could sue the company.

SEE AN EXPERT

Get legal help with your posting requirements. Consult an attorney with expertise in the laws of every state in which your company employs workers to find out the state-specific poster requirements.

EXAMPLE: Delia has worked for your company for two years. Your company doesn't post FMLA information, even though it is covered by the FMLA. Your company also has its own 16-week maternity leave policy but requires employees to follow FMLA procedures to request it. Delia gets pregnant and takes the full 16 weeks of leave. When she tries to return to her original position after the leave ends, you tell her that you filled her position two weeks earlier because she hadn't followed FMLA leave request procedures. Delia objects and says that the FMLA protects her right to return to her original job. You point out to Delia that the FMLA does provide for reinstatement, but only where proper notice and certification are provided. You tell Delia you have assigned her to a downgraded position. Delia threatens legal action. Should you be worried?

You should be quite worried! You were right about the FMLA protecting employees who follow FMLA procedures (as discussed in Chapter 8). But, because the FMLA information wasn't posted for Delia and other employees to see, your company effectively interfered with her FMLA rights.

Written FMLA Policies

Before any individual employee even asks for FMLA leave, your company must notify all employees of their FMLA rights in writing. In addition to the FMLA poster discussed above, your company must include information about FMLA entitlements and employee obligations in its employee handbook or other written guidelines to employees regarding employee benefits or leave.

If your company doesn't have an employee handbook or other written policies on benefits or leave that it distributes to employees, it must give a copy of the general FMLA notice to each new employee upon hire. The general notice is simply the FMLA poster (WH-1420), available as explained in "Posting Requirements," above.

If your company already has a leave policy, you'll want to make sure that it has all the information that's legally required. We've included a sample FMLA policy in Appendix B, which you can use to draft or modify your own company policy.

If your company fails to include FMLA information in its employee handbook or benefits policies or to provide the information to employees as required, it won't be able to take action against an employee who doesn't comply with the requirements of the FMLA or your company's own leave policies. And, your company may be liable for interfering with employee FMLA rights.

Your company's handbook or other written policies should include all company leave policies that interact with FMLA rights, such as attendance policies, notice requirements, and the like. We'll discuss these policies, and how they interact with the FMLA, in subsequent chapters.

Lessons from the *Real World*

An employer that failed to give an employee the required notices under the FMLA interfered with her FMLA rights.

Jacqueline Young worked as a payroll specialist for The Wackenhut Corporation (TWC) for nine years when she went out on maternity leave. TWC failed to give Young the required FMLA eligibility notice, the rights and responsibilities notice, and the designation notice. Because TWC didn't give Young these individualized notices, she was unaware that she had to return to work by a certain date. TWC terminated Young the day after she had exhausted her FMLA leave. Young sued TWC, arguing that the company had interfered with her FMLA rights.

The court agreed with Young, ruling that TWC interfered with her FMLA rights by failing to give her the required notices. The court found that the notices are essential to giving employees the chance to make informed decisions and structure their leave in a way that is protected by the FMLA.

Young v. Wackenhut Corp., No. 10-2608 (D.N.J. Feb. 1, 2013).

Common Mistakes Regarding Employer Coverage—And How to Avoid Them

Mistake 1: **Your company is covered by the FMLA, but managers who don't know it deny leave to eligible employees.**

Avoid this mistake by taking the following steps:

- Figure out whether your company is covered by the FMLA.
- Reevaluate FMLA coverage when there is a change in your company's workforce or structure, such as a merger or expansion.
- Count all employees the FMLA requires you to count (for example, employees on leave, part-time employees, and joint employees).
- Count only those employees the FMLA requires you to count (for example, do not count independent contractors).

Mistake 2: **Your company doesn't meet its obligations as a joint employer.**

Avoid this mistake by taking the following steps:

- Keep track of all workers who are joint employees of your company and another company, including all temps and any employees your company shares with a contractor or subcontractor.
- Figure out whether your company is the primary or secondary employer of joint employees.
- Fulfill your company's responsibilities as a primary or secondary employer.

Mistake 3: **Failing to give all employees general FMLA information.**

Avoid this mistake by taking the following steps:

- Immediately post the required FMLA notice in a conspicuous location at every worksite.
- Make sure that your company's employee handbook includes a detailed and accurate description of employee FMLA rights and duties (use the sample FMLA policy in Appendix B).
- Distribute a copy of the written FMLA notice to all new employees as part of their first-day paperwork.

Is the Employee Covered by the FMLA?

Chapter Highlights

☆ Employees are entitled to FMLA leave if they:
- work at a location with 50 or more employees within a 75-mile radius
- have worked for your company for at least 12 months, and
- have worked at least 1,250 hours in the 12-month period preceding the leave.

☆ You must determine whether there are 50 employees within 75 miles on the date the employee requests leave, not the date the employee's leave is scheduled to begin.

☆ Time that counts toward the 1,250-hour minimum includes:
- any hours the employee worked, whether paid or not
- work-related travel time during the workday
- continuing education or other required work-related activities, and
- hours the employee would have worked if not on military leave.

☆ The following hours don't count toward the 1,250-hour minimum:
- time spent on suspension
- travel time from home to work, and
- time on leave other than for military service (unless your company counts leave time for overtime purposes).

☆ Different hours-of-service rules apply to airline flight crew employees, who are eligible for leave if they:
- have worked or been paid for at least 60% of the applicable total monthly guarantee, and
- have worked or been paid for at least 504 hours in the past 12 months.

☆ You must carefully track employees' hours to determine eligibility; if you don't keep accurate records, records kept by the employee will be used to resolve eligibility disputes.

Now that you know that the FMLA applies to your company, it's time to figure out which employees the law protects. Not every employee who works for a covered employer is entitled to leave. To be eligible, an employee must have worked for your company for at least 12 months and must have worked at least 1,250 hours during the year preceding the leave. In addition, your company must have at least 50 employees within a 75-mile radius of the employee's worksite.

Keeping records of these numbers can get complicated. There are detailed rules on which hours count toward the minimum, how to measure the 75 miles, and when to make these determinations. And it's not a one-time calculation: An employee who was eligible for—and took—FMLA leave in the past might not qualify later on; similarly, an employee who isn't entitled to FMLA leave today might become eligible in the future.

This chapter explains each part of the eligibility process: how to do the necessary calculations, how to track an employee's eligibility, and how to keep proper records that will allow you to quickly determine whether an employee meets these requirements.

Employee Eligibility, Step by Step

To be eligible for FMLA leave, an employee must:
- work at a worksite with 50 or more employees within a 75-mile radius
- have worked for your company for at least 12 months, and
- have worked at least 1,250 hours in the 12 months immediately preceding the leave.

An employee who doesn't meet all three of these requirements is not entitled to FMLA leave.

Step 1: Are There 50 Employees Within 75 Miles?

To figure out whether a specific employee is entitled to FMLA leave, you first need to figure out whether there are 50 or more employees at the employee's worksite or within a 75-mile radius of the worksite. If your company employs thousands of FMLA-eligible workers, but has several employees who work in a remote satellite office that's more than 75 miles from any other company worksite, the employees in the satellite office won't be entitled to FMLA leave.

> **TIP**
>
> **Don't forget to count joint employees.** When figuring out whether there are 50 employees within 75 miles of the employee's worksite, make sure to count joint employees. A joint employee's worksite is the primary employer's office where the employee is assigned or reports, unless the employee has physically worked for at least a year at a facility of the secondary employer, which would then become the joint employee's worksite. For more on joint employers, including primary and secondary employers, see Chapter 2.

Measuring the 75-Mile Radius

If your company has a "campus" of buildings grouped together, they count as one worksite. Similarly, unconnected buildings used by your company within a reasonable geographic vicinity (for example, within the city limits) are considered a single worksite. The 75-mile radius should be measured out from each of the buildings in the worksite. If there are 50 employees within 75 miles of any building in the worksite, all employees who work at the worksite meet this part of the eligibility test.

> **EXAMPLE:** Petra has worked full time at the Main Street outlet of your company, the Grande Baguette bakery chain, for the last four years. Grande Baguette employs 20 people at the Main Street outlet and another 20 people at another location in the city, the First Street outlet. It employs another 20 people at an outlet in a suburban mall that's 77 miles away from Petra's outlet but only 72 miles from the First Street store. Petra is pregnant and has requested leave to begin on the date of her scheduled C-section. Is Petra entitled to FMLA leave?
>
> Yes. Even though there are only 20 employees at the Grande Baguette outlet where Petra works, the two city locations count as one worksite. There are 40 employees at the citywide worksite, and an additional 20 employees at the mall outlet. Because the mall outlet is within 75 miles of one of the city locations, those employees count when determining Petra's eligibility—even though they don't work within 75 miles of her actual location. Because there are 60 employees within 75 miles of the worksite under the FMLA definition, Petra is eligible for leave.

To measure the 75-mile radius, you must use the shortest route on public streets, roads, highways, and waterways from the worksite. Although employees have tried to argue that the 75 miles should be measured "as the crow flies" (that is, in a straight line on a map), courts have determined that this distance must be measured by surface miles using actual routes that could be traveled between worksites.

When to Count the 75-Mile Radius

You must make the 75-mile radius determination on the day the employee requests leave, not the day the employee's leave will begin. If your company had the requisite number of employees on the day the employee requested leave, the employee has met this eligibility requirement, regardless of later reductions in your local workforce.

> **EXAMPLE:** Your company has five stores in downtown Omaha, employing a total of 63 employees. Next month, it plans to close two stores that employ a total of 21 people; after those closures, the company will have only 42 employees. Ted works at one of the stores that will remain open. He asks his supervisor, Margo, for three weeks off beginning six weeks from now, to look after his mother following hip replacement surgery. Margo, who knows about the store closure plans, tells you she is going to deny FMLA leave because there will be only 42 employees when Ted's leave starts.
>
> Fortunately, Margo speaks to you before making this mistake. You correctly point out that the company must determine whether this eligibility requirement is met on the date an employee requests leave, not the date leave is scheduled to begin. Because the company has more than 50 employees in the city at the time Ted makes his FMLA request, he is entitled to leave as long as he meets the other eligibility requirements.

Determining Where an Employee Works

It's not hard to identify the worksite of an employee who works in the same cubicle every day. However, figuring out the worksite for employees who travel or telecommute presents more of a challenge. For employees with no fixed company worksite, the worksite where the employee reports or where work is assigned to the employee is that employee's worksite for FMLA purposes. This is true even if the reporting worksite is temporary and the company's headquarters are many miles away.

> **EXAMPLE:** You are the human resources manager for Nice Catch, a company that owns several fishing vessels operating out of Dutch Harbor, Alaska. Nice Catch is headquartered in Anacortes, Washington. Nice Catch employs 75 workers on its boats in Dutch Harbor and assigns crews from its small dockside office there. In the Anacortes headquarters, Nice Catch employs 22 people.
>
> Maria works on a fishing boat out of Dutch Harbor and has requested leave to care for a baby that she and her partner are adopting. Richie is an accountant in the Anacortes office and needs shoulder surgery to repair a torn rotator cuff, which has interfered with his ability to work. Assuming they meet the other eligibility requirements, are Maria and Richie entitled to FMLA leave?
>
> Yes and no, respectively. Because the boat crews are assigned work out of the Dutch Harbor office, that's their worksite for purposes of calculating FMLA eligibility—even if their fishing boats operate hundreds of miles apart. Because Maria works at a site with more than 50 employees, she is entitled to leave. There are only 22 employees at Richie's worksite, however, so he isn't an eligible employee under the FMLA.

Step 2: Has the Employee Worked for the Company for 12 Months?

To be eligible for FMLA leave, an employee must have worked for your company for at least 12 months. These months need not be consecutive. An employee who has put in a total of 12 months meets this eligibility requirement, even if the employee had a break in service, as long as the employee's break in service lasted for fewer than seven years. If the employee had a break in service of seven years or more, the employer doesn't have to count employment prior to the break in service toward the 12-month requirement, unless the break in service was due to National Guard or Reserve military service obligations or was pursuant to a written agreement, including a collective bargaining agreement, indicating the employer's intent to rehire the employee after the break.

EXAMPLE: Horacio works on one of your company's construction crews. He worked eight months for your company last year, from the beginning of April through the end of November, before he was laid off because of lack of work during the winter. The company rehired Horacio on April 1. On August 1, Horacio has a heart attack and takes several weeks off work for treatment and recovery. Has Horacio met the 12-month requirement for FMLA eligibility?

Yes. Although Horacio has only worked for your company in eight of the last 12 months, he has worked 12 months total: eight months during his first stint with your company and four months immediately before his heart attack. He has met this eligibility requirement.

When to Count the 12 Months

The employee must have worked a total of 12 months as of the date that he or she will begin FMLA leave, not as of the date the employee requests leave. Note that this is different from the 75-mile radius eligibility requirement, discussed above.

EXAMPLE: Anna began working for your company full time 11 months ago. Anna requests leave to undergo back surgery beginning in one month. Is Anna entitled to FMLA leave because she will have worked for you for 12 months by the time her leave starts?

Yes, Anna is entitled to FMLA leave. If she had needed FMLA leave immediately though, she wouldn't be eligible.

Which Time Counts

If an employee works at all during a week, that week counts toward the 12-month requirement. Unlike the hours-worked requirement (discussed below), the 12-month requirement measures how long the employee has been with your company, not how many hours he or she has actually worked.

When determining whether an employee has worked at least 12 months, you should count every week in which the employee shows up on the payroll. It doesn't matter whether the employee works full time or part time or whether the employee works intermittently (that is, the employee works some weeks and not others). Once the employee reaches 52 weeks on the payroll, the employee has met the requirement.

If you have joint employees—that is, employees who are employed both by your company and by another company (such as a temp agency)—count all of the weeks during which they have been employed by either joint company. For example, if an employee of a temporary agency was placed with your company six months ago and worked for the temporary agency for six months before that, that employee has satisfied the 12-month employment requirement.

Time employees spend on leave counts toward the 12-month minimum only if one of the following is true:

- The employee took leave for military service (see Chapter 12 for more information).
- Your company provided compensation or benefits during the employee's leave (such as PTO, group health benefits, and so on).

    EXAMPLE: Brett has worked full time for your company for one year but spent two months of that year on company-approved, paid disability leave. Brett now requests leave for a serious health condition. Is Brett entitled to FMLA leave?
        Yes, because he has worked at least 12 months, including the paid leave time.

A couple of time periods that do not count toward the 12-month requirement are:

- **Suspensions.** If an employee was suspended, that suspension period doesn't count toward the 12 months.
- **Layoff periods.** If you lay off an employee and then recall that employee later, you don't usually count the layoff period when calculating whether the employee has worked for 12 months.

Step 3: Has the Employee Worked Enough Hours?

In addition to having worked for at least 12 months for your company, an employee seeking FMLA leave must have worked at least 1,250 hours in the 12-month period immediately preceding the leave. As with the 12-month requirement, you must calculate whether an employee has worked 1,250 hours as of the date leave is scheduled to begin—not the date the employee requests leave.

Which Hours Count

You must count every hour (or fraction of an hour) worked toward the 1,250-hour minimum. These include:

- hours worked for which the employee was not paid (for example, overtime hours worked by an employee exempt from receiving overtime pay)
- work-related travel time during the workday (for example, when an employee has to travel from his or her usual worksite to a meeting in another location)
- time spent on continuing education or other required work-related activities, and
- hours the employee would have worked if not on military leave (see Chapter 12).

The following hours do not count:

- time during which the employee was suspended
- time the employee spends traveling from home to office and back, unless:
  - your company has an agreement or practice of paying for such time, or
  - state law treats such travel time as paid time (for example, when the employee travels from home to a temporary worksite away from his or her usual worksite)
- time spent on leave other than military service covered by the Uniformed Services Employment and Reemployment Rights Act (USERRA), unless your company counts leave time as "hours worked" for overtime pay purposes. (Learn more about USERRA and how it overlaps with the FMLA in Chapter 12.)

POLICY ALERT

Your company's overtime policies could determine whether employees are eligible for FMLA leave. As noted above, if your company counts leave time as hours worked in determining whether an employee has worked overtime, it must also count leave time toward an employee's total hours worked in the 12-month FMLA period. (See Appendix B for more information on how your company's policies can affect its FMLA obligations.)

Special "Hours of Service" Eligibility Requirement for Airline Flight Crews

The unique challenges faced by airline employers when trying to calculate "hours worked" by flight crew members have led to some changes to the FMLA. In 2010, Congress amended the law to require employers to calculate the "hours of service" for FMLA eligibility in a different manner for airline flight crew employees.

For airline flight crews, which include pilots and flight attendants, the 1,250-hour requirement doesn't apply. Instead, the hours-worked requirement for FMLA eligibility will be met if, in the previous 12 months, the flight crew employee has worked or been paid for:

- at least 60% of the applicable monthly guarantee, and
- at least 504 hours.

The following terms apply to airline flight crews:

- **Applicable monthly guarantee:**
  - For nonreserve flight crew members, this term means the minimum number of hours for which the employer has agreed to schedule the employee for any given month.
  - For reserve status flight crew members, this term means the number of hours for which the employer has agreed to pay the employee for any given month.
- **Hours worked:** This includes the employee's duty hours during the previous 12-month period.
- **Hours paid:** This means the number of hours for which the employee received wages during the previous 12-month period.

Personal commute time, vacation, and medical or sick leave do not count toward the 504 hours of service requirement for these employees.

If Intermittent FMLA Leave Reduces an Employee's Hours

Some employees use their FMLA leave all at once. For example, an employee might take 12 weeks off after the birth of a new child or to recover from a serious car accident. Sometimes, however, an employee needs occasional days, hours, or weeks off or reduced work hours (for example, from full time to part time). The employee may be entitled to intermittent or reduced-schedule leave under the FMLA. (Chapter 7 covers this topic in more detail.)

An unintended consequence of taking leave in this manner can be that the employee's hours fall below the 1,250-hour minimum. But you can't deny FMLA leave based on that reason: As long as the employee still needs the reduced schedule for the same condition that necessitated FMLA leave in the first place, the employee remains eligible.

EXAMPLE: Though her regular schedule requires her to work 25 hours per week, Yvonne has been on an FMLA-qualified reduced schedule of ten hours per week for the past 12 weeks. Yvonne notifies you that she needs to continue her reduced schedule. She has all the necessary paperwork and has not used up all of her FMLA leave time.

In preparation for meeting with Yvonne, you count up her hours for the past 12 months. Because of her reduced schedule, Yvonne has worked fewer than 1,250 hours in the last 12 months. Can you deny Yvonne's request for a continued reduced schedule?

No. As long as Yvonne was qualified when she started leave and needs the reduced schedule for the same condition, she has a right to take the full 12 weeks of leave, as calculated for a part-time employee (discussed in Chapter 7).

The same is true if the employee takes some FMLA leave in a continuous block, then needs more leave for the same condition. Although the employee isn't taking a few hours at a time or working a reduced schedule, this counts as intermittent leave, for which eligibility need not be recalculated in the same leave year.

The rules are different if an employee needs FMLA leave for a different condition. In this situation, you must redetermine the employee's eligibility. If the employee's previous intermittent leave has reduced the employee's hours below the 1,250-hour threshold, the employee is not eligible for leave for an unrelated condition.

EXAMPLE: Let's go back to Yvonne, whose regular work schedule calls for 25 hours a week, but who has been working only ten hours a week for the last three months. Yvonne needed this intermittent leave to care for her father, who has a serious health condition. Yvonne's father is on the mend, but now Yvonne requests two weeks of FMLA leave so she can have knee surgery. Is she entitled to this leave?

No. In the last 12 months, Yvonne has worked ten hours a week for 12 weeks (120 hours), plus 25 hours a week for 40 weeks (1,000 hours), for a grand total of 1,120 hours. If she needed to stay on her reduced-leave schedule to continue caring for her father, she would still be entitled to FMLA leave. But because she wants leave for an unrelated condition, you must recalculate her hours—and she hasn't met the 1,250-hour threshold for FMLA eligibility.

CAUTION

H-1B workers are entitled to FMLA leave. The U.S. Department of Labor has made it clear that employers are required to make FMLA leave available to H-1B workers on the same terms as U.S. citizens in their employ.

Keeping Track of Employees' Work Hours

Because employees' eligibility for FMLA leave depends on how long they've worked for the company and how many hours they've worked, you must keep track of all employees' work hours. After all, an employee's eligibility can change over time. A newly hired full-time employee, for example, won't be eligible until he or she has worked for the company for at least 12 months. After a year, however, the employee may be eligible.

Likewise, an employee who qualified for FMLA leave in the past may not be eligible later on. Maybe the employee hasn't worked enough hours in the previous year or has already used up all his or her FMLA leave.

To make sure that an employee who requests leave is actually entitled to it, keep good records of actual hours worked—and leave taken—for all of your company's employees. If your company's records or a compensation agreement with the employee don't accurately reflect actual hours worked, your company will have to prove that the employee didn't work enough hours to qualify for FMLA leave. Even unpaid time worked by an employee (for example, overtime worked by an exempt employee who is not entitled to overtime pay) counts toward the 1,250-hour requirement, so it is important to keep thorough records of all time employees actually work, whether paid or not.

Most payroll systems provide a running total of hours worked by employees, so you may already have adequate records. If your company keeps time sheets or requires employees to punch a time clock, these records may provide all the documentation you need.

If you don't have some readily available source of documentation, the best practice is to keep a separate chart of hours worked for each employee. This isn't as complicated as it sounds. You can create a simple spreadsheet, like the one below, and update each employee's hours at the end of each pay period. If you have a payroll system, you may even be able to export those numbers directly. This book's companion page includes a downloadable copy of this form. See Appendix C for details on how to access the forms in this book.

SAMPLE 1:

FMLA Hours Worked

Employee Name: _____Employee A_____

Start date	Hours worked in the 12 months prior to requested leave	Dates FMLA leave taken
1/14/16	3,000	3/22/17 – 5/10/17

SAMPLE 2:

FMLA Hours Worked

Employee Name: _____Employee B_____

Start date	Hours worked in the 12 months prior to requested leave	Dates FMLA leave taken
4/25/18	300	Not eligible

Don't forget to track hours worked by employees who aren't entitled to earn overtime pay (called "exempt employees"). Many companies don't routinely record hours worked by exempt employees. After all, these employees are not typically paid by the hour, but instead must put in as many hours as it takes to get the job done.

Unless you have records showing the actual hours worked by exempt employees, however, you must assume that they have worked the required 1,250 hours as long as they've been employed for 12 months. You may also need to know the exact hours worked by an exempt employee if he or she wants to take intermittent or reduced-schedule leave. This type of leave is calculated as a reduction in the hours or days the employee typically works, so you can't figure out how much FMLA intermittent or reduced-schedule leave time an exempt employee is entitled to unless you know how many hours the employee has worked.

Managers' Flowchart: FMLA-Eligible Employees

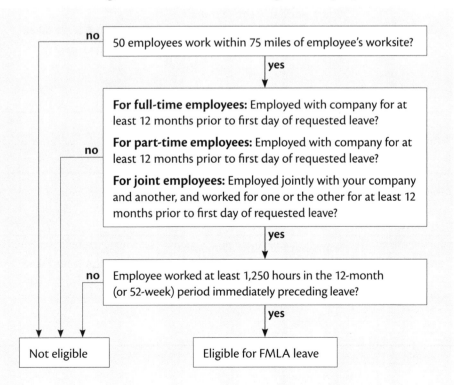

> **TIP**
> **Tracking exempt employees' hours won't change their exempt status.**
> One of the cardinal rules of wage and hour law is to avoid treating exempt employees like nonexempt employees. For example, if you dock an exempt employee's pay for showing up an hour late, you are treating that employee like an hourly worker—and the Department of Labor may require you to pay overtime to that employee and others who hold the same position. When it comes to tracking hours for FMLA purposes, however, you don't have to worry: You can keep records of an exempt employee's hours without inadvertently losing that employee's exemption status.

Common Mistakes Regarding Employee Eligibility—And How to Avoid Them

Mistake 1: **Denying FMLA leave to employees who are eligible, or granting it to those who are not eligible, because work hours aren't properly documented.**

Avoid this mistake by taking the following steps:
- Keep accurate records of employee work hours, including all time that counts toward the FMLA hours requirement (military leave, work hours for which the employee is not paid, and so on).
- Track hours for exempt employees, even if you don't do so for any other purpose.
- Create a chart that keeps a running total of each employee's hours that count toward FMLA eligibility, if your company doesn't have other records you can use for this purpose.

Mistake 2: **Misjudging an employee's eligibility by calculating company size, months worked, and hours worked at the wrong time.**

Avoid this mistake by taking the following steps:
- Calculate whether the employee's worksite has at least 50 employees within a 75-mile radius on the date the employee requests leave, not the date the employee's leave is scheduled to begin.

- Compute the months and hours worked by an employee requesting FMLA leave as of the date the requested leave will start, not the date the employee requests leave.

Mistake 3: Miscalculating how many months an employee has worked.

Avoid this mistake by taking the following steps:

- Count any week in which the employee showed up on your company's payroll.
- Count all time worked toward an employee's 12-month minimum; these months don't have to be consecutive, but don't count time worked before a break in service of seven years or more.
- Count time the employee spent on leave as time worked if your company paid compensation or provided benefits during the leave or the employee was on military leave.

Mistake 4: Miscounting hours worked.

Avoid this mistake by taking the following steps:

- Include all hours that count toward FMLA eligibility, including unpaid hours, compensable travel time, and time spent in continuing education.
- Exclude time spent on leave unless the employee was on military leave or your company counts leave time as hours worked for overtime purposes.
- Allow employees whose hours have dropped below the 1,250-hour minimum due to intermittent leave to continue taking leave for the same condition; if the employee needs leave for a new condition, you must redetermine the employee's eligibility.

Managers' Checklist: Is the Employee Eligible for FMLA Leave?

☐ There are 50 or more employees working within 75 miles of the leave-seeking employee's worksite.

    ☐ I counted telecommuting or other employees not physically present at the worksite where they report or where they receive work assignments.

    ☐ I measured the 75-mile radius based on the most direct surface travel routes, like roads, highways, and waterways.

    ☐ I counted all buildings within a reasonable geographic vicinity as a single worksite and measured the 75-mile radius from those buildings.

☐ The employee worked for the company for at least 12 months (or 52 weeks) prior to the first day of the requested leave.

    ☐ I counted the employee as working in any week in which the employee was on company payroll, even if the employee worked intermittently or part time.

    ☐ I counted the employee as working in any week in which the employee was on leave and getting pay or benefits from my company.

    ☐ I did not count the employee as working in any week in which the employee was suspended or should otherwise have been working but wasn't.

    ☐ I didn't count any time the employee worked prior to a break in service of seven or more years, unless the break was occasioned by National Guard or Reserve obligations or was pursuant to a written agreement indicating our intent to rehire the employee after the break.

☐ Company records show that the employee worked at least 1,250 hours in the 12 months prior to the first day of the requested leave.

    ☐ I counted only the hours that the employee actually worked, whether paid or not.

    ☐ Because my company does not count time on leave when calculating hours for overtime pay purposes, I did not count any hours that the employee was on leave.

    ☐ For airline flight crew employees, I did not apply the 1,250-hour rule, but instead made sure the employee worked or was paid for at least 60% of the monthly guarantee and at least 504 hours in the past 12 months.

Leave for a Serious Health Condition

Chapter Highlights

☆ The FMLA allows an eligible employee to take time off for his or her own serious health condition or to care for a family member who has a serious health condition.

☆ It's not your responsibility to diagnose employees; you just have to know enough about what qualifies as a "serious health condition" to realize when an employee requests or takes time off that might qualify for FMLA protection.

☆ There are six categories of serious health conditions:
- inpatient care
- incapacity for more than three days with continuing treatment by a health care provider
- incapacity relating to pregnancy or prenatal care
- chronic serious health conditions
- permanent or long-term incapacity, and
- certain kinds of conditions requiring multiple treatments.

☆ To take time off for his or her own serious health condition, an employee must be unable to perform the functions of his or her job.

☆ An employee may take time off to care for a spouse, parent, or child with a serious health condition. In-laws, domestic partners, siblings, grandparents, and other family members don't count under the FMLA (but may under state law).

☆ An employee is caring for a family member when the employee provides physical or psychological care, arranges for care or changes in care, provides necessary transportation, or fills in for other care providers.

Eligible employees are entitled to take FMLA leave for their own serious health conditions or to care for family members with serious health conditions. That sounds simple enough, but this has proven to be a fairly complicated standard to apply. Most of the controversy involves the definition of a serious health condition: which illnesses or conditions qualify, how long an employee has to be incapacitated to be eligible for leave, what happens when a minor problem turns into a serious condition, and so on.

This chapter untangles these complications and explains what qualifies as a serious health condition. We cover the definitions and eligibility criteria, and we provide checklists and charts to help you sort through the issues and figure out whether an employee might qualify for this type of FMLA leave.

Your Role in Identifying a Serious Health Condition

After learning that an employee's (or family member's) health condition must be "serious" for an employee to take FMLA leave—and that there's a complex legal definition for that word—some managers start to worry. After all, most managers aren't doctors, and their job responsibilities don't include diagnosing employees, let alone family members of employees. Is every manager going to have to learn how to read X-rays and lab results just to administer the FMLA?

Happily, the answer is no. It's not your job to determine whether an employee really does have a serious health condition; that's for doctors and other health care providers to decide. You simply have to know enough about how the FMLA defines a serious health condition to recognize when an employee's need for leave might be covered. If the FMLA applies, you'll need to give the employee required notices (see Chapter 8), formally designate the time off as FMLA leave (also covered in Chapter 8), and ask the employee to provide a medical certification from a health care provider confirming that the leave is for a serious health condition (see Chapter 9). But you'll only know that it's time to start this process if you're familiar enough with the categories of serious health conditions to recognize that the FMLA might be in play.

EXAMPLE: Cari tells you that she is pregnant. After congratulations and small talk, Cari says she has been having severe morning sickness and might need to take some time off—or, at least, come in late when she's really feeling crummy. Because you're reading this book, you immediately realize that the time off Cari is requesting could be FMLA protected. Should your next step be to question Cari closely about her symptoms, so you can decide whether she is truly incapacitated by her morning sickness?

No. You don't have the right to insist that Cari discuss this type of personal health information with you. (It could even be illegal under the laws of some states.) Instead, you should give Cari the required notices and paperwork to designate her time off as FMLA leave and ask her to provide a medical certification from her health care provider.

This doesn't mean that you have to blindly accept whatever the employee and his or her health care provider tell you, however. If, based on the information you receive, you question whether the employee (or family member) really has a serious health condition, you can request a second opinion (Chapter 9 explains how).

TIP
When an employee takes sick leave, workers' compensation leave, disability leave, or leave to care for a family member, always ask yourself whether the FMLA applies. An employee doesn't have to specifically request "FMLA" leave to be protected by the law: As long as the employee is eligible and takes time off for a covered reason, you should designate the time as FMLA leave. Chapter 8 explains how much information an employee has to provide and how to designate leave; for now, just remember that an employee who is taking another type of leave might also be covered by the FMLA.

What Is a Serious Health Condition?

To qualify for FMLA leave, an employee must have a serious health condition or have a family member with a serious health condition. To be eligible, the employee or family member must have an illness, injury, impairment, or physical or mental condition that involves:

- **inpatient care** at a hospital, hospice, or residential medical care facility
- **incapacity for more than three full calendar days** with continuing treatment by a health care provider
- incapacity due to **pregnancy or prenatal care**
- incapacity or treatment for a **chronic serious health condition**
- **permanent or long-term incapacity** for a condition for which treatment may not be effective (such as a terminal illness), or
- absence for **multiple treatments** for either (1) restorative surgery following an injury or accident, or (2) a condition that would require an absence of more than three days if not treated.

Multiple and Undiagnosed Conditions Count

The FMLA applies to ailments for which health care providers have been unable to offer a definitive diagnosis, as well as to incapacitation that is caused by multiple ailments, even if it doesn't (yet) have a name. As long as someone's medical situation fits into one of the categories above, it's a serious health condition.

Inpatient Care

This is probably the easiest category to recognize as a serious health condition. A condition that involves inpatient care—in other words, an overnight stay —at a hospital, hospice, or residential medical care facility qualifies as a serious health condition covered by the FMLA. An employee is entitled to FMLA leave for the time spent receiving inpatient care and for periods of incapacity or subsequent treatment connected to that inpatient care.

Lessons from the *Real World*

How long is an overnight stay?

Jeffrey Bonkowski worked as a wirecutter and machinist for Oberg Industries, Inc. Bonkowski, who had a number of health conditions, began feeling chest pain, dizziness, and shortness of breath during a meeting with his two supervisors at work. (The meeting was about his recent suspension for sleeping on the job.) Bonkowski left work after his supervisors agreed to continue the meeting the next day.

Bonkowski's wife took him to the hospital that evening, after his condition failed to improve at home. According to Bonkowski, he arrived at the hospital a few minutes before midnight on November 14, was admitted to the hospital early in the morning on the 15th, and was discharged in the early evening on the 15th. Oberg fired him for walking out of the meeting and failing to return to work the next day. Bonkowski sued, claiming that he was wrongfully terminated while on FMLA-protected leave.

Oberg argued that Bonkowski's time off wasn't covered by the FMLA because he hadn't stayed in the hospital overnight and therefore was not receiving inpatient care. The Court agreed, finding that an "overnight" stay requires the patient to stay at the hospital from one calendar day to the next and to spend a substantial amount of time in the hospital. The Court also decided that this time period was to be measured by the hospital's admitting records. Because the admitting records showed that Bonkowski had been admitted and discharged on the same calendar day, the Court threw out his FMLA claim.

Bonkowski v. Oberg Industries, Inc., 787 F.3d 190 (3d Cir. 2015).

A person is incapacitated by a serious medical condition if he or she is unable to work, attend school, or perform other regular daily activities due to the condition, treatment for the condition, or recovery from the condition. This means, for example, that an employee who was hospitalized for an appendectomy would be entitled to FMLA leave not only for the period of time spent in the hospital before, during, and after the operation, but also for time spent at home recuperating from the procedure.

Follow-up treatment after an inpatient stay is also protected. For example, if a person was hospitalized for surgery, return visits to the doctor for post-operative care would also be covered under the FMLA. The person doesn't have to be incapacitated by the treatment or be out for more than three days: As long as the subsequent treatment is connected to the condition requiring inpatient care, it's covered.

> **EXAMPLE:** Jesse takes a nasty fall while cleaning the gutters on his roof and suffers a major concussion. He goes to the emergency room, where they keep him overnight for observation. He spends the next day at home resting, then returns to work. By midmorning, he has a crashing headache. He calls his doctor, who advises him to come in immediately to be checked for complications. All of Jesse's time off—in the hospital, at home, and at the doctor's office—is covered by the FMLA.
>
> If Jesse had never suffered a concussion but simply got a bad headache at work and decided to go to the doctor, his time off might not be protected by the FMLA. Because it isn't subsequent treatment following an inpatient stay, it doesn't qualify as this type of serious health condition. Depending on what the medical cause is, how long the problem lasts, and what type of treatment he gets, however, it might fall into one of the other categories of serious health conditions.

Incapacity for More Than Three Days Plus Continuing Treatment

Someone who is incapacitated for more than three days *and* requires continuing treatment from a health care provider also has a serious health condition under the FMLA. This category of serious health condition has been the most difficult for employers to understand and administer, and it's easy to see why. It covers a lot of gray area because it marks the dividing line between minor ailments such as colds and stomachaches (which are usually not covered by the FMLA; see "Conditions That Are Not Typically Covered," below) and more serious problems that are obviously protected (like a terminal illness or nonelective surgery).

To figure out whether an ailment fits into this category, you must understand how to measure the three-day requirement, who qualifies as a health care provider, and what constitutes continuing treatment.

The "More Than Three-Days" Requirement

To qualify under this category, the employee (or employee's family member) must be incapacitated for *more* than three full consecutive days. The days must be consecutive, but they need not be business days. An employee who is incapacitated Friday through Monday would qualify, for example.

It's not entirely clear what constitutes "more than" three days. Some courts have found that an employee must be incapacitated for at least four days to qualify; others have found that an employee who is sick for any more than 72 hours is covered. Because of this confusion, the best practice is to assume that an employee who is incapacitated for more than 72 hours is covered.

Who Is a Health Care Provider?

Health care providers are defined quite broadly by the FMLA. They include not only medical doctors, but also:

- doctors of osteopathy
- podiatrists
- dentists
- optometrists
- chiropractors (only for manual manipulation of the spine to treat a subluxation of the spine—that is, misalignment of vertebrae—identified by X-ray)
- clinical psychologists
- physician assistants
- nurse providers
- nurse midwives
- clinical social workers, and
- Christian Science providers.

Health care providers who practice outside of the United States also qualify, as long as they are authorized to practice within the laws of the country where they work and the services they provide are within the scope of that authorized practice.

Finally, any health care provider from whom the employer or the employer's group health plan will accept certification of a serious health condition for purposes of substantiating a claim for health care benefits also qualifies. In other words, if your company treats someone as a health care provider for purposes of allowing or disallowing health insurance claims, it must treat that person as a health care provider under the FMLA.

> **EXAMPLE:** Your company's health care plan accepts certifications from chiropractors documenting a wide variety of employee injuries and ailments, including repetitive stress disorders, spinal problems, and neck injuries. Steven sees his chiropractor for pain in his wrists and forearms. After performing a series of tests and physical manipulations, the chiropractor determines that Steven has carpal tunnel syndrome. The chiropractor gives Steven some exercises, gives him braces to wear, and advises him not to do any typing or other activities that will cause strain for three weeks.
>
> Steven asks for FMLA leave and gives you a medical certification from his chiropractor. Because Steven's chiropractor didn't take any X-rays and isn't treating Steven for subluxation of the spine, you intend to tell Steven that he has to get a medical certification from a different type of health care provider.
>
> But wait: Your company's health care plan accepts certifications from chiropractors not just regarding subluxation of the spine, but on a broader variety of conditions and ailments. As a result, Steven's chiropractor qualifies as a health care provider under the FMLA, even though he doesn't meet the usual criteria for chiropractors. If you question whether Steven's condition qualifies as a serious health condition, you are free to request a second opinion (as explained in Chapter 9).

How Much Treatment Is Required

An employee who's out sick for more than three days does not necessarily have a serious health condition under the FMLA. To qualify in this category, the employee's (or family member's) condition must also involve continuing treatment by a health care provider.

Because "continuing treatment" is open to some interpretation, the FMLA regulations provide two definitions. One of the following must be true for the employee or family member to meet the continuing treatment requirement:

- The employee or family member has had at least two treatments by a health care provider, a nurse under the direct supervision of a health care provider, or a provider of health care services under order of, or on referral by, a health care provider. Both treatments must take place within 30 days of the first day of incapacity, absent extenuating circumstances, and the first treatment must take place within seven days of the first day of incapacity. (Extenuating circumstances might include that the provider has no available appointments within the 30-day period.)

- The employee or family member has had at least one treatment by a health care provider, resulting in a regimen of continuing treatment under the provider's supervision. Again, the treatment must take place within seven days of the first day of incapacity.

For both of these definitions, "treatment" means an actual in-person visit to the health care provider, not a telephone call or email exchange. And, in both cases, the necessity of treatment visits or a regimen of continuing treatment must be determined by the health care provider. In other words, the patient's decision to make a second appointment within the 30-day period doesn't convert a minor ailment into a serious health condition.

A continuing regimen of treatment refers only to treatments that require the participation of a health care provider. For example, taking prescription medications or engaging in therapies that require special equipment (such as an oxygen tank) qualify as a regimen of continuing treatment. However, taking over-the-counter medications or staying in bed does not—even if that's just what the doctor ordered—because you could have made these decisions on your own.

> EXAMPLE 1: John has a sore throat, stuffy nose, and cough. He calls his HMO's advice line, and a nurse provider tells him that there's a nasty cold going around and that he should stay in bed and drink lots of water. John doesn't have a serious health condition: He didn't visit the doctor at all, and he isn't following a continuing regimen of treatment.
>
> EXAMPLE 2: Consuela has the same symptoms as John and goes home sick late Tuesday morning. Her symptoms worsen, and she decides to visit her doctor on Thursday. The doctor finds that she has strep throat and prescribes a ten-day

course of antibiotics. Consuela is down for the count until Saturday evening, when she starts to feel better. Consuela has a serious health condition: She was incapacitated for more than three days, visited her doctor once, and had a continuing regimen of treatment.

EXAMPLE 3: Because most of her employees have been sick, Marta finally comes down with the dreaded bug. Marta had several bouts with pneumonia as a child, so she goes to her doctor as soon as she realizes that she's sick. The doctor finds that she doesn't yet have pneumonia, but he also doesn't like the way her lungs sound. Marta doesn't want to take antibiotics unless it's absolutely necessary, so her doctor asks her to come back for a follow-up appointment in several days to make sure her lungs have cleared up. At the second visit, Marta sounds fine; she returns to work after four days off. Marta has a serious health condition: She was incapacitated for more than three days, and she made two visits to the doctor.

Lessons from the *Real World*

Leave necessary to determine that a condition isn't serious might be protected by the FMLA.

James Woodman was a truck driver for Miesel Sysco Food Services. When Woodman suffered chest pains, he went to his doctor, who recommended a series of tests to determine their source and whether Woodman had suffered a heart attack. The doctor also recommended that Woodman take time off until the problem was diagnosed.

Ultimately, the tests showed that Woodman had not suffered a heart attack. His celebration was short-lived, however: Soon afterwards, the company fired him for taking unauthorized leave. Because he didn't have a heart attack, the company said, he also didn't have a serious health condition, so his absence wasn't covered by the FMLA.

The Michigan Court of Appeals disagreed with the company's conclusion, however. The FMLA's definition of treatment includes examinations to determine whether a serious health condition exists, which is precisely what Woodson required, as determined by his doctor.

Woodman v. Miesel Sysco Food Service Co., 657 N.W.2d 122 (Mich. App. 2002).

Pregnancy or Prenatal Care

Incapacity due to pregnancy or for prenatal care qualifies as a serious health condition. The employee need not be out for more than three days nor actually visit a doctor to fall into this category. As long as she is unable to work or perform other regular, daily activities because of her pregnancy, she has a serious health condition. For example, a woman who suffers severe morning sickness or is ordered by her doctor to spend the last month of her pregnancy on bed rest qualifies under this part of the definition.

Visits to the doctor for prenatal care also fall within this category. The woman need not be incapacitated or suffering from medical complications to qualify; even routine check-ups qualify for leave.

Lessons from the *Real World*

Back pain, morning sickness, and pregnancy-related migraines add up to a serious health condition.

Charity Wierman claimed that she was fired from her job as manager of a convenience store for taking time off that was protected under the FMLA. Wierman was pregnant and suffered from back pain, morning sickness, and pregnancy-related migraines. The court found that this was sufficient evidence to put her employer on notice that she had a serious health condition and that her absences might be protected by the FMLA.

Ultimately, Wierman lost her FMLA claim, however. Although she was fired shortly after her employer gave her FMLA paperwork to complete, her employer showed that she was fired not for her time off, but for stealing company property: consuming the pastries and fountain drinks that the store sold. *Wierman v. Casey's General Stores*, 638 F.3d 984 (8th Cir. 2011).

Chronic Serious Health Condition

Chronic serious health conditions are also covered by the FMLA. A chronic serious health condition:

- requires periodic visits for treatment, defined by regulation as at least two visits per year with a health care provider or nurse acting under a provider's supervision
- continues over an extended period of time, and
- may cause episodic, rather than continuing, incapacity.

These conditions needn't cause incapacity for more than three days, nor must they involve continuing treatment. Instead, this category is intended to encompass long-lasting conditions that require ongoing management and treatment, such as diabetes, epilepsy, or asthma.

> EXAMPLE: Raymond has multiple sclerosis (MS), a disease of the central nervous system that can cause loss of vision, extreme fatigue, muscle weakness, loss of coordination, and other neurological problems. He sees his doctor every three months. He is generally able to care for himself and work, with the help of a cane to walk steadily and medications to control his symptoms. On occasion, however, his symptoms become more severe and confine him to his bed. Raymond's daughter, Cheryl, requests time off to care for her father when his symptoms become exacerbated. Is her leave protected by the FMLA?
>
> Most likely, assuming she meets the requirements for caring for a family member (discussed below). Because Raymond's MS requires periodic treatment, is a permanent condition, and causes episodic incapacity, it qualifies as a chronic serious health condition.

Some mental conditions—such as major depression and bipolar disorder—might also qualify under this category. Often, these conditions are long-term, episodic, and require ongoing treatment, but they can be largely controlled with medication. Again, you won't have to make the final call; you'll just need to recognize the possibility when the employee requests leave.

Permanent or Long-Term Incapacity

Someone who is incapacitated permanently or for the long term by a condition that is not necessarily amenable to treatment has a serious health condition, as long as he or she is under the supervision of a health care provider. Actual treatment is not required to qualify under this part of the definition; it is enough that the person's care is supervised by a health care provider.

Examples of conditions that might fall into this category are Alzheimer's disease, terminal cancer, or advanced amyotrophic lateral sclerosis (also known as ALS or Lou Gehrig's disease).

Multiple Treatments

Someone who is absent for multiple treatments has a serious health condition if the treatments are for:
- restorative surgery after an accident or injury, or
- a condition that would require an absence of more than three days if not treated.

Examples of conditions that might qualify in the first subcategory include surgery to reset a broken limb or repair a torn ligament. The second subcategory includes treatments for severe arthritis, dialysis for kidney disease, and cancer treatment. (Of course, cancer might qualify as a serious health condition under other categories as well—for example, if hospitalization and/or surgery were required.)

> EXAMPLE: Geri has been diagnosed with breast cancer. She had a lumpectomy and is undergoing chemotherapy. Every Tuesday afternoon, she goes in for treatment. The treatment takes several hours, and she often feels too nauseated to return to work afterward. As her therapy progresses, her reaction to the treatment becomes more severe; she sometimes has to take all or part of Wednesday off, and sometimes she even feels sick Monday afternoon and Tuesday morning, in anticipation of her treatment. All of this time—the time she actually spends getting chemotherapy and the time during which she is incapacitated by her treatment—is FMLA-protected leave.

Substance Abuse

Substance abuse may qualify as a serious health condition, if it meets one of the definitions described above. However, the employee may not take FMLA-protected leave for the effects of substance abuse (for example, because the employee is using drugs or hung over). The company is only required to provide FMLA leave for treatment by a health care provider or a provider of health care services on referral by a health care provider.

An employee who takes FMLA leave while getting treatment for substance abuse may not be fired solely for taking FMLA leave; that would violate the law. However, if the employer has an established, communicated policy providing that employees may be fired for substance abuse, and it applies the policy consistently to all employees, it may fire an employee for substance abuse even if the employee is out on FMLA leave seeking treatment.

Although the FMLA does not prohibit you from firing an employee for substance abuse even if the employee is seeking treatment, state law may. In California, for example, employers with at least 25 employees must allow employees to take time off to enter rehabilitation treatment as a reasonable accommodation. Before you terminate an employee who is on leave for rehab or other treatment for substance abuse, it's a good idea to get some legal advice.

Conditions That Are Not Typically Covered

The FMLA does not create hard-and-fast rules that particular illnesses or diseases are always, or never, serious health conditions. Instead, the facts of each situation are considered individually. After all, one person might breeze through a bout of bronchitis without missing more than a day of work but another with the same illness might have to be hospitalized for complications. In this situation, the first person would not have a serious health condition, but the second would.

Is It a Serious Health Condition?		
Category	**Requirements**	**Examples**
Inpatient treatment	Overnight stay in a hospital, hospice, or residential medical care facility	Inpatient surgery Hospitalization Overnight hospital stay for observation
Incapacity for more than 3 days and continuing treatment	Incapacity for more than three days and either: • at least two visits to a health care provider within 30 days, or • one visit to a health care provider and an ongoing regimen of treatment	Pneumonia Migraine Chicken pox Mononucleosis Viral infection
Pregnancy/ prenatal care	Incapacity due to pregnancy or prenatal care	Severe morning sickness Doctor's appointments for prenatal care, including OB-GYN visits, sonograms, visits or treatment for complications of pregnancy Medically required bed rest
Chronic serious health conditions	Condition that: • requires periodic visits for treatment (at least two per year) • continues over an extended period of time, and • may cause episodic, rather than continuing, incapacity	Epilepsy Asthma Diabetes Multiple sclerosis Sickle cell anemia
Permanent/ long-term incapacity	Permanent or long-term incapacity, under the supervision of a health care provider	Cancer Alzheimer's disease Stroke ALS
Multiple treatments	Treatments for: • restorative surgery after an accident or injury, or • a condition that would require an absence of more than three days if not treated	Arthritis treatment Dialysis Chemotherapy Radiation therapy Surgery to reset a broken bone, repair a torn ligament, or treat burns

Nevertheless, there are certain ailments that don't typically qualify as serious health conditions. These include:

- cosmetic treatments (other than for restorative purposes), unless complications arise or inpatient care is required
- colds and flu
- earaches
- upset stomachs and minor ulcers
- headaches other than migraines, and
- routine dental or orthodontic problems or periodontal disease.

This doesn't mean you can automatically exclude these conditions from FMLA coverage. It depends on the facts. One person's headache might be the result of eye strain or sinus congestion; another's might be a symptom of a brain tumor. Breast enhancement plastic surgery would not be covered if it is purely cosmetic, but reconstructive surgery after a mastectomy or breast reduction surgery necessary to relieve severe back pain, is likely covered.

Leave for Employee's Own Serious Health Condition

When an employee takes time off for his or her own serious health condition, an additional qualification applies: The employee must not only have a serious health condition as defined above, but must also be unable to perform the functions of his or her job.

An employee is unable to perform the functions of the position if the employee cannot work at all or cannot perform one or more of the essential functions of the job, as defined by the Americans with Disabilities Act (ADA). Under the ADA, essential functions are the fundamental duties of the position: those tasks that the person holding the job absolutely must be able to do.

It can be tough to figure out which job duties are essential, unless you already have a job description that designates those functions. If you don't, you'll need to consider which functions are absolutely necessary to doing the job successfully and which are not.

RESOURCE

Need help drafting job descriptions? For detailed guidance on identifying a job's essential functions and using them to create a legal, effective job description, see *The Job Description Handbook*, by Margie Mader-Clark (Nolo).

The Equal Employment Opportunity Commission (EEOC), the federal agency that enforces the ADA, looks at the following factors in determining whether a function is essential:

- the employer's own assessment of which functions are essential, as demonstrated by job descriptions written before the employer posts or advertises for the position (this caveat is intended to discourage employers from designating essential functions solely to disqualify particular applicants with disabilities from holding the job)
- whether the position exists to perform that function
- the experience of workers who actually hold that position
- the time spent performing that function
- the consequences of not performing that function
- whether other employees are available to perform that function, and
- the degree of expertise or skill required to perform the function.

If an employee must be out of work to receive treatment for a serious health condition (for example, for prenatal care, nonelective surgery, or a doctor's appointment for follow-up care), the employee is considered unable to work for that period of time.

EXAMPLE: Clara tore a ligament in her leg while playing soccer. She had surgery to repair the ligament, and her doctor told her not to walk much on that leg for several weeks. Clara is a receptionist for a large company. Her job involves greeting visitors, answering phones, receiving packages and mail, and so on. Because Clara can perform the essential functions of her job while seated at her desk, she probably isn't eligible to take several weeks off under the FMLA. Although the time she actually spends in surgery and follow-up care would be covered, the weeks of recovery would not.

If Clara's job duties required her to walk around the building—for example, to collect or deliver mail, get refreshments for visitors, and so on—the company would have to decide whether these are essential duties or not, using the criteria listed above. If Clara held a much more physical job (for example, if she worked as a bike messenger or a laborer in a warehouse), she would clearly be unable to perform her job's essential duties and would be entitled to FMLA leave.

 RELATED TOPIC

Other laws may apply. An employee's serious health condition might also qualify as a disability under the Americans with Disabilities Act (ADA) and similar state laws, and/or it might be the result of an on-the-job injury that's covered by workers' compensation. Chapter 12 explains what these laws require and how they might overlap with the FMLA.

Leave for a Family Member's Serious Health Condition

An employee is also entitled to take leave to care for a family member who has a serious health condition, as defined above. To figure out whether an employee qualifies for this type of leave, however, you must also understand which family members are covered by this provision of the law and how the FMLA defines "caring for" a family member.

Who Is a Family Member Under the FMLA

An employee may take time off to care for a spouse, child, or parent with a serious health condition. Here is how the FMLA defines these terms for this provision; different definitions apply to military family leave (see Chapter 6):

- **Spouse.** A spouse is a husband or wife to whom the employee is legally married—domestic partners or live-in partners aren't covered. Same-sex spouses and common law spouses are covered, as long as the marriage was valid in the state where it took place. Those who married out of the country may take FMLA leave for a spouse as long as the marriage was valid in the country where it took place, and it could have been entered into in at least one state.

CAUTION

The FMLA doesn't cover domestic partners, but state law might. Some states' family and medical leave laws cover more family members. For example, the California Family Rights Act (CFRA) allows employees to take time off to care for a domestic partner. Consider both the FMLA and your state's law when evaluating an employee's request for leave. Chapter 11 and Appendix A cover this issue in more detail.

- **Child.** An employee may take FMLA leave to care for a biological child, adopted child, stepchild, foster child, or legal ward with a serious health condition. An employee may also take time off to care for a child for whom the employee intends to assume or has assumed the role of parent by providing day-to-day care or financial support. No biological, adoptive, or formal legal relationship is necessary. (In legal terms, this is called serving "in loco parentis," or in the place of a parent.) Children are covered only until they reach the age of 18, unless they are incapable of taking care of themselves because of a physical or mental disability. These criteria must be assessed as of the date leave is scheduled to begin; if the child is under 18 on that day, the employee is entitled to leave.

  > **EXAMPLE:** Sarah's sister, Frances, is a single mother. After being convicted of selling drugs, Frances was sentenced to three years in prison. While Frances is serving her time, Sarah is taking care of Frances's son, Terry. Terry gets the measles, and Sarah asks for FMLA leave to care for him. Because Sarah is Terry's aunt, and nephews aren't covered by the FMLA, you deny her request. Did you do the right thing?
  >
  > No. Although Sarah is Terry's aunt, she is also assuming a parental role while Frances is in prison. This relationship is covered by the FMLA.

- **Parent.** An employee may take FMLA leave to care for his or her biological parent, adoptive parent, stepparent, or foster parent with a serious health condition. This right also extends to time off to care for someone who stood in loco parentis to the employee when the employee was a child, whether or not that person has a biological, adoptive, or legal relationship with the child. For example, an employee may take time off to care for a grandmother who provided day-to-day parental care for the employee as a child. In-laws are not covered.

We Are Family—Not!

Contrary to the famous song by Sister Sledge, sisters and brothers do not qualify as family members under the FMLA (unless they are "next of kin" to a covered servicemember, as explained in Chapter 6). This means an employee may not take FMLA leave to care for a seriously ill sibling unless the employee has acted as a child or parent to the sibling. For example, an employee who raised her younger brothers and sisters after their parents died would probably be entitled to take FMLA leave to care for them. Your state might have a leave law that covers siblings, however; see Appendix A.

Proving a Family Relationship

Employers are entitled to request reasonable documentation confirming that a familial relationship exists when an employee takes leave to care for a family member. This proof might be in the form of a birth certificate, papers documenting the placement of a foster child, or simply a written statement from the employee (this might be the only documentation an employee has regarding a common law spouse or a child for whom the employee acts as a parent, for example). If the employee provides an official document as evidence, the company must return it to the employee.

We have provided a form you can use to request this confirmation. A sample appears below; you can find an electronic version of this form at this book's online companion page; see Appendix C for details. (The form we provide includes the additional family members for whom the employee may be able to take military family leave; see Chapter 6 for more information.)

Caring for a Family Member

To take FMLA leave to care for a family member, it isn't enough that the employee takes time off to spend with a family member, even if the family member is gravely ill: The employee must actually provide care. For purposes of the FMLA, care includes:

FMLA Leave to Care for a Family Member

I, ____Jerry Singer____ , have requested time off work to care for __Melissa Singer__ . I have read the definitions below and I confirm that this person qualifies as my ___child___ .

I have attached a copy of the following documents confirming this relationship:

Birth certificate

(*List any documents you can provide, such as a birth certificate, papers confirming an adoption or foster care placement, marriage certificate, next of kin designation, and so on. If you don't have any documents, please write that in the space provided.*)

Date:____10-10-xx____   Signature: *Jerry Singer* _____

Definitions

Spouse: A husband or wife to whom you are legally married.

Parent: Your legal parent, or someone who had day-to-day responsibility for supporting you financially or taking care of you when you were a child.

Child: Your biological child, adopted child, stepchild, foster child, or legal ward, or a child whom you have the day-to-day responsibility to support financially or take care of.

- In the case of leave for a serious health condition, children qualify only until they reach the age of 18, unless they are incapable of taking care of themselves because of a physical or mental disability.
- In the case of leave for a qualifying exigency or military caregiver leave, children of any age qualify.

Next of kin: You qualify as next of kin to a covered servicemember, for purposes of military caregiver leave, if:

- you are a blood relative to a servicemember who has designated you as next of kin for purposes of military caregiver leave, or
- if the servicemember has not designated anyone next of kin and you are the nearest blood relative to a servicemember, other than a parent, spouse, or child. For purposes of determining who is the nearest blood relative, everyone in the highest applicable level of priority qualifies, as follows:
  - blood relatives who have been granted legal custody of the servicemember
  - siblings
  - grandparents
  - aunts and uncles, and
  - first cousins.

- **physical care** (such as changing bandages, administering medication, preparing meals, helping with hygiene, assisting with physical therapy or exercise, and so on)
- **psychological care** (providing comfort and reassurance to a family member who is hospitalized or bedridden at home, for example)
- **providing necessary transportation** (to doctor's appointments, for example)
- **arranging for care or changes in care** (for example, making arrangements for a family member to move into an assisted living facility or hiring home health care aides to care for a family member), and
- **filling in for others providing care** (an employee might provide care two days a week, when the family member's usual caregiver takes time off, or might share caretaking responsibilities with other family members).

Lessons from the *Real World*

Son may take FMLA leave to help his sister decide whether to remove their mother from life support.

Charles Romans was a fire and safety officer at a Michigan home for juvenile delinquent boys. He requested time off under the FMLA to go to the hospital where his mother was a patient and help his sister decide whether to remove his mother from life support. His employer denied him time off, and the district court upheld this decision. The court found that he didn't need to provide care because his sister was already doing so.

The federal Court of Appeals for the 6th Circuit disagreed, however. The Court of Appeals relied on the FMLA regulations, which state that an employee can qualify as "needed to provide care" for a family member, even if other family members are also available to do so. The Court of Appeals also pointed out that FMLA leave is available to make arrangements for changes in care, not merely to provide physical care. As the Court put it, "A decision regarding whether an ill mother should stay on life support would logically be encompassed by 'arrangements for changes in care.' To be sure, this is the kind of decision, like transfer to a nursing home, that few people would relish making without the help of other family members, and the regulations do not force them to do so."

Romans v. Michigan Dept. of Human Services, 668 F.3d 826 (6th Cir. 2012).

Lessons from the *Real World*

Calling on the phone does not constitute care.

H. Charles Tellis worked for Alaska Airlines in Seattle as a maintenance mechanic. He told his manager that he needed a couple of weeks off because his wife was having difficulties with her pregnancy. The manager suggested that he take FMLA leave and told him to pick up the appropriate forms at the company's benefits office.

Tellis started his leave and requested the forms. The next day, his car broke down. He decided to fly to Atlanta, where he owned another car, and drive back home. This trip took him four days. While he was gone, his wife gave birth; his sister-in-law took care of the family while he was gone. Alaska Airlines eventually terminated Tellis's employment, based in part on his absence.

Tellis sued, arguing that his time off was covered by the FMLA because he was caring for his wife. The 9th Circuit Court of Appeals disagreed: It found that he did not provide any actual care while he was on his trip. Although Tellis claimed that he gave his wife moral support and comfort by phoning her from the road, the court found that this was not what the FMLA means by caretaking.

Tellis v. Alaska Airlines, 414 F.3d 1045 (9th Cir. 2005).

Unless it is needed for the family member's comfort and assurance, simply spending time with a family member does not qualify as care. For example, an employee who takes time off to visit his ailing parents would not be entitled to FMLA leave unless he was needed to actually care for his parents while there.

The employee need not be the only person or the only family member available to provide care. For example, an employee could take time off to care for her son who suffered a serious injury on active duty, even if the son's wife was also available to care for him.

TIP

"Kin care" laws may also apply. Some states allow employees to take time off to care for a seriously ill family member or to take a family member to appointments with the doctor or dentist. Often called "kin care" laws, some of these statutes allow an employee to take unpaid leave for this purpose, while others require employers to allow employees to use their own sick leave for these types of time off.

Managers' Flowchart: Serious Health Conditions

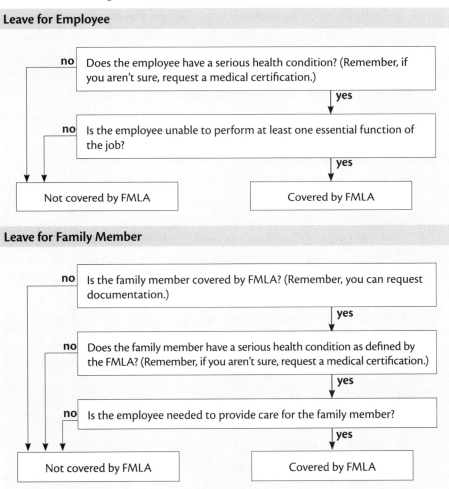

Leave for Employee

no — Does the employee have a serious health condition? (Remember, if you aren't sure, request a medical certification.)

yes

no — Is the employee unable to perform at least one essential function of the job?

yes

Not covered by FMLA

Covered by FMLA

Leave for Family Member

no — Is the family member covered by FMLA? (Remember, you can request documentation.)

yes

no — Does the family member have a serious health condition as defined by the FMLA? (Remember, if you aren't sure, request a medical certification.)

yes

no — Is the employee needed to provide care for the family member?

yes

Not covered by FMLA

Covered by FMLA

Common Mistakes Regarding Serious Health Conditions—And How to Avoid Them

Mistake 1: Denying FMLA leave for conditions that are covered.

Avoid this mistake by taking the following steps:

- Ask an employee to submit certification (see Chapter 9) whenever a serious health condition might be present. It's not your job to diagnose a serious health condition: Leave that to the health care provider.

- Remember that seemingly minor ailments can be serious health conditions. Even colds, stomachaches, and dental problems can qualify as serious health conditions if they meet the criteria.
- Keep in mind that the "more than three-days rule" doesn't apply to every type of serious health condition. An employee with a chronic serious health condition or pregnancy complications is entitled to leave even if the employee isn't incapacitated for more than three days in a row.

Mistake 2: **Denying FMLA leave to care for covered family members.**

Avoid this mistake by taking the following steps:

- Ask the employee to provide documentation of the familial relationship.
- Understand that "parents" and "children" refer not only to legal parents and children, but also to those whom the employee takes care of or who took care of the employee when he or she was a child.
- Don't distinguish between biological children and adopted or foster children.

Mistake 3: **Failing to designate time off for an illness, injury, or disability as FMLA leave, if appropriate.**

Avoid this mistake by taking the following steps:

- Make it your practice to automatically think of the FMLA when an employee takes time off for any physical or mental ailment. If it is a serious health condition, you will want to designate that time as FMLA leave.
- Consider whether an employee who goes out with a workers' comp injury is covered by the FMLA. (The answer will almost always be "yes," for reasons explained in Chapter 12.)

Leave for a New Child

Chapter Highlights

☆ Eligible female and male employees are equally entitled to take parenting leave under the FMLA for the birth, adoption, or foster placement of a child.

☆ Female or male employees who adopt or serve as foster parents of a child may take FMLA leave to:
- attend adoption or foster proceedings
- attend counseling sessions
- meet with attorneys
- meet with doctors
- attend court hearings, or
- attend to other placement-related matters.

☆ You can request documents certifying an employee is a new biological, adoptive, or foster parent before granting parenting leave.

☆ Employees must conclude their parenting leave within one year of the date of birth, adoption, or foster placement of the child.

☆ Married parents who work for the same company are entitled to a combined 12 weeks of leave for the birth, adoption, or foster placement of their child. This limit doesn't apply to unmarried parents, who are each entitled to a full 12 weeks of parenting leave.

Your professional experience likely confirms what studies show: Providing parenting leave enhances employee loyalty, morale, and productivity. Perhaps this is one reason why the parenting leave provisions of the FMLA have generated so little controversy and have resulted in relatively few complaints to the Department of Labor. Employers and employees alike benefit when employees are able to take some time off to care for a new child.

But, just because nearly everyone agrees on the value of parenting leave doesn't mean that everyone understands exactly how the rules work. The basic parenting leave provision of the FMLA provides that qualifying employees of either sex are entitled to up to 12 weeks of leave for the birth, adoption, or foster placement of a child. As with other parts of the FMLA, however, things get more complicated when you take a closer look at the details.

Some of the confusion surrounds the definition of "parent" and "spouse," while some is a result of the interplay between parenting leave and medical leave related to pregnancy or caring for ill children. For example, a female employee may request leave for the birth of her child, as well as leave for a pregnancy-related medical condition—two different categories under the FMLA, which can affect when the female employee is entitled to take leave. On top of these complications, if a child's parents work for the same company, the FMLA treats married parents and unmarried parents differently.

In response to the confusion on the part of employers and employees about who qualifies as a "parent" under the FMLA, the Department of Labor provides clarification. Under the FMLA, a "parent" includes a biological parent, adoptive parent, stepparent, foster parent, or anyone who stands "in loco parentis." Essentially, this last category covers anyone who assumes the status of parent toward a child by taking on parental duties. No legal recognition of the parent/child relationship (such as a birth certificate, adoption decree, or foster placement document) or blood relationship is required. In short, if an employee takes on or intends to take on the role of parent in a child's life, even a child not related to the employee or the employee's spouse, that employee is a "parent" for FMLA leave purposes. And, this is true even if both of the child's biological or legal parents are present in the child's life. As the DOL puts it, the FMLA regulations do not limit the number of parents a child may have for FMLA purposes!

Who Is a Parent Under the FMLA?

Under the DOL's clarification, a "parent" is anyone who intends to act and/or does act as a child's parent. An employee meeting this definition is entitled to take the birth, adoption, and foster placement leave described in this chapter, as well as leave to care for a child suffering from a serious medical condition (covered in Chapter 4). The question of who qualifies as a parent ultimately depends on the particular facts of the situation. The main factors to be considered when an employee claims parental status are:

- the age of the child
- the degree to which the child is dependent on the employee
- the amount of support (either financial, day-to-day care, or both) the employee provides to the child, and
- the extent to which the employee exercises duties commonly associated with parenthood.

This means that an employee whose same-sex partner gives birth to, adopts, or fosters a child may be a parent of that child, in addition to the child's two biological parents, and/or the spouse of the opposite sex biological parent. The key factor is the intent of any of the nonbiological parents to take on the status of the child's parent. Some examples of potential parents for FMLA purposes include:

- unmarried same- or opposite-sex partners of biological, adoptive, or foster parents
- grandparents or other relatives of the child, and
- same-sex spouses.

Of course, an employee who simply agrees to babysit for his or her partner's child while the partner is on vacation will not be considered a parent under the FMLA if the employee does not generally take on parental duties on a day-to-day basis.

This chapter explains the FMLA's parental leave entitlement. It covers leave for birth, adoption, and placement of a foster child; timing requirements; and how to calculate leave rights when an employee needs both parenting leave and leave for a serious health condition. This chapter also describes the rules that apply when both parents work for your company.

Leave for Birth

Any employee defined as a "parent" under the FMLA is entitled to leave for the birth of a child. Parental leave for the birth of a child isn't limited to the birth itself; it's also for bonding with and caring for the newborn. And in contrast with leave for a serious medical condition, employees requesting parenting leave don't have to show that the child is ill or requires care.

At times, it can be hard to distinguish between parenting leave and leave for a serious medical condition, such as when an employee needs leave because of a serious medical condition associated with her pregnancy or childbirth or when a newborn becomes ill. This chapter shows you how to draw this distinction in situations when you might have to do so.

Multiple Births in the Same Year

An employee who has more than one child in the same year does not get additional leave. For example, if an employee gives birth to twins, she does not get 12 weeks of FMLA parenting leave for each child. She gets 12 weeks total.

As discussed further below, employees taking parenting leave are not entitled to intermittent or reduced-schedule leave, so a parent can't divide up his or her leave time, unless your company agrees. For example, a father who had two children at different times in the year (perhaps with two different mothers) can't take six weeks of leave for each birth; he would be entitled only to 12 weeks at once.

Conditions That Don't Count

When an employee's child is stillborn or the mother miscarries, the FMLA does not provide for parenting leave. Of course, if the employee is the mother, she may have serious medical and/or psychological conditions that entitle her to take FMLA leave.

TIP
It's okay to show compassion, as long as you are consistent. When you know that an employee has suffered a loss or trauma, it is both decent and natural to extend sympathetic treatment. Some companies voluntarily offer bereavement leave, for example, even though it isn't required by the FMLA. If your company offers extra leave or benefits in difficult times, such as relaxation of attendance or punctuality rules, just be sure to offer the same treatment to all employees in similar circumstances.

If an employee needs leave to care for a sick newborn or for a wife or partner who is suffering from pregnancy-related illness, that's a request for leave to care for a family member with a serious health condition, not a request for parenting leave. Leave for serious health conditions is covered in Chapter 4.

Leave for Adoption

In addition to biological parents, adoptive parents are entitled to leave to spend time with a newly adopted child or to deal with the adoption process. Often, an employee in this situation needs time off before the adoption is finalized, for example, to attend court proceedings, meetings with attorneys, counseling sessions, consultations with doctors, or for other matters related to the adoption process. The FMLA allows an employee to take this time off (provided other eligibility requirements are also met). The employee is entitled to adoption leave whether the adoption is conducted through a licensed placement agency, private arrangement, or otherwise.

Leave for Placement of a Foster Child

A new or soon-to-be foster parent is also entitled to FMLA leave to spend time with the foster child and to deal with the foster placement process. Foster care is 24-hour care of a child by someone other than the child's parent or guardian. Foster placement is made either by an agreement between the state and the foster parent or by court order. In either case, the state must be involved for a child's placement to qualify as foster care under the FMLA. Informal custody arrangements, even for emergency child care, don't qualify unless the state plays a role in the placement. (An employee who provides care and financial support for a child may still qualify for leave under the "in loco parentis" provision, though.)

As with the adoption of a child, an eligible employee is entitled to take FMLA leave to attend to matters related to the placement of a foster child with that employee, whether the need for leave arises before or after the actual placement. A foster parent may need time off to attend hearings, examinations, and other proceedings, for example.

Lessons from the *Real World*

An employee was entitled to FMLA leave when trying to get custody of his biological daughter in an adoption proceeding.

Dwayne Kelley worked for Crosfield Catalysts. He had raised Shaneequa Forbes as his daughter, even though her birth certificate listed Barbara and Michael Forbes as her parents. Kelley "had reason to believe" that the girl was his biological daughter.

When the state child welfare department filed a court action to take custody of Shaneequa away from him, Kelley requested time off work to pursue custody. Crosfield denied the request based on the belief that Kelley could not "adopt" his own child and so was not entitled to adoption leave. Kelley took four days off anyway to appear at the custody hearing. Crosfield fired him, and he filed a lawsuit under the FMLA.

The trial court agreed with the employer and dismissed the case. However, the court of appeals reversed the dismissal, holding that Kelley should have the opportunity to show his FMLA rights were violated.

Kelley v. Crosfield Catalysts, 135 F.3d 1202 (7th Cir. 1998).

Parental Certifications

When an employee requests parenting leave, you can ask that employee to give you documentation showing that he or she is in fact the parent of a newborn or newly placed child. Such documentation might include:

- a birth certificate
- an adoption decree or court order
- a foster placement certification or court order, or
- a written statement by the employee, showing the employee's intent to take on the role of "parent" as defined by the FMLA.

(See "Proving a Family Relationship," in Chapter 4, for more information on these certifications, including a sample form you can use for this purpose.)

Timing of Parenting Leave

Although a parent is entitled to leave to bond with a new child, the child must indeed be "new." That means the employee must conclude the leave for the birth, adoption, or foster placement of a child within one year of the child's birth or adoptive or foster placement. "Placement" occurs when the parent gets the right to custody of the child. The one-year deadline is not extended when legal or governmental action has delayed the adoptive or foster parent from getting physical custody of the child.

This is a rigid deadline. Even a legitimate need for leave that arises more than one year after birth, adoption, or foster placement will not qualify under this provision of the FMLA. Of course, if the child has a serious health condition that requires the parent's care, the parent may still qualify for FMLA leave to take care of the sick child, even after the first year is over.

EXAMPLE 1: Your employee, Pang, took custody of a foster child on May 2, 2017. On March 28, 2018, Pang asks to take ten weeks of FMLA parenting leave. You grant the request.

You really didn't need to grant that much time because Pang had only a little over four weeks of time left in the one-year period following the child's placement. That was all the time off that she was entitled to within the FMLA deadline for parental leave.

EXAMPLE 2: Your employee Jess and his partner had a baby on March 5, 2017. On March 27, 2018, Jess informs you that he needs to take three weeks off to care for the baby, who has developed severe bronchitis. Because more than a year has passed since the child's birth, you inform Jess that he has no leave time available for the birth of his child.

You blew it! The baby's illness is not "birth-related" and is not subject to the one-year deadline for such leave. Rather, the baby's illness is a serious medical condition, and Jess may qualify to take FMLA leave as long as he meets other eligibility requirements.

Lessons from the *Real World*

An employee is not entitled to FMLA leave to travel to retrieve adopted children more than one year after adoption.

Bernardo Bocalbos, a naturalized U.S. citizen who was born in the Philippines, worked as an assistant actuary for National Western Life Insurance Co. In 1992, Bocalbos adopted his brother's children, who lived in the Philippines. In March 1995, after finally receiving the necessary visas for the children, Bocalbos requested FMLA leave to travel to the Philippines to retrieve the children. The request was granted. Prior to Bocalbos's departure, his supervisor informed him that he had to take certain actuarial exams by May 1995 or he would be terminated. Bocalbos signed a memorandum stating he understood this requirement. In April 1995, Bocalbos left for the Philippines and returned to work in June 1995. Bocalbos did not sit for the required exams prior to his departure. National Western terminated him for failing to take the exams by May 1995. Bocalbos sued National Western for retaliating against him for taking FMLA leave.

The court of appeals sided with National Western, holding that the leave Bocalbos took three years after the adoption of the children was outside the FMLA deadline for adoption-related leave, so he was not protected.

Bocalbos v. National Western Life Ins. Co., 162 F.3d 379 (5th Cir. 1998).

Foreign adoptions like the one in the above "Lessons from the Real World" are increasingly common. Madonna and Angelina Jolie are the most famous people who have adopted children born in foreign countries, but your company's employees may choose to add to their families in this fashion, too. If an employee must take time off to travel to take custody of a newly adopted child and does so within one year of the finalization of the adoption, the FMLA protects the employee's right to this leave.

Where an employee has already taken leave for the placement of a foster child and later adopts that child, the FMLA does not give the employee additional leave for the adoption. The FMLA permits leave only for the "newly placed" foster or adoptive child within one year of the original placement. So even if the adoption doesn't happen for more than a year, the employee can't get additional parenting leave time.

Intermittent or Reduced-Schedule Leave

The FMLA does not require your company to offer intermittent and reduced-schedule parenting leave to employees, with one possible exception: Employees who become foster parents can take leave for each child that is placed with them in the same year. Although such employees still have a maximum of 12 weeks of leave to use in a year, they may take this leave in separate increments if more than one child is placed with them within a single year.

EXAMPLE 1: Brenda, whose delivery date is December 21, 2017, requests four weeks of parenting leave following the birth of her child. She then plans to return to work for a couple of weeks and wants an additional three weeks of leave to bond with the baby in February 2018. You grant the leave immediately following the birth but deny the additional leave. Have you done the right thing?

Yes. As long as Brenda has a normal pregnancy and delivery and no post-delivery complications, she is not entitled to the February leave, because that would be intermittent leave.

EXAMPLE 2: Tomas becomes a foster parent on February 1, 2017, and takes six weeks of FMLA leave to spend with his foster child. He enjoys the experience so much that he decides to take in another foster child, who will be placed with him on August 5, 2017. He asks for another six weeks of parenting leave. You deny his request because he has already taken parenting leave during the year. Was this the right call?

Not in this situation. Even though parents usually can't divide up their parenting leave, an exception applies when they receive more than one foster child in a year. Although the employee's total leave entitlement doesn't increase, the employee can divide this leave in separate parts for multiple foster child placements.

However, your company has the option of agreeing to provide intermittent or reduced-schedule parenting leave at the employee's request, even though the FMLA does not require it. Your company may impose restrictions on this type of leave that are different from those mandated by the FMLA because you're agreeing to provide more than the law requires. For example, although the FMLA requires employers to allow intermittent leave in increments of one hour or less for serious health conditions and military leave, you may require employees who use intermittent leave for parenting to take it in larger increments (for example, a full day at a time).

POLICY ALERT

If your company has a policy of offering intermittent or reduced-schedule leave for parenting leave, follow it. Your company is bound to follow its own leave policies, even if they exceed FMLA obligations.

EXAMPLE: A few years after her first request, Brenda makes a request similar to the one described in the example above, but this time your company has a policy of granting occasional days off or reduced workdays to employees with newborns. Brenda specifically requests FMLA leave in two time segments, one in December and one in February. You deny Brenda the second block of time off because it is not available under the FMLA. Are you correct?

No. Because your company policy allows for intermittent leave for childbirth, you must abide by the policy.

This limitation doesn't apply to a woman who has a serious health condition as a result of pregnancy or childbirth or a spouse or partner caring for a woman with such a condition. In those situations, the leave is not parenting leave, so the employee is entitled to intermittent and reduced-schedule leave. Likewise, if a child has a serious health condition, the employee isn't restricted by this provision and is eligible for intermittent or reduced-schedule leave (see "Intermittent and Reduced-Schedule Leave" in Chapter 7).

SEE AN EXPERT

State family and medical leave laws may require your company to provide intermittent or reduced-schedule parenting leave. Appendix A includes information on each state's family and medical leave laws. If you have questions about how to comply with your state's requirements for parenting leave, consult with an employment attorney.

Substitution of Paid Leave

Your company can require its employees who request parenting leave to use accrued paid vacation, personal leave, or family leave under its own policies and count the time against the employee's FMLA leave. So, for example, an employee with two weeks' vacation time on the books could be required to use it up, and that time off would count against the employee's 12-week entitlement to FMLA leave.

However, the rule is different for sick or medical leave, because parenting leave is not "sick" time. So, your company can't require employees requesting parenting leave to use up accrued paid sick or medical leave. If the leave requested is to care for a spouse, newborn, or newly placed child with a serious health condition, on the other hand, paid sick or medical leave may be substituted if your policy allows employees to use sick leave to care for family members.

Even if your company doesn't require an employee to substitute paid vacation, personal, or family leave for parenting leave, it must allow an employee to use this time to get paid during FMLA leave, upon the employee's request, as long as the employee meets the requirements of your paid leave policy. (For more on paid leave, see Chapter 8.)

Parents Who Work for the Same Company

Parents who work for the same company are entitled to parenting leave, but the amount of time they get depends on their marital status. If the parents are married, they get a combined 12 weeks of leave in connection with the birth, adoption, or foster placement of their child or to care for a seriously ill parent. This rule applies even to spouses who work at different worksites or in different divisions of your company. This rule also applies to same-sex spouses. Spouses are allowed to use the combined leave at the same time.

Spouses who are eligible for military caregiver leave—26 weeks of leave in a single 12-month period to care for a family member who suffered a service-related serious illness or injury (see Chapter 6 for details)—have to share their leave entitlement, as well. These spouses are entitled to a combined total of 26 weeks of leave for parenting, caring for a parent with a serious health condition, and caring for a military family member with a serious illness or injury.

If the parents are not married, they each get 12 weeks of leave (or 26 weeks, for military caregiver leave). This rule seems to favor unmarried couples, but the reason for the rule is actually to avoid discouraging employers from hiring married couples by lessening the burden on those employers when their married employees have children together.

> EXAMPLE: Dan and Anabelle both work for your company and are married to each other. Dan works in the downtown headquarters, while Anabelle works in the warehouse in a nearby suburb. They are both eligible for FMLA leave. Three months ago, Dan and Anabelle adopted a child. Anabelle requests seven weeks of leave in connection with the adoption. You grant the requested leave.
>
> During Anabelle's leave, Dan asks for five weeks off to bond with the child, two of which will overlap with Anabelle's leave. You grant his request. Were you right to do so?
>
> Yes. You accurately noted the time off for each of the parents and calculated the total combined FMLA parenting leave to be taken. Dan was entitled to the five weeks of parenting leave that was left after Anabelle's leave was subtracted from the combined 12 weeks.

Unmarried couples are each entitled to the full 12 weeks of FMLA parenting leave. However, unlike married couples, they are not entitled to FMLA leave to care for each other when one has a serious medical condition. So if an unmarried pregnant employee needs care for a serious medical condition and you also employ her partner, her partner is not entitled to FMLA leave to provide that care. Your state's family and medical leave law might require you to grant leave to care for a domestic partner, however. (Appendix A provides information on each state's family and medical leave laws.)

EXAMPLE 1: Jared and Betsey are domestic partners who are both employed by your company. The couple has announced that Betsey is pregnant. Before Betsey's due date, Jared requests ten weeks of parenting leave to begin after the baby's birth. You grant his request and wish the couple well.

Shortly after the baby's birth, Betsey calls in and asks for five weeks of parenting leave. You deny that request, telling Betsey that she and Jared get a combined 12 weeks of parenting leave and he has already been granted ten weeks.

Wrong. Because they are not married, Jared and Betsey are each entitled to 12 weeks of FMLA leave in connection with the birth of their child.

EXAMPLE 2: Jared phones in two months after the baby's birth to ask to take two weeks of FMLA leave to take care of Betsey, who has developed severe postpartum depression and been prescribed medication that affects her ability to function.

Because you have read this guide, you know that you can deny this request and tell Jared that unmarried partners are not entitled to leave to care for each other under the FMLA.

In the last example, if Jared and Betsey had been married, Jared would be entitled to the requested leave to care for his spouse during her illness. However, that means that in the first example, Betsey would be entitled to only two weeks of parenting leave because Jared already took ten weeks.

RELATED TOPIC

State laws may also apply. Several types of state laws might also protect employees who take leave for a new child. For example, some states require employers to offer parenting leave (similar to that provided by the FMLA) to a wider range of employees than does the FMLA. And some state family leave laws cover the same territory as the FMLA, but with additional requirements. Appendix A provides a summary of each state's laws; Chapter 12 explains what to do when a state law overlaps with the FMLA.

Combining Parenting Leave With Leave for a Serious Health Condition

As you've now learned, employees are entitled to two types of nonmilitary leave under the FMLA: leave for a serious health condition and parenting leave to care for and bond with a new child. Sometimes, these two rights may seem to overlap. For example, a pregnant mother may need time off before her pregnancy, when she experiences morning sickness or is confined to bed. Or a newborn may become ill, requiring a parent's care.

Pregnancy

Incapacity due to pregnancy, including leave needed for prenatal care, is considered a serious health condition under the FMLA. In fact, all leave taken by a pregnant woman before delivery because of her pregnancy is leave for a serious medical condition, not parenting leave. (See Chapter 4 for more information on pregnancy leave.)

There are a couple of reasons why it's important to figure out whether an employee is taking leave for pregnancy (a serious health condition) or parenting:

- **Unlike parenting leave, FMLA leave for pregnancy may be taken on an intermittent or reduced-schedule basis.** If you lump pregnancy and parenting leaves together and deny a request for intermittent leave for pregnancy as a result, you violate the FMLA.

- **If married parents both work for you, they are subject to the combined 12-week "cap" on parenting leave, as explained above.** However, an employee's leave for her own pregnancy doesn't count toward this combined 12 weeks, nor does a husband's leave to care for his pregnant wife. For example, if a pregnant employee took five weeks off due to incapacity, she and her husband would still be entitled to a combined total of 12 weeks off for parenting leave. There is a limitation, though: Each person still has an overall cap of 12 weeks of FMLA leave (or 26 weeks, for military caregiver leave). In this example, the pregnant employee could take a maximum of seven weeks of parenting leave, because she already used five weeks of her annual allotment.

EXAMPLE 1: Back to your married employees, Dan and Anabelle, who took five and seven weeks of parental leave, respectively. A few days after Dan's request for parenting leave, Anabelle asks for three weeks off to care for the child, who has developed pneumonia. You deny this request and tell Anabelle that she and Dan have taken all 12 weeks of parenting leave available under the FMLA.

Oops! Your mistake was assuming that Anabelle's request for time to care for the sick child was part of the 12-week combined parenting leave, instead of leave for a serious health condition. With a medical certification, Anabelle is entitled to the three weeks off. The difference between her total FMLA leave for the year (12 weeks) and the time she actually took off during the combined parenting leave (seven weeks), leaves her with five weeks of FMLA leave for any qualifying reason other than parenting leave.

EXAMPLE 2: A few weeks after returning from his final week of parenting leave, Dan develops a severe cough. He calls in one morning to inform you that his doctor has diagnosed him with bronchitis and ordered him to stay home and off his feet for at least a week to give the antibiotics a chance to work. You ask for a note from his doctor and grant the leave on the condition that you receive the medical certification.

Congratulations! You learned from your earlier error. Dan's illness is an FMLA-qualifying condition separate and apart from the parenting leave he took earlier and he, too, is entitled to 12 weeks of FMLA leave, less the time he actually took off already (five weeks). So, Dan has seven weeks of leave left for any FMLA-qualifying reason except parenting leave.

In addition to granting leave to a pregnant woman incapacitated by a pregnancy-related medical condition, the FMLA also requires your company to allow a husband to take time off to care for his wife who is suffering such incapacitation. As with any other leave for a serious medical condition, the spouse must provide care to the pregnant employee and should provide a medical certification. Of course, this means that a normal pregnancy that doesn't incapacitate the mother doesn't entitle her spouse to take leave to spend time with her.

Lessons from the *Real World*

An employee was not entitled to FMLA leave to be with his pregnant wife when she had not suffered medical complications.

After his pregnant wife experienced false labor, Steve Aubuchon orally requested leave from his job with Knauf Fiberglass to be with her. Aubuchon did not inform Knauf that his wife had any medical complications or that she was incapacitated. Knauf denied the request. Aubuchon nevertheless missed several weeks of work, and Knauf fired him for unauthorized absence. He filed a lawsuit claiming that Knauf violated the FMLA.

The court of appeals ruled in the company's favor. Because Aubuchon failed to provide notice to Knauf that his wife had experienced complications during her pregnancy or that she was incapacitated, Aubuchon's leave was not protected and Knauf did not violate the FMLA by firing him.

Aubuchon v. Knauf Fiberglass, GmbH, 359 F.3d 950 (7th Cir. 2004).

Because domestic partners and other unmarried couples don't qualify as each other's family members under the FMLA, an employee isn't entitled to take FMLA leave to care for a nonmarital pregnant partner even if she has a serious medical condition. But the employee is entitled to take FMLA leave to care for their newborn child.

Caring for a Child

Leave to care for an ill newborn or newly adopted or foster child is separate and apart from parenting leave because it is to care for a family member with a serious health condition. So if a child becomes ill, you assess the employee's entitlement to leave under the FMLA in the same manner as any other leave request for a serious health condition. (See Chapter 4.)

Lessons from the *Real World*

If an employee wasn't entitled to take FMLA leave to care for his common-law wife, he was entitled to take leave to care for his premature infant.

Ingram Construction Company fired Mark Willard for taking time off to care for his common-law wife and newborn child following the baby's premature birth. Willard sued Ingram for violating the FMLA.

The court of appeals held that, while Willard may or may not have met the requirements of a common-law marriage, he was certainly entitled to take FMLA leave to care for his newborn. The legal relationship between Willard and the mother of the child didn't affect his right to take parental leave.

Willard v. Ingram Constr. Co., Inc., 194 F.3d 1315 (6th Cir. 1999).

Common Mistakes Regarding Leave for a New Child—And How to Avoid Them

Mistake 1: Miscalculating the FMLA leave available to spouses who both work for your company.

Avoid this mistake by taking the following steps:

- Make sure both parents are eligible for FMLA leave in the first place, for example, that they have worked enough hours in the past year. See Chapter 3 for more on these requirements.
- Make sure the two married parents get no more, and no less, than 12 weeks of combined parenting leave.
- Calculate the FMLA leave time each parent has left for other purposes after the combined parenting leave is taken.
- Distinguish between parenting leave and other types of leave that a soon-to-be or new parent might take (for pregnancy disability, to care for a pregnant spouse, for disability relating to childbirth, or to care for a seriously ill new child, for example).

Leave for a child's or spouse's serious health condition doesn't count toward the combined 12-week cap.

- Limit spouses who are eligible for military caregiver leave to a combined total of 26 weeks of leave in a single 12-month period for parenting, caring for a parent with a serious health condition, and providing military caregiver leave.

Mistake 2: Denying FMLA leave because the employee has already taken parenting leave.

Avoid this mistake by taking the following steps:

- Allow intermittent parenting leave only if your company's policies allow it or the employee is entitled to separate increments of parenting leave for multiple foster child placements in a single year.
- Recognize the difference between parenting leave and leave for a serious health condition. If a child becomes seriously ill, leave to care for that child does not qualify as parental leave under the FMLA; it's leave to care for a family member with a serious health condition.

Mistake 3: Discriminating against fathers in granting or denying parenting leave.

Avoid this mistake by taking the following steps:

- Grant parenting leave to FMLA-eligible fathers for birth, adoption, or foster placement, just as you would to female employees.
- Make no assumptions about who will or should actually be providing care for a new child. Remember, an employee doesn't have to show that he is needed to provide care for a new child, as he would have to show to care for a family member with a serious health condition—and you can't deny parenting leave simply because the child's mother is already at home.

Managers' Checklist: Leave for a New Child

☐ I confirmed that the employee requesting parenting leave is eligible for FMLA leave (see Chapter 3).

☐ I have informed the employee that he or she must substitute paid company vacation, personal, or family leave for unpaid FMLA leave, and

   ☐ I have subtracted the paid leave from the employee's available FMLA leave for the leave year.

☐ I have noted the deadline by which the employee must take the full 12 weeks of parenting leave (one year after birth, adoption, or foster placement).

For Pregnancy Leave:

☐ If the employee is requesting leave for her own pregnancy before delivery, I have:

   ☐ requested medical certification of a serious medical condition

   ☐ designated the leave as leave for the employee's own medical condition and notified the employee, and

   ☐ noted in the employee's FMLA file that the employee may still request parenting leave within the one-year deadline.

☐ If a pregnant employee is requesting leave to begin before delivery, I have:

   ☐ asked if the leave is for her own medical condition (including prenatal care) or for parenting

   ☐ if for her own medical condition, I have followed the steps in the preceding list entry, and

   ☐ if for parenting, I have denied the request for leave prior to delivery.

☐ If an employee is requesting leave to care for his pregnant spouse, I have:

   ☐ requested appropriate certification of a serious medical condition

   ☐ designated the leave as leave for the spouse's serious medical condition and notified the employee, and

   ☐ noted that the employee may still request parenting leave within the one-year deadline.

Managers' Checklist: Leave for a New Child (continued)

For Parenting Leave:

- ☐ If the employee is requesting parenting leave, I have confirmed that the leave is:
  - ☐ to begin after the birth of the child
  - ☐ not for the employee's own medical condition, and
  - ☐ full time and not intermittent or reduced-schedule leave, unless company policy or state law permits such leave.
- ☐ I have requested appropriate certification of the parental relationship.
- ☐ If the employee is requesting parenting leave for adoption or foster placement, I have:
  - ☐ requested appropriate certification of adoption or placement, and
  - ☐ allowed time off before adoption or foster placement if necessary to attend proceedings or meetings related to placement.

Where Both Parents Work for Your Company:

- ☐ For parents who are married and are both seeking parenting leave, I have:
  - ☐ confirmed in writing to the parents that they get no more than a combined total of 12 weeks of parenting leave and leave to care for a parent with a serious health condition, and
  - ☐ subtracted the parenting time from each employee's FMLA time and noted the remainder for use for other types of FMLA leave.
- ☐ For parents who are not married and are both seeking leave, I have:
  - ☐ confirmed in writing to the parents that each parent has a full 12 weeks of parenting leave available
  - ☐ subtracted the parenting time from each employee's FMLA time and noted the remainder for use for other types of FMLA leave.

Military Family Leave

Chapter Highlights

☆ Employees may use their 12-week entitlement of FMLA leave to handle qualifying exigencies arising from a family member's covered active duty in the military.

☆ Qualifying exigency leave is available only if the family member is a member of the National Guard, Reserves, or regular Armed Forces deployed to a foreign country.

☆ Adult children qualify as family members under this provision.

☆ There are eight categories of qualifying exigency:
- short-notice deployment
- military events and related activities
- child care and school activities
- financial and legal arrangements
- counseling
- rest and recuperation
- postdeployment activities, and
- care for a parent who is incapable of self-care.

☆ An employer and employee may agree that other circumstances also constitute a qualifying exigency; they must also agree on the length and timing of the leave.

☆ For some types of qualifying exigency leave, there are limits on how much leave an employee may take or when the leave must be taken.

☆ Employees may take up to 26 weeks of military caregiver leave in a single 12-month period to care for a family member who incurs or aggravates a serious illness or injury on active duty.

☆ For purposes of military caregiver leave, adult children count as family members; siblings, grandparents, or other blood relatives may also be entitled to leave, if they are the injured servicemember's next of kin.

☆ Military caregiver leave is available to care for members of the regular Armed Forces as well as members of the National Guard and Reserves; veterans suffering from service-related injuries or illnesses are covered, too.

☆ Military caregiver leave is a once per-servicemember, per-injury requirement; it does not renew every year like other types of FMLA leave.

☆ An employee who is eligible for military caregiver leave may take no more than 26 weeks off in a single 12-month period for all FMLA-qualified reasons, combined.

I n 2008, Congress amended the FMLA to add new leave entitlements for employees with family members serving in the military. As originally passed, these provisions allowed employees to take time off to care for family members who suffered serious illness or injury in active military service; they also created "qualifying exigency" leave, which employees could take to handle certain practical matters arising out of a family member's call to active duty.

In 2010, Congress amended these provisions to expand the situations in which employees can take military family leave and the family members for whom they can take such leave. All of these amendments were intended to help employees manage their family responsibilities at a time when our country had significant troops in Afghanistan and elsewhere, and tens of thousands of servicemembers have returned home wounded or ill from their service.

As amended, the FMLA includes two categories of military family leave:

- **Qualifying exigency leave.** Employees may take FMLA leave to deal with certain issues arising from a family member's covered active duty or call to covered active duty in the military as a result of deployment to a foreign country. Although this type of leave was originally available only if the family member was in the National Guard or Reserves, Congress later extended it to apply to family members in the regular Armed Forces as well. This leave counts toward the employee's total 12-week leave entitlement for serious health conditions and bonding with a new child.

- **Military caregiver leave.** Employees may take up to 26 weeks of leave in a single 12-month period to care for a family member who suffers a serious injury or illness while on covered active duty. A servicemember who aggravates a preexisting injury or illness while on active duty is covered. And, a veteran who was discharged (under conditions other than dishonorable) in the past five years and is suffering a service-related serious illness or injury is covered as well.

These military family leave entitlements apply only to covered employers (that is, employers who meet the criteria covered in Chapter 2). And, both are available only to employees who are otherwise eligible for FMLA leave: those who work within 75 miles of at least 50 employees, have worked for at least 12 months, and have worked at least 1,250 hours during the previous year, for the employer (these requirements are covered in detail in Chapter 3).

Beyond the basic FMLA coverage and eligibility requirements, however, each of the military family leave provisions comes with its own definitions, criteria, and requirements, not to mention its own certification forms and notice provisions. In this chapter, we explain how these leave rights work, including which employees may use them, when an employee may take leave, and how much leave an employee may use. In later chapters, you'll find information on how to combine military family leave with existing FMLA leave to determine an employee's total leave entitlement (Chapter 7); notice provisions (Chapter 8); and certification requirements (Chapter 9) that apply to these military family leave provisions, as well as other types of FMLA leave.

Leave for a Qualifying Exigency

Employees may take FMLA leave to handle certain qualifying exigencies relating to a family member's covered active duty or call to covered active duty in a foreign country. Leave for a qualifying exigency is an additional type of FMLA leave for which an employee may take a total of 12 workweeks off per year, along with leave for the employee's serious health condition (see Chapter 4), for a family member's serious health condition (see Chapter 4), or to bond with a new child (see Chapter 5). In other words, this provision doesn't create a right to additional leave. Instead, it creates another type of leave for which the employee might use some of his or her existing 12-week entitlement.

Generally speaking, the qualifying exigency provision gives employees the right to take time off when a family member's current or impending military service raises particular issues that the employee needs to handle, from child care to legal matters to formal military events and activities. But not every event or situation is covered, nor is every family member or every type of military service.

Covered Active Duty

There are many different ways to serve in the military, and not all of them are covered by this type of FMLA leave. Employees are entitled to leave under this provision only for family members whose service meets the following criteria (explained in more detail below):

- The family member must be a member of the National Guard, Reserves, regular Armed Forces (or, in some circumstances, a retired member of the regular Armed Forces or Reserves).
- The family member must be serving, or called to serve, on active duty during deployment to a foreign country.
- For those in the National Guard or Reserves only, the family member must be serving or called to serve:
  - in support of a contingency operation, and
  - under a federal call or order to active duty.

Members of the National Guard, Reserves, or Regular Armed Forces

Employees whose family members are on active duty in the regular Armed Forces (that is, whose family members are career military personnel) are eligible for qualifying exigency leave. Employees may also take leave for family members who are in the National Guard or Reserves and are called to active duty.

Certain retired military members are also covered. Leave is available for family members who are retired from the regular Armed Forces and are called to active duty. In addition, leave is available for family members who are members of the retired Reserve, are retired after completing at least 20 years of active service, and are ordered to active duty.

Covered Active Duty During Deployment in a Foreign Country

Employees are eligible for qualifying exigency leave only if their family members are on active duty in a foreign country. This also includes deployment to active duty in international waters.

Active Duty in Support of a Contingency Operation

For an employee whose family member is serving in the National Guard or Reserves (not the regular Armed Forces), the family member must be on active duty in support of a contingency operation. A contingency operation is a military operation that:

- the secretary of defense has designated as an operation in which members of the armed forces are or may become involved in military actions, operations, or hostilities against an enemy of the United States or an opposing military force, or

- results in the call or order to, or retention on, active duty of members of the uniformed services pursuant to particular sections of the United States code or any other provision of law during a war or national emergency declared by the president or Congress. (You can find a list of the provisions of the U.S. Code that qualify at 29 C.F.R. § 825.126(a)(2).)

Generally, the family member's active duty orders should indicate whether the person is called to serve in support of a contingency operation. You may require the employee to submit a copy of the family member's active duty orders or other official documents about the family member's service along with the employee's certification; see Chapter 9 for more information.

Federal Call to Active Duty

For an employee whose family member is serving in the National Guard or Reserves (not the regular armed forces), the family member must be subject to a federal call to covered active duty; a state call to active duty isn't covered unless it has been ordered by the president of the United States in support of a contingency operation.

> EXAMPLE: Lawrence works for your company in Northern California. His wife, Saundra, works part time for another employer while their young children are in school; she gets off work at 1 p.m., in time to pick up the kids. Saundra is a member of California's National Guard.
>
> Pursuant to an order by the governor of California, Saundra is mobilized to assist firefighters in evacuating residents and creating firebreaks in response to a wildfire in Southern California. Lawrence requests time off to care for the kids in the afternoon for a week. Because Saundra is in the Guard, you allow Lawrence to take the time off and count it, as qualifying exigency leave, against his 12-week FMLA entitlement. Was that the right call?
>
> No. Although Saundra was mobilized, it wasn't a federal call to active duty, because the president didn't order it in support of a contingency operation. That means Lawrence's time off isn't FMLA leave. Had the fire been so severe that it was declared a national emergency by the president, who mobilized Saundra and other troops in response, Lawrence's time off might have qualified as FMLA leave.

Family Members

As explained in Chapter 4, the FMLA allows employees to take leave only to care for certain family members with a serious health condition. Those family members include parents, spouses, and children who are either under the age of 18 or older and incapable of caring for themselves.

The qualifying exigency entitlement uses the same categories of family members and defines "spouses" and "parents" in the same way as for other FMLA entitlements. However, the term "child" is defined differently. For purposes of qualifying exigency leave, family members include the employee's children regardless of age or incapacity. This change was necessary to make the provision meaningful. Because minors are generally not members of the military (and certainly wouldn't already be retired from military service), an employee would never be able to take qualifying exigency leave to handle matters arising from a child's call to active duty unless adult children were encompassed by the law.

Qualifying Exigencies

The FMLA regulations identify eight categories of qualifying exigencies. For some of these exigencies, the amount of leave available is limited, or restrictions apply to when the employee may take leave. In addition, the regulations create a ninth category for additional activities, which applies to any situation that the employer and employee agree is a qualifying exigency.

Short-Notice Deployment

An employee may take leave to address any issue arising from the fact that a family member is notified of an impending call or order to covered active duty within seven or fewer calendar days before the date of deployment. This type of leave may be taken for a maximum of seven calendar days, beginning on the day the family member is notified of his or her impending deployment. Because the regulation refers to calendar days rather than work days, an employee may be entitled to only a few days of FMLA leave pursuant to this provision.

Military Events and Related Activities

An employee may take leave to attend an official ceremony, program, or event sponsored by the military and related to the family member's active duty service. An employee may also take leave to attend family support or assistance programs and informational briefings sponsored or promoted by the military, military service organizations, or the American Red Cross, as long as those programs or briefings are related to the family member's active duty.

Child Care and School Activities

An employee may take time off for the following reasons relating to a family member's call to active duty:

- to arrange alternative child care for the family member's child, if the family member's active duty requires a change
- to provide child care for the family member's child on an urgent, immediate need basis (not regularly or every day) if necessitated by the family member's active duty
- to enroll the family member's child in, or transfer the child to, a new school or day care facility when the need arises from the family member's active duty, or
- to attend meetings with school or day care staff (such as disciplinary meetings, parent-teacher conferences, or meetings with a school counselor) regarding the family member's child, if the employee's attendance at the meetings is necessary because of circumstances arising from the family member's call to active duty.

When an employee takes qualifying exigency leave for child care and school functions, two definitions of "child" are in play. The child who is actually in school or day care must meet the traditional FMLA definition of a child. In other words, the family member's child must be either under the age of 18 or, if the child is older, he or she must be incapable of self-care due to a disability. However, the employee can take time off when an adult child is called to active duty and that adult child's own children need care. In that case, the employee would be taking leave to care for a grandchild.

> EXAMPLE: Rosalva works for your company. Her son, Carlos, is a divorced parent who shares custody of his young son, Javier, with his ex-wife Nancy. Carlos and Nancy live near each other and cooperate closely on raising their son. Currently,

Carlos takes care of Javier from Sunday evening until Wednesday evening, while Nancy works. Nancy takes Javier the rest of the week, while Carlos works.

Carlos, a member of the National Guard, is deployed to Afghanistan. Rosalva asks you for time off to rearrange Javier's schedule. Rosalva anticipates that she may need a few days off for a couple of weeks to care for Javier, until she and Nancy can decide whether to enroll him in day care or make some other arrangements. She may also need time to get her home set up to care for Javier. You sympathize with Rosalva's situation, but regretfully inform her that she can't take FMLA leave because the FMLA doesn't cover care for grandchildren.

Although your instincts would have been correct for other types of FMLA leave, here they were misguided. For purposes of qualifying exigency leave, employees may take time off to handle child care and school issues for their adult children's kids.

Financial and Legal Arrangements

There are a number of financial or legal issues that might need attention when a family member is called to active duty. An employee can take time off for things like preparing or updating a will or living trust, preparing or executing financial and health care powers of attorney, transferring bank account signature authority, obtaining military identification cards, or enrolling in the Defense Enrollment Eligibility Reporting System.

An employee may also take time off to act as the family member's representative for purposes of getting, arranging, or appealing military service benefits for the family member. This leave is available while the family member is on active duty or has been called to active duty, and for up to 90 days after the family member's active duty status terminates.

Counseling

An employee may take leave to attend counseling, provided by someone other than a health care provider, for himself or herself, for the family member, or for the family member's child, as long as the need for counseling arises from the family member's call to active duty.

Rest and Recuperation

An employee may take time off to be with a family member who is on short-term, temporary rest and recuperation leave during deployment. The employee may take a maximum of 15 days off for each rest and recuperation leave.

Postdeployment Activities

An employee may take time off to attend arrival ceremonies, reintegration briefings and events, and other official programs sponsored by the military for up to 90 days following the termination of the family member's active duty status. Employees may also take leave to handle issues arising from the death of a family member while on active duty status, such as recovering the family member's body and making funeral arrangements.

Parental Care

A new category of qualifying exigency leave was created in 2013: time off to assist a military member's parent who is incapable of self-care. This type of leave is available to employees with a military family member (as defined in "Family Members," above) whose parent—including an adoptive parent, stepparent, foster parent, or someone who stood in loco parentis to the military member when he or she was a child—is unable to take care of himself or herself.

A parent is incapable of self-care when he or she requires active assistance or supervision with at least three "activities of daily living" (physical tasks, such as grooming, bathing, hygiene, dressing, and eating) or "instrumental activities of daily living" (basic skills required to live independently, such as shopping, cooking, cleaning, using the phone, paying bills, and so on).

This type of leave is available to:

- arrange alternative care for the parent, if the military member's service necessitates a change in care
- provide care for the parent on an urgent, immediate need basis (similar to the provision for leave to provide child care)
- admit or transfer the parent to a care facility, or
- attend meetings with staff at a care facility, including meeting with social services or hospice providers.

Additional Activities

In addition to the eight categories detailed above, an employer and employee may agree that other events arising out of a family member's call to active duty also constitute qualifying exigencies for which the employee may take leave. For this type of leave, the employer and employee must also agree on the timing and the length of the leave.

Qualifying Exigency Leave

Category	Description	Limits on timing of leave	Limits on amount of leave
Short-notice deployment	To address issues arising from call to duty within seven or fewer days of deployment	May be used only for seven calendar days after notification of deployment	Seven calendar days maximum
Military events and related activities	To attend military program, ceremony, or event; or to attend family support and assistance programs and information briefings sponsored by the military, military service groups, or Red Cross		
Child care and school activities	To arrange alternative child care; provide urgent child care; enroll or transfer child to new school or day care; or attend school meetings and conferences		
Financial and legal arrangements	To handle financial and legal matters relating to the family member's absence, such as wills, powers of attorney, and bank account transfers; to act as the family member's representative in hearings on military service benefits	Leave to act as family member's representative may be taken only while family member is on active duty status and for up to 90 days after termination of active duty status	
Counseling	To attend counseling for oneself, family member, or family member's child		
Rest and recuperation	To spend time with family member who is on short-term, temporary R&R leave during deployment		15 days of leave maximum, per service member's R&R leave
Post-deployment activities	To attend ceremonies, briefings, and events relating to family member's return; to address issues arising from the death of a family member on active duty	Leave for return of family member may be taken only for up to 90 days after termination of active duty status	
Parental care	To arrange alternate parental care; provide urgent parental care; admit or transfer the parent to a care facility; or attend meetings with staff at the parent's care facility		
Additional activities	As agreed upon by employer and employee	As agreed upon by employer and employee	As agreed upon by employer and employee

EXAMPLE: Duquan works for your company. His father, David, runs a kennel out of his home, taking care of dogs while their owners are on vacation. David, a member of the Reserves, is called to report for active duty in ten days. Duquan asks for time off to help his father with the dogs in his care; some owners are not due back until after David deploys. Duquan will help his father try to contact the owners or arrange other care for the dogs until the owners return.

You recognize that Duquan's request doesn't fall under any of the seven enumerated categories of qualifying exigency leave. However, you decide to grant Duquan's request as an "additional activity." After consulting with his father, Duquan tells you that he will need to take four days off; one to learn the ropes from his father, and the other three to care for the remaining dogs until their owners return. You agree, and designate those four days as FMLA leave for a qualifying exigency.

Intermittent or Reduced-Schedule Leave

Leave for a qualifying exigency may be taken intermittently or on a reduced schedule. As you can see from the categories of qualifying exigency leave above, this type of leave may have to be taken at a particular time, often for just a few hours at a time. For example, parent-teacher night, military ceremonies, or hearings on a family member's benefits take place at a given date and time, typically without regard for the employee's work schedule. But these events won't take more than a few hours.

Substitution of Paid Leave

As for other types of FMLA leave, an employee may choose—or you may require the employee—to use paid leave during FMLA leave. The employee's reason for leave must be covered by your company's paid leave program. For example, unless your company's policy allows employees to use sick leave to attend a child's school activities, you wouldn't have to allow (and couldn't require) an employee to substitute paid sick leave for time off used to attend school meetings. Also, you can require the employee to meet all other requirements of your paid leave program, such as having to provide a certain type or amount of notice. For more information on substitution of paid leave, see Chapter 8.

Leave to Care for an Injured Servicemember

The FMLA also gives employees the right to take up to 26 weeks of unpaid leave in a single 12-month period to care for a family member who has a serious injury or illness incurred in the line of duty. Unlike the qualified exigency leave provisions, this caregiver leave entitlement gives employees more leave than they would otherwise have under the FMLA.

In 2010, Congress expanded this leave entitlement in two ways:

- An employee can take leave to care for a family member with a serious illness or injury that was aggravated by service in the line of duty. This means that preexisting conditions that are worsened by military service may be covered along with illnesses or injuries first incurred while on duty.
- An employee can take leave to care for a family member veteran suffering a service-related serious illness or injury, as long as the family member was in the service during the five years before the employee's leave.

Like leave for a serious health condition, an employee's right to take leave for a family member's service-connected serious illness or injury depends heavily on medical facts. Military facts also come into play: The illness or injury must be incurred or aggravated "in the line of duty on active duty," a determination that is generally made by the military, not by private employers. This means that, as is true of a serious health condition, your role is not to determine whether an employee's family member has a serious military-related illness or injury, but to recognize when this type of leave might be implicated. Then, you can ask the employee to submit a certification from the family member's health care provider, filling in the necessary blanks. (Certifications are covered in Chapter 9.)

Which Servicemembers Are Covered

Employees may take leave only to care for a covered servicemember with a serious illness or injury, incurred or aggravated in the line of duty on active duty, and for which the servicemember is: undergoing medical treatment, recuperation, or therapy; is otherwise in outpatient status; or is on the temporary disability retired list.

As you have probably guessed, each of these requirements has its own definition.

Covered Servicemembers

Covered servicemembers include those who are in the regular Armed Forces, the National Guard and Reserves, and members of the regular Armed Forces, Guard, or Reserves who are on the temporary disability retired list. It also includes veterans who were released or discharged from military duty, under conditions other than dishonorable, during the five years before FMLA leave is taken.

Serious Illness or Injury

A serious illness or injury is one that may render the servicemember unfit to perform the duties of his or her office, grade, rank, or rating. For a veteran, a serious illness or injury is one that meets one of the following four definitions:

- a continuation of a serious illness or injury (as defined above) incurred or aggravated when the veteran was in the military, which rendered the servicemember unable to perform the duties of his or her office, grade, rank, or rating
- a physical or mental condition for which the veteran has received a Veterans Affairs Service-Related Disability Rating (VASRD) of 50 percent or greater, at least in part because the condition requires caregiver leave
- a physical or mental condition that substantially impairs the veteran's ability to obtain or maintain a substantially gainful occupation due to a disability related to military service (or would create such an impairment without treatment), or
- an injury (including a psychological injury) for which the veteran has been enrolled in the Department of Veterans Affairs Program of Comprehensive Assistance for Family Caregivers.

Note that these definitions differ from the basic definition of a "serious health condition," for which FMLA leave may otherwise be available. Although a serious illness or injury will often also qualify as a serious health condition, that won't always be the case. As explained in Chapters 7 and 8, if an employee's leave qualifies under both provisions, you must designate it only as military caregiver leave.

In the Line of Duty on Active Duty

The serious illness or injury must have been incurred or aggravated in the line of duty on active duty. These are military terms of art that the Department of Labor declined to define in greater detail. Generally speaking, a person is on active duty when serving full-time duty in the active military service of the United States. "Line of duty" is a term sometimes used to differentiate injuries or fatalities for which the servicemember or his or her family may receive benefits (for example, health care or survivor benefits) from those for which benefits are not available. For example, injuries caused by the servicemember's own intentional misconduct or willful negligence may not be considered "in the line of duty." An injury need not be combat related to qualify as "in the line of duty," though.

The same rule applies to veterans. However, conditions that arise or manifest only after the veteran leaves active duty, or even after the veteran leaves the military, are also covered. For example, post-traumatic stress disorder (PTSD) caused by military duty would be covered if it otherwise met the above definition of a serious illness or injury, even if it did not appear until after the veteran was discharged from military service.

As is true of serious health conditions, this is not a determination you need to make. Instead, the family member's health care provider is asked to determine whether the injury or illness occurred in the line of duty on active duty when completing the certification form (see Chapter 9). If the health care provider can't make this call, he or she may rely on determinations by an authorized representative of the Defense Department.

Treatment or Recuperation Requirements

For leave to care for a current servicemember, one of the following three criteria must be met:

- The servicemember is undergoing medical treatment, recuperation, or therapy.
- The servicemember is otherwise in outpatient status.
- The servicemember is otherwise on the temporary disability retired list.

For leave to care for a veteran, the veteran must be undergoing medical treatment, recuperation, or therapy for a serious illness or injury.

Covered Family Members

An employee may take caregiver leave under this part of the law only if the injured or ill servicemember is the employee's family member. As is true for all other FMLA provisions, this definition includes the employee's spouse, parent, or child. However, like the qualifying exigency provision, the caregiver entitlement extends by necessity to adult children. If an employee's adult child suffers a serious injury while on active duty, the employee is entitled to take leave under this provision.

Employees are also entitled to leave under this provision if they are "next of kin" to a covered servicemember. If a servicemember has designated a blood relative as his or her next of kin for purposes of military caregiver leave, the designated person qualifies as next of kin. However, if the servicemember has not designated someone, the servicemember's next of kin is his or her nearest blood relative (other than a parent, child, or spouse) in the following order of priority:

1. blood relatives who have been granted legal custody of the servicemember
2. siblings
3. grandparents
4. aunts and uncles, and
5. first cousins.

If the servicemember has not designated someone as next of kin, all blood relatives within the same level of the highest priority relationship are considered the servicemember's next of kin. For example, if a servicemember has two siblings, and no blood relative has been granted legal custody of the servicemember, both siblings would be considered the servicemember's next of kin.

The purpose of these rules is to make sure that someone, or more than one person, is available to care for an injured or ill servicemember. A spouse, parent, child, and next of kin (or more than one next of kin) may all take leave to care for the same servicemember, if necessary. However, this probably won't be an issue for most companies, which are unlikely to employ more than one family member.

> **EXAMPLE:** Tory lost a leg and suffered other injuries in a bomb blast while serving in Iraq. She returned home and received inpatient treatment, followed by outpatient care with daily rehabilitation appointments. Tory didn't designate

anyone as her next of kin for purposes of military caregiver leave. She is married, her mother lives nearby, and she has three brothers. One of her brothers, Eddie, works for your company and requests military caregiver leave several days a week to take his sister to her rehab sessions and help her with her exercises. He plans to work until 11 a.m., when he will go to his sister's home, help her get dressed, prepare her lunch, take her to her appointment, bring her home, and assist her with her home exercises. He estimates that he'll need to take off five hours a day, three days a week, for a couple of months.

You're planning to tell Eddie that he can only use his 40 hours of accrued vacation time to care for his sister. After all, Tory's husband can help out, her mother lives nearby and is already retired, and what about those two other brothers? Plus, are siblings even covered by the FMLA? Luckily, you remember the new military caregiver provision: In this situation, and for this type of time off, Eddie is entitled to FMLA leave. As long as he is providing care and the other requirements are met, he may take time off. Tory's husband, mother, and other two brothers are also entitled to military caregiver leave (although none of them work for your company).

As is true of FMLA leave to care for a family member with a serious health condition, you may ask an employee who takes military caregiver leave to provide documentation of a family relationship. For more information, see "Proving a Family Relationship," in Chapter 4, which also provides a form you can use for this purpose.

How Much Leave an Employee May Take

For this provision only, an employee is entitled to 26 weeks of leave in a 12-month period, rather than the 12 weeks allowed for other types of FMLA leave. Unlike other types of FMLA leave, however, military caregiver leave isn't an annually renewed entitlement. Instead, it's available once per servicemember, per injury. The employee may be entitled to another 26-week leave only in one of the following three circumstances:

- The servicemember suffers a different serious injury or illness in the line of duty on active duty. For example, if the servicemember recovered, then suffered another serious injury or illness during a subsequent deployment, the family member would be entitled to a second 26-week leave. If the servicemember later manifested a second injury or illness from the initial event, that would also entitle the employee to a second leave. However, multiple injuries sustained in a single incident don't entitle the employee to more than one leave period, if the injuries manifest immediately.

EXAMPLE: Two years ago, Song's son, Michael, was injured by an incendiary device in Iraq. He lost part of his right leg and suffered some burns. Song took 26 weeks of military caregiver leave to take care of him. Recently, Michael has begun suffering from post-traumatic stress disorder relating to the incident. Song requests FMLA leave to get her son into an outpatient program, take him to his therapy appointments, and care for him when he is too debilitated to leave the house. Should you grant her request?

Yes. Even though she already took military caregiver leave for Michael, Song is entitled to another period of leave. Michael's PTSD is a separate injury because it manifested at a later time. Song would not be entitled to more leave for injuries that were all apparent right away—for example, for Michael's amputation and his burns. Because the PTSD wasn't apparent until two years later, she is entitled to more leave.

- **The servicemember becomes a veteran.** According to guidance issued late in 2016 by the federal Department of Labor, an employee may be entitled to a second period of leave to care for the same military family member suffering from the same injuries once the family member becomes a veteran. For example, if Janelle suffers a traumatic brain injury while on active duty, her husband would be entitled to take military caregiver leave to take care of her. If Janelle was discharged honorably a year later, and her injury continued to meet the definition of a serious injury under the FMLA, her husband may be entitled to a second 26-week period of leave in a second 12-month period to provide care for her. (Because this guidance, issued in the Department's Field Operations Handbook, is recent, you should talk to a lawyer if you are facing this relatively rare situation.)
- **A different family member suffers a serious injury or illness in the line of duty on active duty.** If, for example, an employee's two children both serve in the military, and the employee takes time off in 2016

to care for one who is injured, the employee would be entitled to an additional 26-week leave period if the other child was injured in 2018.

Even if the employee is entitled to more than one leave period based on these rules, the employee may never take more than 26 weeks of leave in one 12-month period. This limit applies even if the two events entitling the employee to leave occur during the same 12 months. And, the employee's total leave entitlement—for military caregiver leave and all other types of FMLA leave—is 26 weeks in a year. So, for example, if an employee already used six weeks of leave for the adoption of a child, the employee may use only 20 weeks of military caregiver leave in the same 12-month period. Calculating the employee's leave entitlement is covered in Chapter 7, as are the rules for determining when the 12-month leave period begins.

Military caregiver leave doesn't carry over to a subsequent 12-month period. Any part of the 26 weeks the employee doesn't use in 12 months is lost.

Limits on Leave Available to Married Couples

Spouses who work for the same employer are entitled to a combined 26 weeks. As explained in Chapter 5, you may limit a married couple to no more than 12 weeks of combined leave for parenting and caring for a parent with a serious health condition. This type of limit also applies to military caregiver leave: Spouses who work for the same employer can be required to limit their total leave for military caregiver purposes, parenting, and caring for a parent with a serious health condition to 26 weeks in a 12-month period. See Chapter 5 for a discussion of how much combined leave each spouse may take and how much leave is available for purposes not subject to the combined restriction (such as leave for the employee's own serious health condition).

Intermittent or Reduced-Schedule Leave

Like leave for a serious health condition, military caregiver leave may be taken intermittently or on a reduced schedule when medically necessary. The certification form asks the family member's health care provider to indicate the medical necessity of intermittent or reduced-schedule leave; see Chapter 9 for more information.

Substitution of Paid Leave

An employee may choose, or you may require the employee, to substitute applicable paid leave for military caregiver leave. As is true of other types of FMLA leave, the employee's reason for leave must be covered by your company's paid leave program, and your company may require the employee to comply with your company's policies—for example, requiring a certain type or amount of notice—for using paid leave.

Common Mistakes Regarding Military Family Leave—And How to Avoid Them

Mistake 1: **Failing to recognize employee requests for military family leave as FMLA requests.**

Avoid this mistake by taking the following steps:

- Train yourself to think of the FMLA whenever an employee mentions a family member's military service, past or present, as a reason for time off.
- Ask questions to determine whether the time off might count as qualifying exigency or military caregiver leave.
- Use certifications to determine whether an employee's leave meets the medical and military requirements of military caregiver leave.
- Remember that more family members—including parents of adult children, siblings, and grandparents—may qualify for military family leave than for other types of FMLA leave.

Mistake 2: **Miscalculating how much leave is available for military family purposes.**

Avoid this mistake by taking the following steps:

- Count a qualifying exigency just like any other FMLA leave that is part of the employee's 12-week entitlement; if the employee has already used up his or her FMLA leave for the year, none is available for qualifying exigencies.
- Give employees their full 26 weeks of military caregiver leave. No matter how your company calculates its leave year for other purposes, the clock for an employee's military caregiver leave

always starts on the first day of such leave, as explained in Chapter 7.

Mistake 3: Mishandling qualifying exigency leave.

Avoid this mistake by taking the following steps:

- Keep track of the limits on timing and duration for particular types of qualifying exigency leave.
- Allow qualifying exigency leave for grandparents, if an adult child is called to active duty and his or her children need care.
- Be consistent in which types of activities your company agrees to count as qualifying exigency leave; if you grant exceptions for some activities and not others, make sure you have a good reason.

Managers' Checklist: Military Family Leave

☐ Whenever an employee takes or requests time off relating to a family member's military service, I have determined whether the employee is eligible for either qualifying exigency or military caregiver leave.

☐ If the employee requests time off to care for an injured or ill family member, I have determined whether the employee qualifies for military caregiver leave.

    ☐ I have determined whether the employee meets the general eligibility requirements for FMLA leave.

    ☐ If the employee is not the spouse, parent, or child of the servicemember, I have determined whether the employee is the servicemember's next of kin.

        ☐ I have requested documentation of the family relationship, if appropriate.

        ☐ I have requested the servicemember's next of kin designation, if appropriate.

    ☐ I have asked whether the servicemember or veteran is or was a member of the regular Armed Forces, National Guard, or Reserves.

    ☐ I have provided the employee with a certification form to be completed by the servicemember's health care provider.

Managers' Checklist: Military Family Leave (continued)

☐ If the employee requests time off to handle matters arising out of a family member's military duty, I have determined whether the employee is eligible for qualifying exigency leave.

  ☐ I have determined whether the employee meets the general eligibility requirements for FMLA leave.

  ☐ I have determined whether the employee has any FMLA leave left to use in this leave year.

  ☐ I have determined whether the family member is a current member the National Guard, Reserves, or regular Armed Forces, or a retired member of the regular Armed Forces or Reserves.

  ☐ I have determined whether the employee is a covered family member for purposes of qualifying exigency leave, and I have requested documentation of the family relationship.

  ☐ I have determined whether the employee's reason for leave may fall within one of the eight categories of qualifying exigency.

    ☐ If not:

      ☐ I have determined whether or not our company will agree to treat the reason for leave as a qualifying exigency.

      ☐ If our company will treat the leave as qualifying exigency leave, we have reached an agreement with the employee on the length and timing of the leave, and we have put this agreement in writing.

    ☐ If so, I have provided the employee with a certification form.

How Much Leave Can an Employee Take?

Chapter Highlights

☆ Employees eligible for military caregiver leave may take up to 26 weeks of FMLA leave in a single 12-month period, beginning on the first day of leave.

☆ Employees eligible for all other types of leave are entitled to 12 weeks of FMLA leave in a 12-month leave year.

☆ The 12-month leave year may be measured in one of four ways:
  • the calendar year
  • any fixed 12-month period, such as the fiscal year, the year starting on the anniversary of the employee's hire, and so on
  • twelve months counted forward from the date an employee begins FMLA leave, or
  • twelve months counted backward from the date an employee uses any FMLA leave.

☆ Your company must use the same calendaring method for all employees, except those using military caregiver leave. Your company may change calendaring methods with 60 days' advance notice.

☆ Each week of leave is based on the employee's normal workweek, including any overtime the employee is required to work.

☆ Employees eligible for military caregiver leave may take no more than 26 weeks of combined leave, for all FMLA-covered reasons, in a single 12-month period, of which no more than 12 weeks may be for purposes other than military caregiver leave.

☆ Only leave time the employee actually needs can be counted against the employee's available FMLA leave time.

☆ If needed for any reason other than parenting, FMLA leave may be taken intermittently or on a reduced schedule.

☆ Employees may take intermittent or reduced-schedule leave in the shortest increments of time used for other types of leave or in one-hour increments, whichever is shorter.

Y ou've come a long way. You've determined that your company is covered by the FMLA. You've confirmed that the employee seeking leave is FMLA qualified and that the reason for leave falls within the FMLA. Now it's time to figure out how much leave the employee has—or has left—to use.

Most provisions of the FMLA require your company to give eligible employees up to 12 workweeks of leave in a 12-month period. But when does that period start and end? What if the employee took leave last December and wants more leave this July—does the employee get another 12 weeks of leave because it's a new calendar year, or does the employee have to wait a full 12 months? How much leave is available to an employee who works odd hours, part time, or overtime? What if the employee wants to take only one day or one hour off a week, rather than 12 weeks at once?

The military caregiver provision, which allows eligible employees to take up to 26 weeks of leave in a single 12-month period, can complicate the calculation. When does this 12-month period start and end—is it the same as for other types of FMLA leave? What does a "single 12-month period" mean? What if an employee needs regular FMLA leave after taking military caregiver leave? How do you calculate how much total FMLA leave an employee gets?

If you don't know the answers to these questions off the top of your head, you aren't alone. In this chapter, we'll give you the information you need to determine exactly how much FMLA leave is available to your employees. We explain how to measure the 12-month leave year, how to calculate 12 (or 26) weeks of leave in the 12-month leave year, how to handle requests for intermittent leave or reduced-schedule leave, how to calculate leave for employees who work part time, and more.

Counting the 12-Month Leave Year

Each eligible employee is entitled to 12 weeks of FMLA leave in a 12-month period for his or her own serious health condition, to care for a family member with a serious health condition, to bond with a new child, or to handle qualifying exigencies relating to a family member's call to active military duty. Under the military caregiver provision, employees are entitled to 26 weeks of FMLA leave in a single 12-month period to care for a family member who suffers or aggravates a serious illness or injury on active military duty.

Believe it or not, these two 12-month periods may be different. The 12-month period for military caregiver leave always begins when the employee's leave begins. However, for the other types of FMLA leave (those that allow for 12 weeks off), employers may choose among four different methods of measuring the "leave year" during which an employee may take leave. This means you may have to track two different leave years for a single employee.

> **TIP**
>
> **FMLA leave cannot be carried over from one leave year to the next.** No matter how your company measures the 12-month leave year, employees can't carry over FMLA leave. An employee is never entitled to more than 12 weeks of any type of leave (or 26 weeks of military caregiver leave) in a given leave year.

Calculating the Leave Year for Military Caregiver Leave

Military caregiver leave is different than other types of FMLA leave in a number of important ways. Perhaps most notably, it allows employees to take up to 26 weeks off, rather than the 12 weeks allowed for all other types of FMLA leave. And, it's not a renewable annual entitlement: As explained in Chapter 6, this is a "per-servicemember, per-injury" right that, absent unusual circumstances, an employee may use only once.

Here's another difference: The 12-month leave year for military caregiver leave always begins on the employee's first day of leave. As the Department of Labor has explained, the purpose of this rule is to make sure that employees can use their full 26 weeks of military caregiver leave. If the 12-month leave year was the same for military caregiver leave as for other types of FMLA leave, the employee may have already used some FMLA leave for other purposes, which would reduce the total amount of military caregiver leave available to the employee. Because military caregiver leave will typically be a one-time entitlement, the DOL wanted to make sure employees get the full benefit provided by law.

Calculating the Leave Year for Other Types of FMLA Leave

The FMLA gives companies four different ways to define the leave year for all other types of FMLA leave:

- the calendar year
- any fixed 12-month period, such as the company's fiscal year, a year starting on the anniversary of an employee's hire, or a year defined by state law
- the 12-month period counted forward from the date that the employee begins FMLA leave, or
- a "rolling" 12-month period counted backward from the date that the employee uses any FMLA leave.

Employers may choose any of these methods. Whichever method you decide to use, it's important to consistently apply the same method to all employees. If you don't, employees can choose whichever method is most advantageous to them.

The Calendar Year or a Fixed-Period Year

If your company chooses to measure the leave year by either a calendar year or another fixed 12-month period (like the fiscal year), an eligible employee is entitled to up to 12 weeks of FMLA leave at any time in the selected leave year. A major disadvantage for companies that use one of these methods is that an employee could take 24 weeks of continuous leave in a row, if the leave spans the end of one year and the beginning of the next. It's difficult for many employers to have an employee out for that long.

> **EXAMPLE:** Your company measures the FMLA leave year by the calendar year: From January 1 to December 31, each eligible employee is entitled to 12 weeks of FMLA leave. Your employee, Megan, begins her 12-week FMLA leave on October 1. As of January 1, Megan is entitled to 12 weeks of FMLA leave for the new leave year. This means she will be able to take a solid 24 weeks of FMLA leave in a row.

Counting Forward

If your company chooses the third method, an eligible employee is entitled to 12 weeks of FMLA leave in the year beginning on the first day that the employee takes FMLA leave. From that day forward, the employee has 12 months to take the full 12 weeks of FMLA leave. The next 12-month period begins when leave is next taken after the initial 12-month leave year ends. For example, if an employee began leave on February 15, 2017, the employee would have until February 14, 2018 to use up the 12 weeks of leave. If the employee again wanted leave beginning June 20, 2018, the clock would start over. (Note that this is the method required for all military caregiver leave, as explained above.)

This is a relatively simple method for your company to use, because you can administer it easily on a case-by-case basis. However, it may allow employees to take more than 12 weeks of leave in a given 12-month period in the same manner that the first two methods do.

> **EXAMPLE:** Your company counts the leave year by going forward one year from the date FMLA leave is first taken. Megan begins a six-week FMLA leave on December 1, 2016. On October 20, 2017, Megan requests to take her remaining six weeks of leave, returning on December 1, 2017. On January 2, 2018, Megan requests a full 12-week FMLA leave. So, Megan will get 18 weeks of FMLA leave between October 20, 2017 and March 27, 2018.

The "Rolling" Leave Year

A "rolling" year is just what it sounds like—an employee's leave eligibility rolls out throughout the year, as leave is taken. If your company calculates the leave year using this method, an eligible employee is entitled to 12 weeks of FMLA leave in the year measured backward from the first day that FMLA leave is taken. Each time the employee takes leave, any part of the 12-week entitlement that was not used in the immediately preceding 12 months is available for future leave.

This is less complicated than it sounds. Essentially, when an employee requests leave, you look back to the last 12 months to see if the employee has already used 12 weeks of leave. Below is a sample worksheet to keep track of hours used under the rolling year method. You can find a digital copy of this form (and all other forms in this book) at this book's online companion page; see Appendix C for details.

Chart for Calculating Leave Under Rolling Leave Year Method

FMLA Leave Tracking for___Jane Edwards___

Date Leave Commenced	Amount of Leave Taken	Eligibility for Additional Leave
2/12/16	4 wks.	Currently eligible—8 wks.
4/22/16	4 wks.	Currently eligible—4 wks.
9/07/16	4 wks.	Eligible beginning 2/12/17
3/20/17	4 wks.	Eligible beginning 4/22/17
7/17/17	2 wks.	Currently eligible—2 wks.

The main advantage of this method is that it does not allow employees to take FMLA leave totaling more than 12 weeks in any 12-month period.

> EXAMPLE: Jane comes to you on February 7, 2018 asking for two weeks of FMLA leave. You look back to the last twelve months, from February 7, 2017 to February 7, 2018 to see how much FMLA she has used. Jane used four weeks on March 20, 2017 and two weeks on July 17, 2017. Because Jane has used six weeks of FMLA leave in the last 12 months, she still has six weeks of available FMLA leave. You should grant her request.

Choosing a Leave Year Method

For military caregiver leave, the 12-month leave year always begins on the first day an employee takes leave; your company can't choose the leave year. For all other types of FMLA leave, however, your company may choose among the four options discussed above. Be sure to define the leave year in your company's written FMLA policy and clearly describe which method the company will use. (See Appendix B for a sample FMLA policy.) If your company's chosen method is not stated in its policies, employees will be allowed to use the method most favorable to them, whether or not it's the best method for the company.

If, after reading this, your company decides to choose a new calculation method, it can do so. However, if employees are on leave or have requested leave, the company must provide 60 days' notice of the change of method to all employees. During that 60-day period, the employee can continue to utilize the method of his or her choice. Once the 60 days has passed, your company may begin using its selected method for all FMLA leaves.

Lessons from the *Real World*

Employees are entitled to rely on old leave year calculation method if their employer doesn't give 60 days' notice in writing of change in method.

Carl Thom, Jr., worked for American Standard as a molder. After he injured his shoulder off duty, he requested FMLA leave for surgery and recovery from April 27, 2005 to June 27, 2005. American granted his request in writing. At the time Thom made his request, he believed that American used the calendar year method for calculating the leave year, which meant his 12-week leave entitlement would have extended through July 14, 2005. However, unbeknownst to Thom, American had changed its leave year calculation method to the rolling leave year method on March 1, 2005, but provided no notice to Thom of the change. Under the rolling leave year method, Thom's leave entitlement expired on June 13, 2005 (due to five weeks of leave taken in October of 2004).

On June 14, American called Thom because he had not returned to work on June 13. When Thom tried to give American a doctor's note stating that he would be returning to work on June 18 (still well before the agreed return date), American told him he was fired for unexcused absences after June 13.

The court found that American hadn't given proper notice (60-days' notice in writing) to Thom of the change in its leave year calculation method. And, the court found that American had not acted in good faith because it applied the rolling leave year method after allowing Thom to rely on its prior calendar year method and used Thom's ignorance of the changed policy to terminate him. Thom won the case, and the court instructed the jury to award double damages against American for violating the FMLA.

Thom v. American Standard, Inc., 666 F.3d 968 (6th Cir. 2011).

POLICY ALERT

Your policy determines the leave year. If your company does not designate a leave year calculation method, uses different methods with different employees, or changes methods without proper notice, each employee will get to choose his or her favored method.

Applying the Leave Year Consistently

Regardless of which method your company uses to calculate the leave year, it must use the same method for all employees who request FMLA leave. It cannot choose different methods for different employees. If one department uses a different method from another and an employee sues to challenge the method used, a court will use the method most beneficial to the employee.

Military caregiver leave is an exception to this rule. Employers must use the "counting forward" method to calculate the leave year for this type of leave, as explained above. However, this doesn't mean employers must use the counting forward method for other types of FMLA leave. As long as employers choose one method for all other types of FMLA leave and use it consistently, they don't lose their right to choose the leave year calculation method.

Another exception applies to certain employers who do business in more than one state. Some states require employers to use a particular method for calculating the leave year under their own medical leave laws. If your company has employees in a state with this type of law, it must apply the method required in that state. However, if your company does business in other states that don't have this same requirement, it is free to use a different (but uniform) method for employees in those other states. In this limited situation, using two different methods to calculate the leave year—one in the state where it is mandated and the other in all other locations—won't give employees the right to choose whichever leave method works best for them.

SEE AN EXPERT

Multistate employers may need some expert help. You can find information on each state's family and medical leave laws in Appendix A, but if you have to integrate various state laws with the FMLA, you'll appreciate some advice from a lawyer.

How Many Weeks May an Employee Take?

Employees are entitled to 12 total weeks of FMLA leave, unless they need military caregiver leave, for which they can take up to 26 weeks off. If an employee needs both types of leave within a single leave year, the calculations can get a bit tricky.

Employees Who Don't Use Military Caregiver Leave

Employees are entitled to a combined total of 12 weeks of FMLA leave to care for a family member with a serious health condition, for their own serious health conditions, to bond with a new child, or to handle qualifying exigencies relating to a family member's call to active military duty. If an employee needs leave for more than one qualifying reason during the 12-month leave year, all of that leave counts toward the employee's 12-week total. In other words, the employee gets 12 weeks of leave per year, not per qualifying reason.

> **EXAMPLE:** Your company uses the calendar year method for measuring the leave year. Max takes three weeks of FMLA leave in March to recover from hernia surgery. In August, he takes nine weeks of FMLA leave after his wife has a baby. In November, Max's father, a retired member of the Reserves, is called to active duty in Afghanistan, and Max requests FMLA leave to help him get his legal and financial affairs in order. You tell Max that he has no FMLA leave available until January, but Max replies that he should still have 12 weeks available, because he hasn't used any FMLA leave for a qualifying exigency.
>
> Nice try, Max! Employees get 12 total weeks of FMLA leave in a 12-month period, for all qualifying reasons (except military caregiver leave, for which employees can take up to 26 weeks). They don't get 12 weeks for each type of FMLA leave.

Employees Who Use Only Military Caregiver Leave

Employees are entitled to up to 26 weeks of leave in a single 12-month period for military caregiver leave. As explained above, the 12-month "clock" starts on the first day of an employee's leave. Any leave the employee doesn't use during the 12-month leave year is lost; the employee can't take it later.

An employee is entitled to only one 26-week leave per servicemember, per injury. Unless another family member suffers a service-related injury, the same family member suffers a different service-related injury, or the service-member becomes a veteran and continues to need care, the employee does not get any additional time off (see Chapter 6). Even an employee who is in the unfortunate position of qualifying for two periods of military caregiver leave may take no more than 26 weeks off in a single 12-month period, regardless of when the employee became eligible for the second period of caregiver leave.

> **EXAMPLE:** Ellen comes from a military family. Her father served in the Army, her husband serves in the Marine Corps, and all three of her children are members of the National Guard. Ellen requests FMLA leave to begin May 5, to care for her husband who was seriously injured on active duty in Iraq. Ellen takes 22 weeks of leave and returns to work on October 6.
>
> On February 1, Ellen's son Craig, who had been called to active duty in Afghanistan, is returned home after contracting malaria. Craig is severely weakened by the disease; his doctor predicts that he'll be hospitalized for at least several weeks, after which he will need assistance with daily tasks until he regains his strength. Ellen asks you for another eight weeks of leave. Because she is one of the unlucky few to have more than one family member suffer a serious illness or injury on active duty, you begin a new 12-month leave clock and inform her she is entitled to another 26 weeks of leave. Were you correct?
>
> Nope. Although Ellen is entitled to another single 12-month period for her son, she may not take more than 26 total weeks of leave in 12 months. Ellen has four weeks of her original 26-week entitlement remaining, and that's all the FMLA leave she may take until May 5, when her first single 12-month period ends.

Employees Who Use Both Military Caregiver Leave and Other Types of FMLA Leave

What about an employee who needs military caregiver leave and FMLA leave for a different purpose—such as the employee's own serious health condition—in the same leave year? These employees may not take more than 26 total weeks of FMLA leave, for any purpose, in a 12-month period. And, no more than 12 of those weeks may be used for all other types of FMLA leave combined. In other words, an employee's eligibility for military caregiver leave doesn't give that employee more than 12 weeks to use for other FMLA-qualifying reasons.

> EXAMPLE 1: Benito's wife was seriously injured while serving in the military. He has taken 20 weeks of leave, starting on September 1, to care for her. His son now has a serious medical condition requiring surgery and rehabilitation. Benito requests ten weeks of leave, starting on April 15, to care for the boy. Do you have to grant that request under the FMLA?
>
> No. As the spouse of an injured servicemember, Benito is entitled to a maximum of 26 weeks in a 12-month period for all FMLA leave. That 12-month period began on September 1, and he's used up 20 weeks of it. So, Benito has only six weeks of any type of FMLA leave left until September 1 of the following year.
>
> EXAMPLE 2: Now assume that Benito has taken only eight weeks of leave to care for his wife since she was injured on September 1. Benito provided care for the first few weeks after her injury, then his mother-in-law took over as the primary caregiver. Benito has taken a few days off here and there, when his mother-in-law was unavailable. When Benito's son requires surgery, he asks for 16 weeks of leave, to begin April 15. Must you grant this request?
>
> Still no. Even though Benito has used up only eight weeks of his 26-week entitlement for military caregiver leave to care for his wife, he is still entitled to only 12 total weeks of FMLA leave for all other purposes. His request for time off for his son's serious health condition is subject to this 12-week limit. Although he would be entitled to 18 additional weeks to continue caring for his wife, if necessary, he may not use all of this leave for other FMLA purposes.

If this doesn't already seem complicated enough, remember that two different leave years might be in play. For military caregiver leave, the leave year begins on the date the employee first takes leave. For all other types of FMLA leave, your company may use a different leave year. These situations can turn into brain teasers, although the basic rules remain the same:

- Employees who are eligible for military caregiver leave may take no more than 26 total weeks of FMLA leave in the single 12-month period. No more than 12 of those weeks may be for all types of FMLA leave other than military caregiver leave.
- FMLA leave, whether military caregiver leave or any other type, does not carry over from one year to the next. Leave that is not used during the leave year is lost.

Here are some examples that illustrate how to calculate leave entitlements when two different leave years are in play. As you read these examples, keep in mind that time off must be designated either as military caregiver leave or as another type of FMLA leave, but not both. In many instances, military caregiver leave would also qualify as leave for a family member's serious health condition. However, the revised regulations state that this time must be counted and designated as military caregiver leave only, to give employees the full benefit of this time off. (Chapter 8 explains this rule—and how to designate FMLA leave—in more detail.)

EXAMPLE 1: **Calendar Leave Year.** Josie's company uses a calendar year for FMLA leave. Josie takes eight weeks of leave when she adopts a new child, starting February 15. On August 1, Josie starts taking military caregiver leave to care for her brother, who has returned from Iraq with serious combat-related injuries. (Josie is his next of kin.) She is entitled to 26 weeks of leave in the 12-month period beginning on August 1. But, through December 31, Josie is entitled to only four additional weeks of FMLA leave for any other purpose.

Starting on January 1 of the following year, Josie will begin a new leave year for all other types of FMLA leave, and will again be entitled to 12 weeks. However, the 26-week limit for all types of leave will continue to apply to the 12-month leave year for military caregiver leave. For example, if Josie uses her entire 26-week allotment of military caregiver leave, she won't be entitled to any more FMLA leave for any reason until August 1 of the following year. At that point, she will once again be eligible for 12 weeks of FMLA leave for other purposes for the remainder of the regular FMLA leave year.

EXAMPLE 2: **Counting Forward.** Terrence's company uses a counting forward method to calculate the FMLA leave year. Terrence hasn't used any FMLA leave in years. On May 1, he begins taking military caregiver leave to care for his daughter, who contracted a serious illness while on active duty. He takes 20 weeks off to care for her, returning to work on September 18.

On December 15, Terrence's mother has a heart attack. Her doctors decide that she needs surgery, for which she is hospitalized for two weeks. She is immobilized and needs care for a couple of months afterwards. Because Terrence's company uses the counting forward method, he is entitled to 12 weeks of FMLA leave for other purposes (including his mother's serious health condition) in the year that begins on December 15. However, he only has six weeks of leave left to use in the 12-month period that ends on May 1 of the following year, because he already used 20 weeks of military caregiver leave. Terrence may use six weeks now to care for his mother; on May 1, he will become entitled to use his remaining six weeks, if necessary.

EXAMPLE 3: **Rolling Leave Year.** Caroline's company uses a rolling leave year for FMLA leave. Caroline took ten weeks of FMLA leave for childbirth and caring for her new child, starting on January 1. She returned to work on March 12. Her husband was seriously injured while on active duty, and Caroline took ten weeks of military caregiver leave starting on June 1.

On October 1, Caroline asks for four weeks off to care for her baby, who needs surgery. Because her company uses the rolling leave year, however, Caroline has only two weeks of FMLA leave to use for other purposes. She already used ten weeks of leave in the past 12 months, and she won't be eligible for more FMLA leave until January 1. If Caroline needed that time to continue providing military caregiver leave for her husband, however, she would have 16 weeks of leave left.

Counting Time Off as FMLA Leave

Under the FMLA, eligible employees are allowed to take off 12 workweeks (or 26 workweeks for military caregiver leave) in the 12-month leave year. If an employee takes FMLA leave all at once, you won't need to consider the employee's hours or schedule in determining how much leave is available. Whether the employee works part time or full time or puts in plenty of overtime, an employee who takes a whole week off at once has used up one week's worth of FMLA leave (subject to the rules set out below).

If an employee takes intermittent or reduced-schedule leave, however, you'll need to figure out how many total hours of FMLA leave are available to the employee. In this situation, the employee's work hours determine how much leave the employee can take. We explain how to make these calculations in "Intermittent and Reduced-Schedule Leave," below.

Whether an employee takes FMLA leave all at once or a little bit at a time, you'll need to know what time off counts as FMLA leave. Here are the rules:

- **Time spent working is not FMLA leave.** If an employee is on full-time FMLA leave but continues to work (perhaps putting in a few hours at home), the hours worked don't count as part of the employee's FMLA leave time. This is true even if your company does not require the employee to work on leave, but the employee voluntarily does it anyway. So, be sure that employees on FMLA leave are not working. Follow up with managers and supervisors to make sure they understand the rule and they tell employees not to work on leave.

- **Extra time taken off at your request isn't FMLA leave.** If the employee agrees to take off more time than he or she actually needs—for example, if an employee agrees to take a full day rather than a couple of hours so that you can hire a temporary employee to perform the employee's duties for the day—you can't count the difference between the time off and the time actually needed against the employee's FMLA leave entitlement. These extra hours were a convenience to you and can't be held against the employee. But, if it's not possible for the employee to leave work or return to work midshift, the entire period of absence counts as FMLA leave. For example, it would be impossible for an employee who works as an airline attendant to rejoin a flight in midair; in this situation, the entire shift counts as FMLA leave, even if the employee didn't need all of that time off.

  > **EXAMPLE:** Hal usually works an eight-hour shift, five days a week. Hal requests three hours off every Tuesday to care for his sick father. You instruct Hal to take all of Tuesday off, so that your company can put a different employee into his original schedule. You log Hal's eight hours off as FMLA leave. Was this correct?
  >
  > No. Only the three hours off that Hal needed can be counted as FMLA leave time. The other five hours may be designated as paid time off or other leave under your company's policies but do not reduce Hal's available FMLA leave time.

- **Holidays don't affect the count for full weeks of FMLA leave.** All full workweeks are counted; it doesn't matter that a holiday falls within one of the weeks that an employee is out on FMLA leave. However, if an employee takes less than a full week of leave, a holiday that falls within that partial week of leave is not counted against the employee's available FMLA time.

- **If the company is closed for at least a week, that time doesn't count as FMLA leave.** If your company shuts down operations entirely and employees are not required to come to work for a week or more, that week will not count as one of the employee's FMLA leave workweeks. For example, a company that closes its doors for two weeks in August can't count those weeks as FMLA leave for any employee.

Counting Time Off for Airline Flight Crews

Special rules apply to airline flight crew employees. These employees are entitled to 72 total days of FMLA leave during any 12-month period. Eligible airline flight crew employees are also entitled to 156 days of military caregiver leave in a single 12-month period. These entitlements are based on a uniform six-day workweek, regardless of time actually worked or paid, multiplied by the FMLA 12-week leave entitlement (or the 26-week leave entitlement for military caregiver leave). For example, if an eligible pilot took six weeks of leave to care for her sick child, the pilot would use 36 days (6 days x 6 weeks) of her 72-day entitlement.

Intermittent and Reduced-Schedule Leave

Sometimes an employee doesn't need a full workweek off at a time or doesn't need to take all of his or her FMLA leave at once. An employee may, for example, request permission to take hours or days off "as needed" to care for an ill family member when the usual caretaker is unavailable. This "intermittent leave" is allowed under the FMLA. Intermittent leave is leave taken in separate blocks of time for a single qualifying reason, such as a course of treatment spread over months or flare-ups of a chronic illness.

An employee may also need a reduced work schedule, for example, during recovery from surgery or illness. The FMLA allows an eligible employee to take "reduced-schedule" leave when he or she needs to work fewer hours per week or per day than usual, typically while the employee or a family member is recovering from or being treated for a serious health condition.

When an employee uses one of these types of leave, figuring out how much leave the employee is entitled to and how long it will take to use up the

12-week or 26-week allotment can be challenging. It gets especially tricky for part-time employees or those with irregular work schedules because you have to measure the leave taken based on the employee's normal workweek. In this section, we explain how to calculate intermittent and reduced-schedule leave for employees working all types of schedules.

> **RELATED TOPIC**
>
> **See Chapter 10 for information on managing intermittent leave, including rules that allow flexibility in scheduling.** When Congress passed the FMLA, it recognized that providing intermittent leave could impose a significant burden on employers. The law gives companies a couple of options for easing the load, including the right to transfer an employee who needs intermittent leave to a different position and the right to require employees to schedule foreseeable intermittent leave in a manner that isn't unduly disruptive. These rules—and tips for making sure employees don't abuse the right to take intermittent leave—are covered in Chapter 10.

When Can an Employee Take Intermittent or Reduced-Schedule Leave?

An employee may take intermittent or reduced-schedule leave if it's medically necessary for a serious health condition (the employee's own or that of a family member) or military caregiver leave. Employees may also take intermittent or reduced-schedule leave to handle qualifying exigencies arising from a family member's call to active duty. As explained in Chapter 5, the FMLA doesn't require you to provide intermittent or reduced-schedule parenting leave, but you're permitted to do so as long as you do it consistently.

Here are some examples of conditions that qualify for intermittent or reduced-schedule leave:

- **An employee is receiving chemotherapy and radiation treatment for cancer.** The weekly treatment renders him unable to work, so he reduces his schedule by one afternoon per week to receive treatment and recover afterward.
- **An employee's mother has multiple sclerosis.** Some days, she is able to care for herself; other days, she needs assistance. The employee can take intermittent leave to care for her mother when necessary.

- **An employee has back surgery to repair a herniated disk.** The employee returns to work part time for several weeks, until he is strong enough to work full time. Afterward, the employee takes a couple of hours off each Friday to go to physical therapy, as well as an hour every other week for a doctor's appointment to check his progress. This employee is using both reduced-schedule leave and intermittent leave.

Lessons from the *Real World*

An employee suffering from flare-ups of a chronic condition is entitled to intermittent leave.

Kathleen Victorelli, an employee at Shadyside Hospital, requested leave when she experienced an episode of stomach pain, nausea, and vomiting as a result of peptic ulcer disease that her doctor had diagnosed two years earlier. The hospital refused the request. Victorelli took the leave anyway, and the hospital fired her. She sued, claiming that Shadyside had violated the FMLA.

The court held that Victorelli's peptic ulcer disease was a chronic medical condition that entitled her to intermittent leave when her condition flared up. *Victorelli v. Shadyside Hosp.*, 128 F.3d 184 (3rd Cir. 1997).

Leave Must Be Necessary

An employee may not take intermittent leave simply because that's what he or she prefers. It must be medically necessary or necessitated by a qualifying exigency arising from a family member's call to active duty. Qualifying exigency leave may often be intermittent. For example, if an employee must attend counseling sessions, school functions, or military events, those activities will probably take up only a few hours at a time. This time will count as intermittent FMLA leave.

Intermittent leave is available for a serious health condition or for military caregiver leave only if medically necessary. This means that the employee must need the leave in separate increments rather than all at once.

How can you tell whether intermittent leave is medically necessary? By getting a medical certification. On the certification form, the employee's (or family member's) health care provider must state that intermittent leave is necessary. The provider must also indicate the expected duration of leave and, if intermittent leave is necessary for medical treatment, the dates and duration of the treatment. For more on the medical certification form, see Chapter 9. Chapter 10 explains how to use the information in the form—and in subsequent recertifications, if necessary—to make sure an employee uses intermittent leave appropriately.

EXAMPLE: Eric tells you that he needs to reduce his work schedule from 40 hours per week to 30 hours per week to recover from surgery. You request medical certification and give him a preliminary designation of the leave as FMLA qualified, subject to withdrawal if the certification is inadequate (see "Counting Time Off as FMLA Leave" in Chapter 8).

When you get the medical certification, you discover that the surgery is elective cosmetic surgery to reduce eyelid puffiness. You withdraw the preliminary FMLA designation and deny Eric's request for FMLA leave to recover from this surgery. Have you violated the FMLA?

No. Elective surgery and recovery from it don't count as serious health conditions under the FMLA.

Eric has the surgery on a Saturday and returns to work on Monday, a little bruised and bandaged but able to work. However, on Wednesday, Eric calls in to explain that he has a postoperative infection and his doctor has placed him on a regimen of antibiotics and a restricted work schedule of 25 hours per week for two weeks.

Because you have read this book, you send Eric notice that this reduced-schedule leave may qualify as FMLA leave, because the postsurgery complications are FMLA qualified (even though the initial surgery wasn't).

Employees Must Be Able to Perform the Essential Functions of the Job

Because an employee on intermittent or reduced-schedule leave continues to work, the employee must still be able to perform the essential functions of his or her job. (See Chapter 4 to learn what an "essential function" is.) In contrast, an employee who takes FMLA leave all at once for a serious health condition must be unable to perform at least one essential job function. These opposing requirements are based on the different types of leave: An employee on intermittent leave must still be able to do the job while at work, but an employee on full-time FMLA leave won't be working at all.

Lessons from the *Real World*

An employee who cannot perform the job's essential functions is not entitled to intermittent leave or reinstatement.

Minnie Hatchett worked as a business manager for Philander Smith College. A skylight fell on her head, injuring her to such a degree that she couldn't perform certain essential functions of her job. She asked permission to continue working part time, but the college refused the request and told her she had to go on full-time leave. At the end of her FMLA leave, Hatchett still could not perform all the essential functions of her job, so the college offered her some alternative positions. She rejected them, so the college terminated her employment. Hatchett sued the college for violating the FMLA.

The court sided with the college, finding that an employee who cannot perform the essential functions of her job is not entitled to reduced leave schedule or reinstatement under the FMLA.

Hatchett v. Philander Smith Coll., 251 F.3d 670 (8th Cir. 2001).

Applying the 1,250-Hour Eligibility Requirement

An employee on intermittent or reduced-scheduled leave doesn't become ineligible for FMLA leave if his or her hours drop below the 1,250-hour requirement because of the FMLA-protected schedule. As long as the employee worked 1,250 hours in 12 months at the time of initially requesting the intermittent or reduced-schedule leave, the employee's leave is protected for absences relating to the original condition requiring intermittent leave. In other words, you don't recalculate the employee's eligibility.

This rule applies only to intermittent leave taken for the same condition. If an employee properly qualifies for intermittent leave and then needs FMLA leave for a different reason within the same 12-month period, you should recalculate the employee's eligibility at the time of the second request. In doing so, you needn't count the employee's leave hours as hours worked. The odd result of this rule is that an employee might be eligible for one type of FMLA leave (intermittent leave that began when the employee met the eligibility requirements) but not for others.

EXAMPLE 1: Telly, one of your company's part-time employees, has worked 25 hours per week for five years. For the first 12 weeks of 2017, Telly needs to reduce his hours to 20 per week so he can care for his wife, who is receiving cancer treatment. Your company uses the calendar leave year calculation. In July of 2017, Telly's wife takes a turn for the worse, and he asks to resume his reduced leave schedule effective July 1. You count up his time for the last 12 months and discover that he's only worked 1,240 hours. Should you deny his leave request?

No. Because Telly needs intermittent leave for the same condition, you can't redetermine his eligibility during the leave year. Although his hours have dropped below the eligibility threshold, he is still entitled to leave.

EXAMPLE 2: Now assume that Telly needs to take time off, starting July 1, 2017, for his own serious health condition. May you deny this request?

Yes. Because Telly is requesting leave for a different condition, you must redetermine his eligibility. He hasn't worked 1,250 hours at the time his leave is scheduled to begin, so he isn't qualified to take this leave.

And, the employee must meet the 1,250-hour test at the start of each FMLA leave year. Once the employee has used up his or her FMLA leave, you will need to recalculate the employee's leave eligibility as of the next request for leave. When making this calculation, the employee's leave time does not count as hours worked.

Part-Time Employees

Under the FMLA, a part-time employee or an employee with variable hours is entitled to leave in proportion to the amount of time he or she normally works. In other words, the leave time allowed for those employees is prorated. Usually, you will not need to calculate the pro rata time unless the employee is requesting intermittent or partial leave: whether an employee normally works 15 hours in a workweek or 50 hours, an employee who takes a whole week off has used one week's worth of leave time. On the other hand, if the employee uses only a few hours here and there, you have to figure how much total leave time the employee has available.

EXAMPLE 1: Leslie, who normally works 30 hours per week, needs 15 hours off each week due to a serious medical condition. Because Leslie is reducing her schedule by 50%, she will take half a week of FMLA leave each calendar week and will use up all her FMLA leave in 24 calendar weeks.

EXAMPLE 2: Keith usually works the same shift, six days a week. He takes four calendar weeks and two days of leave. The four calendar weeks count as four full weeks of FMLA leave. In the last week, Keith is taking two days of leave out of his normal six-day work schedule, which equals a one-third workweek of leave. If Keith's regular schedule was four days a week, he would be taking half a week of leave in the last week.

If a part-time employee's schedule varies from week to week, you should measure the FMLA workweek by calculating the average weekly hours worked in the 12 months prior to the start of the FMLA leave. You can use the employee's timesheet or payroll records to come up with this figure. Make sure the employee agrees to the weekly average in a signed document.

EXAMPLE: Manny works between 20 and 35 hours per week, depending on your company's needs. He requests intermittent leave for his asthma, which flares up periodically. You add up Manny's hours for the past 12 months, which total 1,456 hours. Dividing that by 52, you come up with a weekly average of 28 hours for the past year. Manny signs an agreement stating that his weekly average is 28 hours. Using that as Manny's average workweek, you track his FMLA leave. So, when Manny's asthma acts up at work and he takes four hours off, he has used one-seventh of a workweek of FMLA leave.

CAUTION

Make sure part-time employees are eligible for leave in the first place. As explained in Chapter 3, part-time employees must work 1,250 hours in the preceding 12 months to be eligible for FMLA leave. This works out to a bit more than 24 hours a week, 52 weeks a year. You won't have to do the math on intermittent leave availability unless your part-time employees can meet this initial eligibility requirement.

Employees Who Work Overtime

If your company requires an employee to work overtime, the overtime hours are considered part of the employee's normal workweek for purposes of calculating the amount of leave time an employee is entitled to. If an employee chooses to work overtime but is not required to, the overtime hours don't count as part of the employee's normal workweek.

EXAMPLE: Claire and her coworkers all have to work four hours of overtime a week, in addition to their regular 40 hours. In this situation, Claire's usual workweek is 44 hours, and she's entitled to 528 total hours of FMLA leave per year (assuming she's otherwise qualified).

If Claire's overtime was voluntary—that is, the company didn't require it but she decided to work it anyway—then she would have a 40-hour week for purposes of calculating her available FMLA leave.

Exempt Employees

It can be tricky to figure out what constitutes a normal workweek for exempt employees—employees who are not entitled to overtime pay. Most companies don't routinely track hours worked by exempt employees, because those employees don't get paid for putting in extra time. However, an exempt employee's FMLA entitlement is based on the hours the employee usually works, just like any other employee.

Because a salaried, exempt employee usually does not "clock in" or "clock out," when an exempt employee requests this type of leave, your company and the employee must agree in writing on the length of the employee's workweek. If you can't reach agreement, your company must track the exempt employee's hours to calculate how many hours are available for leave.

EXAMPLE: Manny is an exempt manager who regularly works 60 hours per week. His FMLA workweek and intermittent time off are calculated according to a 60-hour workweek. When Manny takes four hours of FMLA intermittent leave one week, that counts as 1/15 of a workweek of his overall entitlement.

TIP

Pay docking rules don't apply to FMLA leave. Generally, employers may not dock the pay of an exempt employee for absences of less than a full day (for example, because the employee is tardy or leaves early). Employers who violate this rule might lose the right to exempt these employees from overtime—and, as a result, have to pay them time-and-a-half for every extra hour worked. There are a few exceptions to this rule, however, and one of them is for FMLA leave. You can track—and not pay an exempt employee for—FMLA leave taken in increments of less than a full day without losing the exemption.

Administering Intermittent or Reduced-Schedule Leave

Because intermittent and reduced-schedule leave differs from full-time FMLA leave in several ways, it must be administered more carefully. After all, you'll have to keep track of how much protected time an employee is using and how much time that employee has available. Here are some of the notable differences:

- **Record keeping.** Because the calculations and calendaring required by intermittent and reduced-schedule leave are more complicated than those required by full-time FMLA leave, it is essential to keep accurate and regularly updated records of these leaves. Below is a sample work-sheet for keeping track of this leave. You can find a blank copy (and all other forms in this book) at this book's online companion page; see Appendix C for details. Note that this worksheet is completed for employees who are *not* using military caregiver leave.

Calculating Intermittent/Reduced-Schedule Leave

A	B	C	D	E
Employee	Regular Workweek	Total Hours Available for FMLA Leave (column B x 12)	Hours of Leave Needed Per Week	Total No. of Calendar Weeks of FMLA Leave Available (column C ÷ column D)
Employee A	30 hrs./wk.	360 hrs.	20 hrs./wk.	18 weeks
Employee B	25 hrs./wk.	300 hrs.	9 hrs./wk.	33.3 weeks
Employee C	62 hrs./wk.	744 hrs.	21 hrs./wk.	35.4 weeks

- **Fitness-for-duty reports.** As explained in Chapter 11, you may ask employees who have been out for their own serious health condition to provide a fitness-for-duty report before returning to work. However, you may not ask an employee on intermittent or reduced-schedule leave to provide a fitness-for-duty report unless you have reasonable safety concerns about the employee's ability to perform his or her duties due to the serious health condition for which leave was taken. A reasonable safety concern is a reasonable belief of significant risk of harm to the employee or others, considering the nature, severity, and likelihood of the potential harm. Even if you have a reasonable safety concern regarding an employee's return to work from intermittent leave, you may only request a fitness-for-duty report once every 30 days and only in connection with an absence.

- **Minimum increments of time.** Employees may take intermittent or reduced-schedule FMLA leave in one-hour increments or the shortest periods of time that your company's payroll system uses to account for other types of leave, whichever is shorter. So, if your company clocks its employees' leave time by the minute, then an employee's intermittent or reduced-schedule leave could be measured in minutes. If your company uses different increments of time for different types of leave, it must use the smallest of the increments to measure an employee's intermittent FMLA leave. An employer cannot require an employee to take more FMLA leave than the employee needs for the purpose of the leave. But, if the employee cannot arrive at or leave work midshift, the entire period of absence counts as FMLA leave. This so-called "physical impossibility provision" (when an employee is unable to start or end work midway through a shift) is to be applied in only the most limited circumstances, and the employer bears the responsibility of restoring the employee to the same or an equivalent position as soon as possible. If it chooses to, an employer may grant intermittent or reduced-schedule FMLA leave in shorter time increments than it grants for other types of leave.

- **Scheduled time versus time actually taken.** If an employee taking intermittent leave returns to work early, only the time the employee actually takes off counts as FMLA leave (even if more time was initially granted).

- **Special rules apply to teachers.** See 29 C.F.R. § 825.601 for special rules that apply to school employees seeking intermittent or reduced-leave schedules.

• **Special rules apply to airline flight crew employees.** An airline employer must account for an airline flight crew employee's intermittent or reduced-schedule leave using increments no greater than one day. For example, if an eligible flight attendant needs to take FMLA leave for a two-hour physical therapy session, the airline employer may require the employee to use a full day (but no more) of FMLA leave.

Flexible Schedules Versus FMLA Leave

Sometimes, an employee who has a medical condition or caretaking responsibilities might request a flexible schedule. In this situation, the employee isn't asking for time off work; instead, the employee wants to work the same total number of hours, but on a different schedule than usual. Because such an employee won't be taking any time off, this does not count as a request for FMLA leave.

> EXAMPLE: Your employee Bud normally works a 9-to-5 workday. He has recently requested a change in his work schedule to 11-to-7 because the antidepressants he is taking make him groggy in the morning. Is this a request for FMLA intermittent/reduced-schedule leave?
>
> No, because Bud is not taking any time off and the schedule change is not needed for medical treatment. However, keep in mind that, if Bud's depression is a disability, you may have to accommodate the schedule change under the ADA. (For more information, see Chapter 12.)

Common Mistakes Regarding Leave Duration—And How to Avoid Them

Mistake 1: Using inconsistent methods to measure the "leave year."

Avoid this mistake by taking the following steps:

• Use the "counting forward" method to measure the single 12-month leave period for all employees using military caregiver leave.

- Make sure everyone in your company uses the same leave year method for all employees seeking other types of FMLA leave.
- If your company changes leave year methods, provide 60 days' written notice to all employees before implementing the change. You must allow employees who already started or requested leave prior to your announcement to use whichever method of calculating the leave year is most beneficial to them.
- Apply the new method to all employees as soon as the 60-day notice period passes.

Mistake 2: Failing to accurately count the leave time taken by employees.

Avoid this mistake by taking the following steps:
- Calculate the total amount of available FMLA leave at the beginning of leave.
- Track all leave time the employee takes—not including time the employee actually spends working, additional time off taken for your company's convenience, and weeks during which your company is shut down.
- Subtract all leave time taken from the employee's available FMLA leave time.

Mistake 3: Failing to accurately calculate available leave time for employees who need intermittent or reduced-schedule leave.

Avoid this mistake by taking the following steps:
- Calculate available leave time based on the employee's usual workweek. Employees who work part time or work overtime hours are entitled to a proportionate amount of leave based on their usual hours worked.
- Keep good records of employee work hours, including hours worked by exempt employees.
- Come up with the average hourly workweek for employees with irregular schedules, based on the 12-month period before they start their leave.
- Get written agreements of average workweek hours from employees with irregular schedules and exempt employees who request FMLA leave.

✓

Managers' Checklist: Duration of Leave

For All Employees Requesting Leave:

☐ I confirmed that my company's method for defining the FMLA leave year is in writing, in our FMLA leave policy.

☐ If our company has not yet defined its leave year or has decided to change methods of defining the leave year, I either

  ☐ provided all employees with notice of this change at least 60 days before they requested leave, or

  ☐ gave employees the benefit of whichever leave year calculation method provided them with the most leave.

☐ I calculated the FMLA leave time available to the employee requesting leave according to my company's leave year method.

☐ For military caregiver leave, I calculated the employee's entitlement using the "counting forward" method.

☐ I recorded all FMLA leave the employee has taken, but I have not included the following types of time off as FMLA leave:

  ☐ time the employee actually spent working

  ☐ time taken off for the company's convenience, and

  ☐ weeks during which the company was shut down.

For Employees Requesting Intermittent or Reduced-Schedule Leave:

☐ I determined that the employee's requested intermittent or reduced-schedule leave is medically necessary, or necessary for a qualifying exigency.

☐ I determined that the employee is able to perform the essential functions of his or her job.

☐ If the employee works the same number of hours each week, I used that schedule to calculate the FMLA leave available to the employee.

☐ If the employee's hours are irregular, I calculated the average hours worked per week by the employee requesting FMLA leave, and

  ☐ I have a written agreement of the average workweek signed by the employee, and

  ☐ I calculated the pro rata time off that the employee is entitled to under the FMLA.

Managers' Checklist: Duration of Leave (continued)

☐ If the employee is exempt from overtime, the employee and I reached an agreement as to the employee's average weekly hours, and

☐ I have the employee's sign-off on this average.

☐ I included all mandatory overtime hours in the workweek hours of the employee requesting FMLA leave.

Giving Notice and Designating Leave

Chapter Highlights

☆ Your company must provide individualized FMLA information to each employee requesting leave who may be FMLA qualified, explaining the employee's rights under the FMLA and the effect of the employee's failure to comply with the FMLA and company rules, and designating the employee's leave as FMLA leave.

☆ Employees requesting FMLA leave must give you 30 days' notice of the need for foreseeable leave, unless one of the following is true:

- The leave is not certain in time.
- There is a change in circumstances.
- As a result of medical emergency, the 30-day notice is not practicable.

☆ An employee requesting FMLA leave that is not foreseeable must provide notice as soon as practicable, usually the same or next business day after learning that he or she needs leave.

☆ Your company is allowed to discipline an employee for failing to provide proper notice of FMLA leave and can delay the leave.

☆ Employees may choose to use accrued paid leave during their FMLA leave—or your company may require them to—but only if the reason for the employee's leave is covered by your paid leave policy.

☆ Your company may require employees to follow its usual procedures to use paid leave during their FMLA leave, but an employee's failure to follow these procedures only limits the employee's right to use paid leave, not the right to use FMLA leave.

☆ The employee requesting FMLA leave must give you sufficient information to determine that the FMLA might apply, but the information doesn't have to be detailed or even refer to the FMLA (unless the employee has already used FMLA leave for the same qualifying reason).

This chapter covers the FMLA's notice requirements: what information you and the employee must provide each other when an employee takes or requests time off that might be protected by the FMLA. The heavier informational burden lies with you, and for good reason: Many employees don't know what the law is or what their rights are. In fact, your employees might never have heard of the FMLA. This means that employees might come to you requesting leave, without knowing their legal right to take it or their legal obligation to give you information so that you can properly determine whether the FMLA applies.

Your company's informational requirements begin with hanging an FMLA poster and providing general information about the law to employees; Chapter 2 explains how to comply with these obligations. Once an employee requests leave, however, additional requirements kick in. You must know enough about the FMLA to figure out whether it applies and ask the employee for more information if necessary. You must give the employee three separate notices about the FMLA: an eligibility notice, a rights and responsibilities notice, and a designation notice. These notices, mandated by the FMLA regulations, provide employees with detailed information about the law and your company's requirements for FMLA leave. You must also designate the leave as FMLA leave and notify the employee that you've done so.

Sounds like a lot of meetings and paperwork, doesn't it? While it is a significant responsibility to comply with all these requirements, there are ways to streamline the process. We tell you how below and give you some approved forms to use.

Counting Time Off as FMLA Leave

When an employee comes to you requesting medical, parenting, or family military leave, the first important duty that you have is to figure out whether the leave might qualify as FMLA leave. If the leave qualifies, you must give the employee the required notices (see "Individual Notice Requirements," below), including a notice that designates the leave as FMLA leave.

If you don't give notice and designate an employee's time off as FMLA leave in a timely fashion, and your error causes the employee harm, your company may be liable for damages, including lost compensation and benefits that the employee has suffered as a result. The employee may also be entitled to other remedies, including reinstatement, promotion, or other relief for the harm caused by your actions.

Of course, if an employee comes to you and says, "I need FMLA leave," or the employee's leave clearly qualifies under the FMLA, you can proceed to giving your required notices and designating the leave. This section covers a couple of situations that can get complicated: substitution of paid leave for FMLA leave and designating FMLA leave retroactively.

Substituting Paid Leave for FMLA Leave

The FMLA allows employees to substitute paid time off provided under the employer's policies—such as vacation, sick, or personal leave—for unpaid FMLA leave, as long as the reason for leave is covered by the employer's policy and the employee meets the other requirements of the employer's paid leave program. It also allows employers to require employees to make this substitution, even if the employee doesn't want to.

In addition, you should designate any time off for which the employee is paid from another source as FMLA leave, if it meets the requirements. For example, an employee who suffers an on-the-job injury and takes time off while receiving workers' compensation benefits is probably also qualified for FMLA leave—and you should designate that time off accordingly.

Paid Leave Provided by Your Company

Whether company-provided paid leave can be used during all or part of an employee's FMLA leave depends on your company's policies. Employees may use, or you may require them to use, any applicable accrued paid leave during their FMLA leave. However, the type of leave must be covered by your paid leave policies. Employees may not choose to use paid leave for reasons that are not covered by your company's paid leave program, and your company cannot require them to.

TIP

It's really overlap, not substitution. Although the law refers to "substitution" of paid leave, that's not exactly accurate. The employee isn't using paid leave *instead* of FMLA leave, but is using the two types of leave at the same time.

EXAMPLE 1: Your company has a paid sick leave policy that employees can use to care for ill children and spouses. Your employee, Kurt, has asked for a two-week leave to care for his father following surgery to treat prostate cancer. You provide Kurt with the necessary FMLA notices and inform him that he must use accrued paid sick leave under your company's policy.

Bad move. Because your company's paid sick leave policy does not cover care for a parent, you can't require Kurt to use paid leave during his FMLA leave. The effect is that Kurt has the right to take unpaid FMLA leave to care for his father, and he retains his accrued paid sick leave under your company's policy.

EXAMPLE 2: Lourdes is eight months pregnant and requests four weeks of leave following the birth of her child. She also requests to use paid sick leave under the company's sick leave policy. You deny her request, because your company's paid sick leave policy does not cover time off to bond with a new child.

Not so fast. Lourdes might need the postdelivery leave for her own serious health condition, which would mean she is entitled to use accrued paid sick leave. Your company may also require her to use it.

Your company may require employees to follow its usual paid leave procedures to get paid for their time off, but you may not deny them unpaid FMLA leave for failing to follow those procedures. An employee's failure to follow company policies for paid leave affects only their right to paid leave, not their right to unpaid FMLA leave.

EXAMPLE: Your company requires employees to give at least one week of advance notice before using paid vacation time. Tim's wife is seriously injured in a car accident while commuting to work on Monday morning. Tim calls you from the hospital and tells you about the accident. He tells you that his wife is in surgery and is expected to recover quickly. He asks about using vacation time while he is out. You tell Tim that he can't use vacation time until a week has passed, because of the company's advance notice rule, but that he is entitled to unpaid FMLA leave. You prepare the necessary notices and send them to Tim's home. Did you do the right thing?

Yes. Your company can require employees to follow its usual paid leave procedures to use paid leave, but it cannot deny them the right to take unpaid FMLA leave if they are otherwise entitled. Tim provided as much notice as is required for unforeseeable FMLA leave (as explained below), so he is covered by the FMLA. If he has to be out for more than a week, he is also entitled to start using accrued vacation time once he has met the one-week notice requirement.

Paid Leave From Another Source

When an employee takes any type of time off to care for a family member, for parenting, for military family leave, or for the employee's own health, you should always consider whether the FMLA applies—and, if so, provide the necessary notices and designate the leave accordingly. Some types of leave slip through the cracks because the employee is covered by another law or program. But any type of leave that falls within the FMLA's parameters should be designated as such and counted against the employee's entitlement, no matter how many other laws apply.

Here are some examples:

- **Workers' compensation.** As explained in Chapter 12, an employee who suffers a work-related illness or injury may be entitled to partial wage replacement while off work to recuperate. This time will almost always also qualify as FMLA leave.
- **Temporary disability.** The laws of a handful of states provide some income to employees who are temporarily unable to work because of a disability. This time may also qualify as FMLA leave.
- **Paid family leave.** In some states, employees can receive some income for time they take off to care for a family member, which might also qualify as FMLA leave.
- **Disability insurance.** If your company provides disability insurance for employees, they might have the right to replacement income while they are out of work. This time off may also be covered by the FMLA.
- **Paid sick leave.** Seven states and the District of Columbia require private employers to provide at least a few days of paid sick leave to their employees each year.

If an employee is entitled to some compensation from another source, paid leave typically may not be substituted for this time off, nor may your company require employees to use paid leave during this time. After all, the employee is already receiving some pay. However, your company and the employee may agree that the employee may use some paid leave to supplement benefits from another source. For example, workers' compensation and state disability insurance typically replace only a portion of the employee's wages. If you and the employee agree, the employee may use paid leave to complete his or her pay.

> **EXAMPLE:** Ted is on workers' compensation leave and is receiving two-thirds of his usual compensation as wage replacement. Because Ted has a serious health condition, all of his time off counts as FMLA leave. You and Ted agree that Ted may use accrued sick leave to make up the remaining third of his preinjury wages. Ted was working 36 hours a week before being injured, so he takes—and your company pays him for—12 hours of sick leave per week while he is receiving workers' compensation benefits.

Designating FMLA Leave Retroactively

Often, an employee takes vacation or sick leave for a reason that's covered by the FMLA, but you don't know about it. For example, an employee who needs time off to care for a dying parent might simply request vacation time, without revealing the reason for the time off. Or, the employee might develop a need for FMLA leave while on paid leave, for example, because the employee becomes very ill while on vacation.

You can designate FMLA leave retroactively if, after an employee has started or even returned from leave, you learn that the leave qualifies under the FMLA. You may make a retroactive FMLA designation as long as the employee agrees to it or your late designation doesn't cause harm to the employee. When making a retroactive designation, you must give the employee all of the notices discussed under "Individual Notice Requirements," below.

You can also retroactively designate FMLA leave when circumstances change so that a leave that wasn't originally an FMLA-qualifying leave becomes qualified. The rules for how much of the original time counts as FMLA leave depend on whether the FMLA-qualifying event developed out of the original reason for leave (for example, when a minor illness takes a serious turn) or not (for example, when an employee suffers an accident during vacation). In the first situation, you may designate all of the employee's time off as FMLA leave; in the second, only leave taken after the FMLA-qualifying event can be designated as FMLA leave.

EXAMPLE 1: Your employee, Ravi, caught a cold that turned into bronchitis. Ravi requests sick leave to recover from the bronchitis. Four days after going out on sick leave, Ravi calls in and says that he's gotten worse and his doctor has diagnosed him with bronchial pneumonia. How do you handle this change of circumstance?

Because you have read this book, you correctly realize that Ravi now has a serious health condition. Because it grew out of Ravi's original health condition, the entire time he has taken off counts as FMLA leave for a serious health condition. You provide Ravi with the required notices and give him a written designation after learning of the diagnosis of bronchial pneumonia.

EXAMPLE 2: Selena requests two weeks' vacation time to go snorkeling in Belize. You grant the request. One week into the vacation, Selena calls to report that she took a nasty spill on her motorbike and had to be hospitalized for a concussion and broken arm. Does the accident change Selena's leave?

Yes. Selena's leave changed from vacation to FMLA leave for a serious medical condition as soon as she got hurt. Only the time off after her injury counts as FMLA leave. The initial week of time off was true vacation time, and does not count against Selena's available FMLA leave.

Individual Notice Requirements

There are four types of notice an employer must give to an employee who requests FMLA leave. We discuss each in turn and refer to the forms and documents that are available online; see Appendix C for details.

General Notice

The first type of notice that you have to give employees requesting leave, the "general notice," is the same notice you have to post in the workplace and distribute to all employees explaining FMLA rights, discussed in Chapter 2. You can use the FMLA poster for this purpose (see Appendix C).

If your company includes the general notice information (that is, the information contained in the DOL FMLA poster) in its employee handbook or in some other written policy that it distributes to all employees and applicants, it has satisfied the general notice requirement. If your company doesn't include the general notice information in its handbook or other disseminated, written policies, it must give each new employee a copy of the general notice information in writing at the time of hire.

Lessons from the *Real World*

An employer can be liable for failing to give an employee information on the FMLA.

Marria Saroli was the controller for Automation & Modular Components, Inc. ("A&M"). Upon learning that she was pregnant, Saroli notified A&M and requested leave. A&M didn't respond or provide Saroli with any FMLA information. Instead, A&M told Saroli that it was hiring a man to manage her department and take over her duties.

Saroli's doctor placed her on immediate leave due to a medical condition related to her pregnancy. She again requested pregnancy leave. This time A&M wrote to her, telling her that she could take only six weeks of leave. Saroli had to extend her leave twice, so it exceeded six weeks. When Saroli tried to return to work, A&M told her that the only job she could return to was one with diminished duties. Saroli resigned and sued A&M for interfering with her FMLA rights.

The court ruled that A&M's failure to give Saroli information about her rights under the FMLA and its failure to respond to her requests for information about pregnancy leave interfered with her FMLA rights.

Saroli v. Automation & Modular Components, Inc., 405 F.3d 446 (6th Cir. 2005).

You can distribute the general notice information electronically on your company's intranet system or in its electronic handbook. But, all *employees and applicants* must have access to it. (This applies to the general posting requirement discussed in Chapter 2, as well.) If the electronic information is not accessible by all employees and applicants, you have to give the general notice information to them in writing or post the information in a conspicuous place where employees and applicants can readily see it.

Eligibility Notice

When an employee requests leave that may qualify under the FMLA, you must tell the employee whether he or she is eligible for FMLA leave. This "eligibility notice" is required at the start of the first leave taken in the leave year and must be provided, for each qualifying reason, within five business days after an employee requests leave, absent extenuating circumstances. For example, an employee requesting leave to care for a spouse injured while on active military duty should get an eligibility notice for FMLA military caregiver leave. If the same employee later requested leave for her own pregnancy, you would have to issue a separate eligibility notice as to that qualifying reason. The eligibility notice may be written or oral, and may be distributed electronically.

If an employee is not eligible for FMLA leave, you have to give the employee a written notice stating at least one reason why the employee is ineligible (for example, that the employee has not worked 1,250 hours for the company in the previous 12 months). If the employee's eligibility for leave for the reason requested changes during the leave year, or the employee requests leave for a different reason, you have to give the employee a new eligibility notice upon his or her next request for leave in that leave year.

> EXAMPLE: Dev requested three weeks of leave earlier in the year to care for his new baby when the baby was kept in the hospital for a medical complication following birth. He has recently requested another six weeks of leave to bond with the baby. Do you have to give him another eligibility notice for leave for the same child in the same leave year?
>
> Yes, because the reason for the original leave—the child's serious medical condition—is different from the reason for the current leave request—bonding.

FORM
You can use the DOL's *Notice of Eligibility and Rights & Responsibilities* form (Form WH-381) to satisfy the obligations described in this section. (See Appendix C for details on how to access this form.)

Rights and Responsibilities Notice

At the same time you give the eligibility notice to the employee requesting leave, you must also give the employee a written "rights and responsibilities" notice that lays out the employee's rights and obligations under the FMLA, as well as the consequences if the employee doesn't fulfill his or her obligations. The written rights and responsibilities notice must tell the employee, as appropriate to the employee's circumstances:

- that the leave may count against the employee's available FMLA leave time
- whether your company requires the employee to provide certification and, if so:
  - what those requirements are, and
  - the consequences of failing to provide required certification
- that the employee has the right to substitute paid leave for FMLA leave, if applicable
- whether your company requires the employee to substitute paid leave for FMLA leave and, if so:
  - any conditions relating to substitution of paid leave, and
  - the consequences of failing to meet those conditions
- that the employee has the right to continue benefits during leave and have them restored upon return to work
- whether your company requires the employee to pay for health insurance benefits during leave and, if so:
  - how the employee's payment for health insurance premiums during leave is to be arranged
  - the consequences of the employee's failure to pay for health insurance benefits during leave, and
  - the employee's liability, if any, for the cost of benefits payments if your company pays them during leave and the employee fails to return to work

- key employee information, and
- that the employee has the right to return from FMLA leave to the same or an equivalent job.

FORM

You can fulfill your notice obligations by providing the employee with the DOL's *Notice of Eligibility and Rights & Responsibilities* form (Form WH-381).

You may, but don't have to, provide a certification form to the employee along with this notice. (See Chapter 9 for more information on certifications.)

CAUTION

Email notice to an employee may not suffice. If the employee's leave has already begun, the FMLA states that the rights and responsibilities notice should be mailed to the employee's address of record. At least one court has rejected an employer's argument that email notice (in that case, a recertification notice; see Chapter 9) was adequate.

If the information in the rights and responsibilities notice changes, you have to notify any employee who subsequently requests leave of those changes within five business days of learning of the employee's need for leave.

> **EXAMPLE:** Dev requested leave to bond with his new baby, which your company granted, and you gave him the eligibility and rights and responsibilities notices. He's been on leave for a week and the company just instituted a new policy requiring employees to substitute paid leave for FMLA leave. You've added the new policy to your employee handbook, which is available to employees via the company's intranet. Do you have to give Dev a new rights and responsibilities notice laying out the details of this new policy?
>
> Not necessarily. You must give him notice of the changes in some form. If he can access the policy while on leave, you can just send him a notice referring to the policy and telling him he can review it in the electronic handbook.

Designation Notice

Within five business days of receiving enough information to determine that a leave request does or does not qualify for FMLA coverage, you must give a written "designation notice" to the employee requesting leave. As with the eligibility notice, you may have more time to give this notice in the event of extenuating circumstances.

The designation notice must contain the following information:

- whether or not the employee's leave is approved as FMLA leave
- how much time will be counted against the employee's available FMLA leave time; if the amount of leave needed is unknown at the time of the designation notice (for example, because the employee will take leave intermittently, as needed), the notice doesn't have to include this information, but
  - the employer must give the employee an accounting of how much time has been counted against the employee's available FMLA time upon the employee's request
  - this accounting doesn't need to be given more often than every 30 days
  - the accounting may be oral, but if so must be confirmed in writing no later than the next payday, and
  - the written confirmation of the accounting may be a notation on the employee's pay stub
- whether the employer requires paid leave to be substituted
- whether the employee has requested that paid leave be substituted
- whether the employer requires a fitness-for-duty certification for return to work (this information may be given orally if the employer's written policies set forth the fitness-for-duty requirement), and
- whether the employer requires that the fitness-for-duty certification cover the employee's ability to perform essential functions of his or her job. If so, the employer must include a list of the essential job functions with the notice. (Fitness-for-duty certifications are covered in Chapter 11.)

FORM

You can use the DOL's *Designation Notice form* (Form WH-382) for these purposes; see Appendix C to access an electronic copy.

As mentioned in Chapter 7, when an employee requests military caregiver leave, the request often also falls under the FMLA category of leave to care for a family member with a serious health condition. However, that FMLA category allows only the usual 12 weeks of leave per leave year. The DOL regulations require you to designate leave to care for a seriously injured or ill servicemember as military caregiver leave only, in order to give the caregiver the full benefit of the FMLA. That way, an employee who uses less than 26 weeks of military caregiver leave still has some leave left for other FMLA-qualified reasons.

> EXAMPLE: Johnny's wife is injured in combat, and Johnny takes 20 weeks of military caregiver leave. Having read this book, you designate that leave as military caregiver leave only. Assuming he hasn't used FMLA leave for any other purpose in the leave year, Johnny still has six weeks of leave left to use for any other FMLA-qualifying reason, such as for his own serious health condition.
>
> Absent this rule, Johnny's leave could have been counted as both military caregiver leave and leave to care for a family member with a serious health condition. Johnny could use his remaining six weeks only for military caregiver leave; he wouldn't have any of his 12-week entitlement left. This is exactly what the DOL is trying to avoid by requiring employers to designate qualifying leave as military caregiver leave only.

You have to give the employee only one designation notice per qualifying reason per year, even if the employee takes the leave intermittently during the year. But, if the information in the notice changes, you must give the employee a written notice of the change within five business days of receiving the employee's first request for leave after the change is made. Also, as noted above, an employee who is using intermittent leave may request an accounting of how much FMLA leave has been used every 30 days. If you choose to give this accounting orally, you must follow up in writing; the written statement may appear as a simple notation on the employee's pay stub.

If You Don't Designate Within the Time Allowed

If you know that an employee's time off is for an FMLA-qualified reason, you are required to provide the designation notice within five business days. Even if you don't designate the leave within this time limit, however, the FMLA regulations allow your company to count an employee's time off as FMLA leave, as long as the employee is actually eligible for FMLA leave and the leave is taken for an FMLA-qualifying reason. However, if the employee is harmed by your late designation, your company may be liable for damages caused as a result. As discussed above, you may be able to avoid this problem by retroactively designating leave as FMLA leave, as long as this doesn't harm the employee, or the employee agrees to the retroactive designation.

Likewise, if you mistakenly designate an employee's time off as FMLA leave when it's not—because the employee is ineligible or the reason for leave isn't covered by the FMLA, for example—that doesn't convert the employee's leave to FMLA leave. In other words, the employee can't claim FMLA rights based on your mistake if the employee isn't eligible for FMLA leave. However, if the employee relies on your failure to properly designate the leave in a way that harms the employee's interests, the employee may still have a valid legal claim.

EXAMPLE: Abdul took eight weeks of leave to help his adult son rearrange his children's care and custody, handle his legal and financial affairs, and deal with other qualifying exigencies when his son's Reserve unit was called to Iraq. Several months later, Abdul asked for time off to care for his wife after hip replacement surgery, scheduled in a couple of months. You incorrectly told Abdul that he'd have his full 12 weeks of FMLA leave time to care for his wife, because the leave for his adult son wasn't FMLA-qualified. Just before Abdul's wife has her surgery, you realize your error and tell him that he only has four weeks of FMLA leave left because his leave for his son counts as qualifying exigency leave. Now Abdul says that he and his wife will incur a lot of expenses hiring a home-care aide that they could have avoided if you'd properly designated his leave. Had he known that he only had four weeks to use, his wife's sister could have planned to care for her. Because Abdul thought he had time off, however, his wife's sister has taken a new job and is unable to help out. Your error doesn't mean that Abdul is entitled to extra FMLA leave; however, your company could be on the hook for the added expense that Abdul will incur as a result of the misdesignation.

Employee Notice Requirements

While most of the obligation to administer FMLA leave falls on you, the employee bears some responsibility. Primarily, an employee requesting leave that might qualify under the FMLA must give you enough information so that you can determine whether the FMLA applies. If the employee doesn't provide you with the necessary information, you may deny the employee's leave request.

If an employer and employee disagree as to whether a leave request is FMLA qualified, the Department of Labor regulations indicate that the dispute should be resolved through discussions, which the employer must document along with the resolution of the dispute.

Lessons from the *Real World*

An employee only has to give enough information for the employer to conclude that the employee may need time off for a serious health condition.

Samuel Cavin worked as a production associate in the assembly department of Honda of America Manufacturing, Inc. Cavin had an accident while riding his motorcycle. He called Honda and told his supervisor about it, explaining that he was in the hospital. Honda claimed that this wasn't enough information to notify the company that Cavin had a serious health condition covered by the FMLA and fired him. Cavin sued Honda for violating the FMLA.

The court ruled that Cavin had provided enough information for Honda to conclude that he had a serious health condition entitling him to FMLA leave.

Cavin v. Honda of America Manufacturing, Inc., 346 F.3d 713 (6th Cir. 2003).

Methods of Employee Notification

The employee's notice may be either oral (including by telephone) or in writing (including by fax or email). An employee's spokesperson may give the notice if the employee is incapacitated or otherwise unable to give the notice.

What does the employee need to tell you? Not much: only enough information to let you know that the need for leave may be covered by the FMLA. Generally, the employee doesn't have to mention the FMLA or the particular rights protected by the FMLA. Nor does the employee have to give you any medical information when making the initial request for leave: It's enough if the employee's notice reasonably informs you that the leave is for a serious health condition, parenting, or military family obligations.

Lessons from the *Real World*

An employee's statement to her employer that she needed time off because she "didn't feel good" wasn't sufficient notice of a serious health condition.

Shortly before Jill Beaver was scheduled to return from an approved vacation to her job at RGIS Inventory Specialists, Inc., she called in and reported to her supervisor that she was ill, "didn't feel good," and that her doctor had ordered her not to fly or return to work for "a couple of days, a few days." RGIS viewed Beaver's extra time off as unauthorized and fired her. Beaver sued RGIS for terminating her while on FMLA leave.

The court sided with RGIS because Beaver hadn't provided sufficient information to alert her supervisor that the FMLA applied to her leave. Beaver's statements to her supervisor were too general for her supervisor to conclude that she might have suffered from a serious health condition.

Beaver v. RGIS Inventory Specialists, Inc., 144 Fed. Appx. 452 (6th Cir. 2005).

It's up to you to recognize the possibility that the leave is covered by the FMLA. For example, if you know that an employee suffers from a chronic medical condition and the employee requests leave without specifying why, you should ask for more information so you can determine whether it falls under the protection of the FMLA. Your knowledge of the chronic medical condition and the leave request is enough to put you on notice under the FMLA. Likewise, if an employee's behavior shows that the employee is suffering from a serious health condition, that may be enough to put you on notice of the need for FMLA leave. Again, you should ask the employee for more information, so you can determine whether the leave qualifies for FMLA protection.

The rules are different when an employee seeks additional FMLA leave for an FMLA-qualifying reason for which he or she has previously taken leave. In this situation, the employee must specifically refer to either the qualifying reason or the need for FMLA leave. This rule recognizes that employees who have already used the FMLA and know their situation qualifies for FMLA leave can be expected to know the rules and provide more extensive notice.

When the employee asks to use accrued paid leave, such as vacation leave, the employee might not tell you the possibly FMLA-qualifying reason for the leave request. As with any request for possible FMLA leave, you are entitled to find out if the type of leave falls within both your company's paid leave policy and the FMLA. If the employee doesn't give you this information, you can deny the employee's request for leave and the employee must then give you sufficient information to establish that the need for leave falls within the FMLA. Otherwise, the employee hasn't shown that he or she is entitled to FMLA-protected leave. For example, if an employee says, "I'd like to take a couple of personal days off," but doesn't indicate what the time off is for, the employer may ask if there is a family or medical need for the leave. While an employer cannot demand detailed medical information, it does have the right to find out if the leave is possibly covered by the FMLA.

Although an employee doesn't have to give detailed medical information when requesting leave, it is not enough for the employee to simply call in "sick" without more information. An employer may request additional information in response to such inadequate notice.

Employees can notify you after returning from leave that they took leave for an FMLA-qualified reason, if that's as much notice as is practicable under the circumstances. Generally, however, it should be practicable for an employee to give notice the same business day or the next business day after the employee learns of the need for leave. If the employee fails to give you enough information to determine that the FMLA applies, then the employee can't later claim that the leave was protected under the FMLA.

Lessons from the *Real World*

An employee's statement that he did not want to apply for FMLA leave "at this time" is not an explicit waiver of FMLA rights.

Robert Righi sent his supervisor at SMC Corp. of America an email explaining that, due to his mother's medical emergency, he needed to take "the next couple of days off" to arrange for her medical care. Righi stated, "I do have the vacation time, or I could apply for the family care act, which I do not want to do at this time."

SMC Corp. argued that Righi had waived his FMLA rights by the latter statement. The court disagreed and held that because Righi's email "left open the *possibility* that Righi might want to use FMLA leave" at some point, the email was sufficient to alert SMC Corp. to the potential that Righi would need FMLA leave.

Righi v. SMC Corp., 632 F.3d 404 (7th Cir. 2011).

Getting More Information From the Employee

If you need more information than the employee gives you to figure out if the FMLA applies, ask for it. Also ask for certification (covered in Chapter 9) and, if applicable, proof of a family relationship (see Chapter 4).

If the employee fails or refuses to tell you why he or she needs leave, you can deny FMLA leave. After all, you won't have enough information to determine whether the leave is FMLA qualified, and it would be unfair and inconsistent to grant FMLA to some employees without proper documentation, while denying it to others.

Even an ambiguous notice from an employee suggesting that the employee might not want to exercise FMLA rights triggers the employer's duty to get more information about whether the leave qualifies under the FMLA.

CAUTION

Don't assume an employee is waiving rights based on an ambiguous leave request. Courts have ruled against employers who assumed employees waived FMLA rights by saying they did not wish to invoke the rights "at this time," or making similar statements. If you are not sure whether an employee's leave request is FMLA qualified, follow up with the employee to get more information. And, ask when the employee will return to work, or get the employee's best estimate of a return date.

Lessons from the *Real World*

An employer may deny FMLA leave when the employee didn't provide enough information for the employer to determine whether he had a serious health condition.

Lee Brenneman worked in the pharmacy department of MedCentral Health System for 27 years. Brenneman had diabetes and needed time off because of a medical problem related to using his insulin pump. He informed MedCentral that he was "having trouble" with his insulin pump, but didn't otherwise explain the problem. Brenneman then took time off.

MedCentral didn't designate his leave as FMLA leave and terminated him for unexcused absence. Brenneman sued MedCentral for violating the FMLA.

The court ruled that Brenneman's request for leave didn't adequately notify MedCentral of a serious medical condition, since his statement that he was having trouble with his insulin pump didn't give his employer enough information to indicate that he had a serious medical condition.

Brenneman v. MedCentral Health System, 366 F.3d 412 (6th Cir. 2004).

How Much Notice the Employee Must Give

Sometimes employees need time off for conditions or events that are foreseeable, such as a scheduled surgery or the birth of a child. Other times, the need isn't foreseeable, such as a hospitalization and treatment following a heart attack. While the FMLA allows employees to take leave in either case, it requires different amounts of notice.

Foreseeable Leave

When the need for leave is foreseeable, an employee requesting FMLA leave must give at least 30 days' notice of the need for leave. An employee who fails to give at least 30 days' notice of the need for FMLA leave has to respond to the employer's request for an explanation of why such notice wasn't practicable.

There are several exceptions to the 30-day notice rule:

- **When the need for leave isn't certain in time.** This situation may arise, for example, where an adoption date isn't certain. In this situation, the employee must give notice as soon as is practicable.
- **When there is a change in circumstances.** This situation may arise, for example, where a medical procedure is changed to accommodate a hospital's schedule. In this situation, the employee must give notice of the change as soon as he or she learns of it, even if he or she already gave notice of the original procedure date.
- **When your company elects to waive the FMLA notice requirement.** Your company may allow employees to give less notice than the FMLA requires.
- **When the employee needs qualifying exigency leave.** For this type of leave, the employee need only give such notice as is practicable, even if the need for leave is foreseeable.

How much notice is "practicable" depends upon the particular circumstances of each employee's situation. Generally, it should be practicable for an employee to provide notice either the same business day or the next business day after the employee learns of the need for leave.

An employee must also make reasonable efforts to arrange medical treatment so as not to unduly disrupt the employer's operations. If an employee fails to do so, the employer can tell the employee that he or she must try to make such arrangements, subject to the approval of the health care provider. Employees who are seeking leave to care for an injured servicemember must also try to work out a schedule for intermittent leave that doesn't unduly disrupt the employer's operations. (See Chapter 10 for more on these requirements.)

Unforeseeable Leave

If the employee's need for FMLA leave is not foreseeable, different notice rules apply. An employee must give notice of the need for unforeseeable leave as soon as practicable, which typically means the same business day or the next business day after the employee learns of the need for leave. Generally, it should be practicable for the employee to give you notice within the deadlines set out in your company's usual and customary leave notice rules, absent unusual circumstances.

Even where an employee's need for FMLA leave is unforeseeable, you are entitled to ask when the employee expects to return to work. The employee may not be able to provide that information immediately, but does have a duty to tell you once an actual or estimated return date is known. And, the employee must respond to your efforts to get more information while the employee is on leave.

Lessons from the *Real World*

An employee on unforeseeable leave can't simply ignore his employer's repeated attempts to reach him during leave.

For more than a week after Robert Righi went out on leave to see to his mother's emergency medical needs, his supervisor left numerous voicemails on his cell and home phones asking Righi to report how long Righi would be out and when he expected to return to work. Righi ignored all but the last message, nine days after he went on leave. His employer fired him the next day for violating its leave policy. The court upheld the termination based on Righi's failure to fulfill his notice obligations.

Righi v. SMC Corp., 632 F.3d 404 (7th Cir. 2011).

The FMLA regulations relax employee notice requirements in "extra-ordinary" circumstances (such as when an employee is physically unable to respond to the employer's efforts to get more information for some period of time). And, when the employee's need for leave is unforeseeable, the employee may not know the exact date of return to work. But, the employee still has an obligation to tell you that the date of return is not yet known.

Your Company's Leave Notification Rules

Your company can require employees to follow its usual and customary leave notification rules, as long as those rules don't discriminate against employees taking FMLA leave and don't require more notice than the FMLA requires. However, your company may require compliance with its usual notice requirements only if there are no unusual circumstances. For example, let's say your company requires employees to call in by 8 a.m. if they are going to be absent that day. You may not deny FMLA leave to an employee who has a heart attack during the night and misses work because he is hospitalized. As long as the employee gives notices as soon as is practicable—all that's required by the FMLA for unforeseeable leave—the employee is entitled to FMLA leave. If an employee doesn't comply with the usual notice rules, and no unusual circumstances are present, you may discipline the employee and delay or deny FMLA leave.

Notice that this contrasts with the rules for using paid leave, discussed above. To substitute paid leave for unpaid FMLA leave, an employee must follow your company's usual notice rules for paid leave. If the employee fails to do so, your company may deny the request for paid leave. Even in these circumstances, however, your company must grant the request for FMLA leave as long as the employee met the FMLA's notice requirements.

Employee Failure to Give Notice

As mentioned above, an employer may delay the start of leave if an employee fails to give adequate notice within the applicable notice period. However, the extent of such a delay depends upon the facts and circumstances of the particular leave request. According to the FMLA regulations, the appropriate delay is the difference in time between when the employee gave notice and when the employee should have given notice.

> **EXAMPLE:** Lila informs you that she is adopting a baby and is scheduled to take custody of the baby in 15 days. You ask her why she didn't give you 30 days' notice and she says it slipped her mind. Because she gave inadequate notice, you can delay the start of Lila's leave by 15 days, to the date 30 days after she gave notice. You are entitled to delay her leave because her failure to give you the required notice was not due to unusual circumstances.

Notice Based on Employer Observations

Sometimes an employee's behavior, appearance, or other facts will alert an employer to the employee's need for FMLA leave. When observable indications, combined with an employee's request for leave, reveal that an employee may have a serious health condition, you should designate the leave as FMLA leave. You can ask the employee for more information if you aren't sure whether the FMLA applies.

SEE AN EXPERT

Consult an attorney when you make an FMLA designation based on employee behavior. It's always a bit dangerous to make assumptions based on an employee's actions. For example, you could be accused of treating the employee as if he or she has a disability, which constitutes disability discrimination under the Americans with Disabilities Act. (See Chapter 12 for more information.) Talking to an attorney can help you make sure you're doing the right thing.

Lessons from the *Real World*

An employer had notice of an employee's serious health condition because the employer had ordered the employee to participate in an employee assistance program.

William Moorer was the administrator and CFO of Baptist Memorial Health Care System, where he had worked for 17 years. Moorer's boss smelled alcohol on Moorer's breath and noted that his performance had started to slip, he was "fidgety" at meetings, and, at one point, slumped in his chair. His boss ordered Moorer to attend the company's employee assistance program, which would require several weeks of leave. Moorer underwent the program and ceased drinking. Nevertheless, Baptist Memorial fired him during the leave. Moorer filed a lawsuit claiming that the company had violated the FMLA by terminating him during an FMLA leave. Baptist Memorial argued that Moorer had never requested FMLA leave.

The court ruled that Baptist Memorial could not claim that it had no notice that the leave it placed Moorer on was FMLA leave. Baptist Memorial had recognized Moorer's serious health condition of alcoholism and need for leave, because it had ordered him into treatment for the condition.

Moorer v. Baptist Memorial Health Care System, 398 F.3d 469 (6th Cir. 2005).

Common Mistakes Regarding Giving Notice and Designating Leave—And How to Avoid Them

Mistake 1: Failing to count FMLA-qualified leave taken as FMLA leave.

Avoid this mistake by taking the following steps:

- Consider whether the FMLA applies whenever an employee takes or requests time off for parenting, military family obligations, illness, or a family member's illness.
- Consider whether the FMLA applies if an employee requests time off and the employee's behavior suggests that he or she might have a serious health condition.

- Ask the employee to provide more information if you aren't sure whether the FMLA applies.
- Count paid leave as FMLA leave, if the reason for leave qualifies under the FMLA. Don't forget workers' compensation leave, disability leave, and paid family leave.
- Count time off (such as vacation or sick leave) as FMLA leave when a new FMLA-covered event occurs during the leave.

Mistake 2: Denying FMLA leave because the employee has not followed company notice rules.

Avoid this mistake by taking the following steps:

- Understand the different rules that apply to paid leave and unpaid leave: As long as the employee provides adequate notice under the FMLA, you may not deny FMLA leave; you may, however, deny paid leave if the employee doesn't follow the notice requirements of your paid leave program.
- Rather than denying FMLA leave, delay leave for the 30-day notice period if the need for leave was truly foreseeable and it was practicable to give more notice. (See Chapter 10.)

Mistake 3: Failing to give individualized FMLA information to employees who need FMLA leave.

Avoid this mistake by taking the following steps:

- Give each employee requesting FMLA leave the three required notice forms for eligibility, rights and responsibilities, and designation.
- Provide the notices in a language the employee understands.
- If the employee is sensory impaired, give the individualized information in a form that the employee can receive and understand.
- Make sure the notice information is tailored to the employee's particular situation (for example, telling the employee that he or she can substitute paid leave, or that he or she must pay health insurance premiums during leave).
- Provide a new notice form whenever the employee will be required to follow different rules (for example, to provide a medical certification or fitness-for-duty report).

Managers' Checklist: Giving Notice and Designating Leave

☐ The employee requesting leave received a general notice in our handbook, in our written policies, or upon hire.

☐ Within five business days of the employee's request for leave, I have given the employee a ☐ written ☐ oral ☐ electronic eligibility notice stating:

  ☐ that the employee is eligible for FMLA leave, or

  ☐ that the employee is ineligible for FMLA leave and providing at least one reason for the employee's ineligibility.

☐ At the same time I provided the eligibility notice, I gave the employee a rights and responsibilities notice in writing informing the employee:

  ☐ that the leave will count against his or her available FMLA leave time

  ☐ of any certification requirements the employee must satisfy

  ☐ of the consequences of failing to satisfy the certification requirements

  ☐ (if applicable) that the employee has the right to substitute paid leave for FMLA leave

  ☐ (if applicable) that the employee must substitute paid leave for FMLA leave, the conditions relating to substitution of paid leave, and the consequences of failing to satisfy those conditions

  ☐ that the employee has the right to continue benefits during FMLA leave and upon return to work

  ☐ (if applicable) that the employee is required to pay health insurance premiums during leave, how the employee's payments will be arranged, and the consequences of failing to pay the premiums

  ☐ of (if applicable) the employee's liability, if any, for the cost of benefits payments if the employee does not return to work after leave

  ☐ of key employee information, and

  ☐ that the employee has the right to return to the same or an equivalent job after returning from FMLA leave.

Managers' Checklist: Giving Notice and Designating Leave (continued)

☐ Within five business days of receiving enough information to determine that a leave request does or does not qualify for FMLA coverage, I have given the employee requesting leave a designation notice informing the employee:

☐ whether the leave is approved as FMLA leave

☐ that the amount of time that will be counted against the employee's available FMLA leave time, if known

☐ (if applicable) that the employee has requested that paid leave be substituted

☐ (if applicable) that the employee is required to substitute paid leave

☐ (if applicable) that a fitness-for-duty certificate must be submitted by the employee for return to work, and

☐ (if applicable) that the fitness-for-duty certificate must cover the employee's ability to perform the essential functions of his or her job, which I have provided to the employee.

☐ If the amount of leave needed was unknown when the employee requested leave, I have given the employee a written accounting of how much time has been counted against his or her available FMLA leave, upon the employee's request.

Certifications

Chapter Highlights

☆ A certification is a document verifying an employee's need to take leave for a serious health condition, military caregiver leave, or qualifying exigency leave.

☆ A certification for a serious health condition must be completed by a health care provider.

☆ A certification for military caregiver leave must be completed by a health care provider in the case of current servicemembers. For veterans, family members may submit documentation from the Department of Veterans Affairs.

☆ A certification for a qualifying exigency relating to a family member's call to active duty must be completed by the employee.

☆ To request a certification, you must do so in writing within five business days after learning of an employee's need for FMLA leave.

☆ The employee must return the certification within 15 calendar days, unless you allow the employee more time or it is not practicable for the employee to do so under the circumstances, despite the employee's diligent, good faith efforts.

☆ Once you receive a certification, you may grant FMLA leave or deny it based on the information on the form. If the form is insufficient or incomplete, you must tell the employee in writing and give the employee at least seven calendar days to provide a complete, sufficient certification. You may take steps to clarify or authenticate a certification for a serious health condition or military caregiver leave.

☆ If you have reason to doubt a medical certification for a serious health condition, you may ask the employee to get a second opinion, at your company's expense. If the first and second opinions conflict, you may request a third opinion, again at the company's expense.

☆ You may verify the information an employee provides in a certification for qualifying exigency leave only by contacting the Department of Defense to verify the family member's duty status and contacting third parties named in the certification as people with whom the employee will be meeting.

☆ You may request a recertification only after the duration of the condition identified in the original certification expires or only once every 30 days, unless the employee requests an extension of leave, circumstances have changed significantly, or you have reason to suspect the continuing validity of the certification.

☆ For chronic or lifelong conditions, you may request recertifications once every six months, in connection with an absence.

When an employee requests time off for his or her own health problem, to care for an ailing family member, or for any reason connected to a family member's military service, you should immediately think, "FMLA." But what if you aren't sure whether the employee's situation qualifies for FMLA leave, or you need more information?

In that situation, you may request a certification: a written statement, completed by the employee, a health care provider, or both, that provides some basic information about the employee's need for leave. You may ask the employee to provide a certification for all types of FMLA leave except leave to bond with a new child. In that situation, you may require the employee to provide proof of a family relationship only, as explained in Chapter 4.

This chapter explains what certifications are, how and when to request them, when an employee must provide them, and what to do if the certification is late, insufficient, or incomplete (or never shows up at all). We also explain your options for challenging or verifying a certification of a serious health condition by asking for a second or even a third opinion, as well as the rules about requesting a recertification of the same condition.

Types of Certifications

There are four types of certifications:
- certification of the employee's own serious health condition
- certification of a family member's serious health condition
- certification of a family member's serious illness or injury entitling the employee to take military caregiver leave, and
- certification of an employee's need to take qualifying exigency leave.

As explained below, each type requires different information, and most must be completed by a health care provider, at least in part.

Certification of the Employee's Own Serious Health Condition

A certification of the employee's own serious health condition must be completed by a health care provider and include the following information:
- the name, address, telephone number, and fax number of the health care provider, along with the health care provider's practice or specialization

- the date the serious health condition began
- how long the condition is expected to last
- information on the health condition for which leave is requested, such as symptoms, diagnosis, hospitalization, doctors' visits, medication, referrals for evaluation or treatment, or any regimen of continuing treatment, and
- information sufficient to show that the employee cannot perform the essential functions of the job (unless the employee is requesting intermittent or reduced-schedule leave), information on any other work restrictions, and the likely duration of the inability or restrictions.

If the employee needs intermittent or reduced-schedule leave, the certification must state that intermittent leave is medically necessary. For intermittent leave for planned medical treatment, the certification must estimate the dates and duration of such treatment and any recovery period. For intermittent leave for a condition that may require unforeseeable absences, the certification must give an estimate of the frequency and duration of the episodes of incapacity.

FORM

The Department of Labor has created a form, *Certification of Health Care Provider for Employee's Serious Health Condition* **(Form WH-380-E),** which employers can use to gather this information. The form is designed to be handed to employees, who can then ask their health care providers to complete and sign it. Using this form is optional, but if you develop your own form instead, you cannot ask for more information than Form WH-380 requests.

CAUTION

State law may prohibit you from using Form WH-380. Some states (including California) have strict laws that protect the privacy of medical information and records. If your state's law prohibits employers from requesting certain types of medical information, you must adhere to those restrictions, even if the FMLA allows you to have that information. And, because Form WH-380 asks the health care provider to give details about the employee's serious health condition, you may not be able to use that form in some states. Before you adopt Form WH-380 or any other medical certification form, talk to a knowledgeable employment lawyer in your state to make sure that it doesn't violate your employees' medical privacy rights.

RESOURCE
All certification forms (and other FMLA forms) are available online.
You can find all of the forms we discuss in this chapter, along with many other FMLA forms, at this book's online companion page. See Appendix C for the link to this page.

Certification of a Family Member's Serious Health Condition

The certification of a family member's serious health condition is similar to the certification of the employee's serious health condition. All of the same information must be provided by the family member's health care provider, with the following differences:

- The certification need not address essential job functions or work restrictions.
- The certification must provide sufficient information to establish that the family member needs care (as defined in Chapter 4), and it must estimate the frequency and duration of leave necessary for the employee to provide that care.
- If the employee requests intermittent or reduced-schedule leave, the certification must state that such leave is medically necessary to care for the family member and must estimate the frequency and duration of the leave.

FORM
The DOL has created an optional certification form for this purpose,
Certification of Health Care Provider for Family Member's Serious Health Condition
(Form WH-380-F).

Lessons from the *Real World*

Asking an employee to provide receipts and other proof of caregiving may violate the FMLA.

Jill Diamond worked for Hospice of Florida Keys as a licensed clinical social worker. She needed intermittent FMLA leave to care for her parents, who both had serious health conditions. She took leave without incident in 2013 and the start of 2014. In March of 2014, Diamond learned that her mother was seriously ill. She made an immediate request for two periods of intermittent FMLA leave to provide care for her mother.

In the same time period, the Hospice got a new HR manager. The manager asked Diamond to provide not only a new medical certification regarding her mother's condition, but also additional documentation—in the form of gas receipts, food receipts, and hospital discharge papers—showing that she actually spent her time off caring for her mother. In an email, the manager told Diamond that her continued time off work was compromising the Hospice's quality of care. Diamond was terminated weeks later for performance issues, some of which the HR manager described to Diamond as relating to her time off work.

Diamond sued the Hospice for retaliation and interfering with her FMLA rights. Although a lower court found in favor of the Hospice, the federal Court of Appeals found that Diamond could go forward with her claims. Among other things, it found that requiring Diamond to provide receipts and other evidence of her whereabouts during FMLA leave could be seen as an effort to discourage her from taking leave, by making it more burdensome to do so.

Diamond v. Hospice of Florida Keys, 677 Fed. Appx. 586 (11th Cir. 2017) (unpublished opinion).

Certification for Military Caregiver Leave for Current Servicemembers

The certification for military caregiver leave must be completed by the employee and by the family member's health care provider.

FORM
You can request this information using the DOL's optional form, *Certification for Serious Injury or Illness of Covered Servicemember—for Military Family Leave* (Form WH-385).

Information to Be Supplied by Employee

The employee must complete the following information on the certification form:

- the name of the employee, the name of the family member for whom the employee will be providing care, and the name and address of the caregiver's employer
- the employee's relationship to the family member
- whether the family member is a current member of the Armed Forces, National Guard, or Reserves, and the family member's military branch, rank, and current unit assignment
- whether the family member is assigned to a military medical facility as an outpatient or to a unit established for the purpose of providing command and control of members of the Armed Forces receiving medical care as outpatients (such as a medical hold or warrior transition unit), as well as the name of the treatment facility or unit
- whether the family member is on the temporary disability retired list, and
- a description of the care to be provided and an estimate of the leave necessary to provide it.

Information to Be Supplied by Health Care Provider

The family member's health care provider must also complete part of the form. For purposes of military caregiver leave, the following health care providers may complete a certification:

- a Department of Defense (DOD) health care provider
- a Department of Veterans Affairs health care provider
- a DOD TRICARE network authorized private health care provider (TRICARE is the military's health care program)
- a DOD non-network TRICARE authorized private health care provider, or
- any health care provider recognized by the FMLA (see "Who Is a Health Care Provider?" in Chapter 4 for more information).

The health care provider must complete the following information on the certification form; if the health care provider is unable to make any of the required military-related determinations, he or she may rely on the decisions of an authorized DOD representative (such as a DOD recovery care coordinator):

- the name, address, and contact information of the health care provider, the type of medical practice and specialty, and whether the health care provider falls into one of the categories listed above
- whether the family member's injury or illness was incurred or aggravated in the line of duty on active duty
- the date on which the injury or illness commenced and its probable duration
- a statement of medical facts regarding the family member's injury or illness sufficient to support the employee's leave request, including classification of the family member's medical status; whether the injury or illness may render the family member medically unfit to perform the duties of his or her office, grade, rank, or rating; and whether the family member is receiving medical treatment, recuperation, or therapy
- information sufficient to show that the family member is in need of care
- whether the family member will need care for a single continuous period of time, and if so, the time necessary for treatment and recovery, along with an estimate of the start and end dates of the need for care
- if the employee requests intermittent or reduced-schedule leave for follow-up treatment, information on the necessity of periodic care and an estimate of the treatment schedule, and
- if the employee requests intermittent or reduced-schedule leave for another reason, information on the necessity of periodic care and an estimate of the frequency and duration of the periodic care required.

If the Employee Receives an Invitational Travel Order or Authorization

Sometimes, the Department of Defense issues a family member an invitational travel order (ITO) or invitational travel authorization (ITA), to travel immediately to the bedside of a seriously ill or injured servicemember, at the Department's expense. You must accept an ITO or ITA in lieu of a certification form for the time period specified in the order or authorization.

The ITO or ITA is considered sufficient certification for that time period, and it entitles the employee to take continuous leave or intermittent leave. The employee need not be the family member named in the ITO or ITA.

You may ask the employee to provide proof of a family relationship to the servicemember, as explained in Chapter 4. If the time specified in the ITO or ITA runs out, you may require the employee to provide a certification then.

Certification for Military Caregiver Leave for Veterans

The certification for military caregiver leave to care for a veteran must be completed by the employee and by the family member's health care provider.

 FORM
The Department of Labor has issued an optional certification form to be used for this purpose, *Certification for Serious Injury or Illness of a Veteran for Military Family Leave* **(Form WH-385-V).**

Information to Be Supplied by Employee

The employee must complete the first part of the form by providing:
- the name of the employee, the name of the veteran who needs care, and the name and address of the employer
- the employee's relationship to the veteran
- information on the veteran's service and discharge
- whether the veteran is in medical treatment or therapy or is recuperating from a serious illness or injury, and
- the care to be provided to the veteran and an estimate of how much leave the employee will need to provide it.

Information to Be Supplied by Health Care Provider

For veterans, the health care provider must give the same information on the certification form as required for a current servicemember. However, the form for veterans uses a different definition of a serious illness or injury, as these individuals are no longer serving in the military and their incapacity must be measured by something other than their inability to perform their military duties. Chapter 6 explains how the FMLA defines a serious illness or injury for veterans.

If the Veteran Is Enrolled in the Department of Veterans Affairs Program of Comprehensive Assistance for Family Caregivers

There are four ways for an employee's family member veteran to qualify as having a serious illness or injury, for purposes of military caregiver leave (see Chapter 6 for details). One way is the veteran's enrollment in the Veterans Affairs Program of Comprehensive Assistance for Family Caregivers. If you request a certification from an employee who needs FMLA leave to care for a veteran, you must accept evidence of such enrollment in lieu of a certification form. This is true even if the employee is not the caregiver named in the documentation.

However, you may ask the employee to provide proof of a family relationship to the veteran, as explained in Chapter 4. You may also ask the employee to provide proof of the date the veteran was discharged and that the discharge was not dishonorable.

Certification of Qualifying Exigency

The certification for qualifying exigency leave is to be completed by the employee only. You may ask the employee to provide the following information:

- a statement of facts regarding the qualifying exigency sufficient to show that the employee needs leave, including information on the type of exigency and any available documents supporting the request for leave, such as a meeting announcement or copy of an appointment schedule
- the date when the qualifying exigency began or will begin
- the start and end dates of leave requested for a single, continuous period of time
- the frequency and duration of leave requested on an intermittent or reduced schedule, and
- contact information for any third parties with whom the employee will be meeting as part of the qualifying exigency, along with a brief description of the purpose of the meeting.

In addition to the certification, you may require the employee to provide a copy of the family member's active duty orders or other military documentation indicating that the family member is on covered active duty or call to active duty status, along with the dates of the family member's service. You may require the employee to provide this documentation only once, unless the employee needs leave arising out of a different call to active duty or for a different family member.

If the employee is requesting leave to spend with a family member who is on short-term rest and recuperation leave during deployment, you may request additional documentation. You may ask the employee to provide a copy of the family member's Rest and Recuperation orders or other paperwork issued by the military indicating that the family member is on leave and the dates of that leave.

 FORM
You may request this information using the DOL's optional form, *Certification of Qualifying Exigency for Military Family Leave* **(Form WH-384).**

Requesting Certification

Although you have the right to request a certification when an employee takes leave for any reason except bonding with a new child, you aren't required to. Because it's optional, some managers don't request a certification or request one only occasionally (for example, if the employee has a history of unexcused absences). The best practice, however, is to request a certification every time an employee wants time off for a covered reason, regardless of the circumstances. This section explains why, how, and when to request a certification.

Why You Should Always Request Certification

You shouldn't pick and choose which employees or conditions will require a certification. Instead, you should always request one when an employee requests leave for a covered reason. Here are three good reasons why.

The Condition Might Not Qualify

Unless you ask for a certification, you don't know whether the employee or family member has a condition qualifying the employee for FMLA leave. Remember, it's not your job—or your right—to diagnose a serious health condition or serious illness or injury. Once an employee tells you that he or she needs time off, you can't simply say, "You don't look that sick to me," or "I'm sure your wife will be up and around in no time." If you want proof, the only way you are legally allowed to get it is through the certification process.

As a practical matter, once an employee requests leave for a covered condition, you have three options: grant the request outright, deny the request outright, or ask for a certification. If you grant the request without proof, you'll never know whether the employee or family member really had a qualifying condition; you might have provided job-protected leave and continued benefits when you didn't have to. If you don't request proof and don't grant FMLA leave, you are inviting a potentially ruinous lawsuit if the employee's request was legitimate.

Requesting a certification every time is the best way to make sure that you provide the leave required by the FMLA, no more and no less.

You Might Want to Challenge the Employee Later

If you don't ask for certification, some courts have held that your company can't later claim that the employee or family member didn't really qualify for FMLA leave. This could deprive you and your company of an important argument if the employee sues for violation of the FMLA. The lesson here is use it or lose it: If you don't ask for a certification, you may have conceded this point. After all, it might be impossible for anyone to conclusively determine whether or not a person actually suffered a claimed illness months or years later, when a lawsuit finally gets to court.

Inconsistency Leads to Discrimination Claims

Some managers pick and choose which employees have to submit certifications and which do not. A manager might ask only employees who have a history of attendance problems to get a certification or might request a certification only for ailments that are not immediately apparent.

The problem with this approach is that it can lead to discrimination claims. Any time a manager decides to treat employees differently, there is a risk that the manager will be accused of discrimination. If, for example, you ask only pregnant employees to provide a certification, you could be accused of gender discrimination. If you ask only employees who have chronic or permanent conditions—as opposed to a one-time need for surgery or time off for an injury—to provide a certification, you could be accused of disability discrimination. To avoid this problem, you should always request a certification.

Lessons from the *Real World*

Company that didn't request a medical certification can't later dispute the employee's serious health condition.

Katherine Thorson worked in the packing and shipping department of Gemini, Inc., a company that manufactures plastic signs. The company had a policy that employees who were absent for more than 5% of their scheduled hours in a rolling 12-month period could be fired for excessive absenteeism.

Thorson left work and went to the doctor on Wednesday, February 2, complaining of stomach cramps and diarrhea. She came back to work the following Monday, February 7, with a doctor's note saying "no work" until February 7. After a few hours, she returned to the doctor with stomach pain. The doctor suspected a peptic ulcer or gallbladder disease and ordered some tests for that Friday. The following Monday, February 14, Thorson returned to work, again with a doctor's note saying "no work" until the 14th. That Friday, she was fired for excessive absences. She was eventually diagnosed with several stress-related conditions.

When Thorson sued for violation of the FMLA, Gemini argued, among other things, that Thorson didn't have a serious health condition because she was not incapacitated. In other words, she didn't really have to miss work because of her condition. The court found that Gemini wasn't entitled to contest this issue because it failed to request a medical certification at the time. Thorson's own doctor's notes said "no work"; if Gemini doubted this statement, it was entitled to request a certification. Because it didn't exercise this right, the court refused to credit evidence from another physician, whose opinion was sought months after the fact for use in the lawsuit, that there was "no obvious reason" why Thorson had to miss work.

Thorson v. Gemini, Inc., 205 F.3d 370 (8th Cir. 2000).

EXAMPLE: Maggie, one of your employees, has bipolar disorder. She and her doctor have been experimenting with a new medication. Unfortunately, before she and her doctor figure out the correct dosage, Maggie has a manic episode and must be hospitalized briefly. Her brother calls you about the situation and says that Maggie will have to stay in the hospital for at least a couple of days, then will be released to be cared for by her family until she's able to return to work.

You usually don't require employees to submit a medical certification. In this situation, though, you think you might ask for one. "She had to be hospitalized for getting overexcited? It sounds like someone just wants some time off work. I don't grant FMLA leave for 'mental health' days, and I bet she'll come back to work pretty quickly once she knows that." Because the FMLA allows you to request a certification, you're well within your rights to make this your first, aren't you?

Not quite. Maggie might claim that your request is discriminatory, because it's based on negative stereotypes about people with mental disabilities (that they are "faking it" or could control their conditions with a little will power, for example).

Procedures and Deadlines for Requesting a Certification

As soon as an employee requests leave for a serious health condition or military caregiver leave, you should request the certification, in writing. The regulations interpreting the FMLA say that employers "should" request a certification within five business days of learning that an employee needs leave, either because the employee has requested leave or because the employee has taken leave for an unforeseeable purpose (emergency surgery, for example). The regulations give you the right to request certification later if you "have reason to question" the duration or appropriateness of the leave. The best practice is not to rely on this language, but instead to give your notice and request a certification right away, every time.

Although the FMLA regulations allow employers to make an oral request in limited circumstances, you want written proof of your request for a certification, including the date you made it. The written request must state not only that you are requesting a medical certification, but also the deadlines for providing the certification and the consequences of failing to provide it.

You may request a medical certification as part of the rights and responsibilities notice you must give to an employee who has requested leave for a purpose covered by the FMLA (see Chapter 8 for more information on this notice). If you instead choose to give the employee a separate written request for a medical certification, you can use our form, "Request for Medical Certification." A sample of this form is below; see Appendix C for an electronic copy.

To: Sarah Beadle

From: Rayna Harmon

Date: August 23, 2018

On August 22, 2018, you informed us that you need to take leave for a serious health condition.

You must submit a medical certification of a serious health condition from your health care practitioner. The certification form is attached to this letter. Please note that you must complete a portion of the form if you are seeking leave to care for a family member.

You must return this form to us by September 7, 2018. If you fail to return this form on time, we may delay the start of your leave, or postpone the continuation of your leave, until we receive your certification. If you are unable to return the form on time due to circumstances beyond your control, please contact me right away.

Feel free to contact me if you have any questions about this requirement.

Sincerely,

Rayna Harmon   *August 23, 2018*

Rayna Harmon   Date

CAUTION

A written policy isn't enough. Many employers have policies explaining FMLA leave in their employee handbooks. (For information on what your FMLA policy should include, see Appendix B.) Typically, these policies cover medical certifications, including the information you must give the employee when you request one. If your company has this type of policy, however, it doesn't take the place of a written request and notice to the employee when the employee requests leave. Courts have found that an employer that doesn't make a specific written request to an employee cannot later challenge the employee's certification (or failure to provide one).

Employee Deadline for Returning the Certification

You must give the employee at least 15 calendar days to return the completed certification form, unless it is not practicable for the employee to meet this deadline under the circumstances, despite the employee's diligent, good faith efforts. You may give more than 15 days, if you wish.

If the employee can't meet this deadline despite reasonable, good-faith efforts to do so, the employee must return the certification as soon as it's reasonably possible. You may delay the start of leave if the employee misses the deadline and hasn't made reasonable, good-faith efforts to meet it. If the employee never provides you with a medical certification you properly requested, the leave is not protected by the FMLA.

Even though you have the right to penalize an employee for missing the deadline to return a certification, that doesn't mean you should exercise it. You must act very carefully—preferably, after talking to a lawyer—if you choose to enforce these rules. If an employee is clearly entitled to the FMLA's protections, some courts have been lenient about these requirements. Particularly if your actions cause the employee harm—for example, because the employee had to delay a medically necessary treatment program—you should anticipate the possibility that a court might take the employee's side.

The best practice, both to avoid legal trouble and to provide leave when your employees need it, is to work with your employees on this issue. Remind employees that you need a certification. If an employee misses a deadline, get in touch with the employee or a family member and explain how important the certification is. Put a note confirming this contact in the employee's FMLA file and be sure to include the name of the person you contacted, the date, and the substance of your discussion.

Rather than immediately taking drastic action, such as postponing or ending an employee's FMLA leave, be a little more flexible about getting the documentation you need. Although you might need to wait a little longer, this is the safest and most humane approach.

Lessons from the *Real World*

An oral request for a medical certification doesn't start the clock.

Ralph Cooper worked for Fulton County, Georgia, for almost 20 years. During his tenure, Cooper had a number of health problems, including depression, for which he was repeatedly absent from work. He was disciplined, suspended, and twice threatened with termination for failing to provide proper medical documentation and contact his supervisor in connection with his absences.

In June 1998, Cooper was absent for several days because he was experiencing chest pains. He was given a letter informing him that he had to provide a doctor's excuse for each day of his absence. On July 8, Cooper provided a doctor's note that accounted for his absences and said he could return to work on July 13. He returned to work as scheduled, only to go home ill several hours later. He told his supervisor he was too ill to work; she reminded him orally to provide a doctor's excuse.

On July 14, Cooper faxed his supervisor a request for leave because he was suffering from blurred vision, having extreme headaches, and passing out. His supervisor called him and again told him to provide a medical excuse. On August 4, the county delivered a letter to Cooper, advising him that he had to provide a medical excuse for his absences by August 10. Cooper got the required excuse from his doctor several days later, but did not immediately deliver it. On August 10, Cooper was sent a letter stating that his employment was terminated effective August 12; Cooper then submitted his medical excuse.

Even with his lengthy history of unexcused absences and failure to comply with employer policies, Cooper won this lawsuit. Why? Because Fulton County didn't give him 15 days' written notice to return the certification. Although the county repeatedly asked him for a doctor's excuse, it did not do so in writing until August 4. Therefore, Cooper had until August 19 to return his certification. By firing him before the time limit expired, Fulton County violated Cooper's FMLA rights.

Cooper v. Fulton County, Georgia, 458 F.3d 1282 (11th Cir. 2006).

After You Receive the Certification

Once you receive a certification, you have several options. You may decide, based on the information provided, that the employee is entitled to FMLA leave. In that situation, you should make sure you've provided the required notices and move on to structuring the employee's time off. (See Chapters 8 and 10.)

The information you receive might lead to the opposite conclusion: that the employee is not protected by the FMLA. This is not as common, but it does happen. For example, the health care provider might describe the condition as a minor ailment which does not incapacitate the patient or might indicate that the employee does not need time off work. In this situation, the employee has not submitted the required proof and is therefore not entitled to FMLA leave. You don't have to request a second opinion; you can simply deny leave based on this information.

> TIP
>
> **Tell the employee what's wrong with the form.** If the information in a medical certification doesn't show that the employee qualifies for FMLA leave, let the employee know. That way, the employee can make sure that the doctor didn't make a mistake in completing the form and will understand why you are denying the leave request. If the employee subsequently gives you a new form indicating that there is a serious health condition, you can always request a second opinion (see "Second Opinions," below).

Even if the form indicates that the employee qualifies for FMLA leave, you might still have doubts. You might wonder whether the illness or ailment described on the form really qualifies as serious. You might doubt that the employee is really using qualifying exigency leave to attend school meetings for a family member's child. You might question the employee's inability to work due to a serious health condition. Perhaps the form is incomplete, or you simply can't read the doctor's handwriting. Later on in this section, we explain your options if you need or want more information after receiving a certification.

Where to Keep Medical Certifications

Employees have a right to privacy in their own medical information and that of their family members. Although you can request limited medical information so you can fulfill your obligations under the FMLA, you still have to maintain the confidentiality of this material by storing it in separate files (that is, not in employees' regular personnel files) and restricting access to it. (For more information, see Chapter 13.)

Certifications in a Foreign Language

You must accept a medical certification from a health care provider who practices in another country, if the employee or family member is visiting there, or the family member lives there, when a serious health condition develops. You must also accept second and third opinions from foreign health care providers; these procedures are described below. If the certification is in a language other than English, the employee must give you a written translation of the certification, upon request.

Incomplete or Insufficient Certifications

If the employee returns a certification that is incomplete or insufficient, you must tell the employee and give him or her a reasonable opportunity to fix the problem. A certification is incomplete if one or more of the required entries has not been completed. For example, perhaps the health care provider didn't fill in some of the blanks on the form, didn't sign and date it, or didn't indicate the duration of the employee's condition. A certification is insufficient if it is complete but the information provided is vague, ambiguous, or nonresponsive.

In these situations, you must tell the employee in writing that the certification is incomplete or insufficient, and you must explain what additional information is necessary to make the certification complete and sufficient. You must give the employee at least seven calendar days to hand in a complete, sufficient certification, unless it isn't practicable for the employee to meet this deadline under the circumstances, despite the employee's diligent good faith efforts. Remember, this rule applies only if the employee hands in a timely certification form. If the employee doesn't provide a certification at all, that isn't considered an incomplete or insufficient certification; it's a failure to meet the certification requirement.

Lessons from the *Real World*

Employer can't deny leave based on inadequate medical certification if it doesn't give the employee a chance to correct it.

Curtis Sims drove a bus for the Alameda-Contra Costa County Transit District (AC Transit) for 25 years. Starting April 18, 1994, he took a couple of weeks off work because of a back injury. He went to two doctors and a chiropractor during this time and was prescribed medication and physical therapy. He returned to work on May 4 and handed in three medical slips, one from each practitioner. Together, the doctors' slips said he was unable to work through May 1; the chiropractor's slip said he could return to work on a trial basis on May 4.

AC Transit placed Sims on a five-day, unpaid suspension following this absence. In July, Sims took two days off for an illness and was fired.

Sims sued, claiming that his FMLA rights were violated when AC Transit counted his April absence against him. AC Transit argued that the last two days of Sims's leave were not protected by the FMLA because, among other things, the chiropractor did not qualify as a health care practitioner. The court found that AC Transit might be right, but it didn't matter: Because AC Transit didn't tell Sims what was wrong with his certification and give him an opportunity to correct it, it couldn't deny him FMLA leave based on that deficiency.

Sims v. Alameda-Contra Costa Transit District, 2 F.Supp.2d 1253 (N.D. Cal. 1998).

Verifying a Certification for a Qualifying Exigency

A qualifying exigency certification is completed by the employee only. As long as the certification is complete and sufficient, you may not ask the employee for additional information. However, if the employee's qualifying exigency involves meeting with a third party, you may contact that third party to verify that the meeting took place, or is scheduled to occur, and the nature of the meeting (for example, that it is a parent-teacher conference or counseling session). You may also contact an appropriate unit of the Defense Department to verify that the employee's family member is on covered active duty or call to active duty status; however, you may not request any additional information. If the employee is requesting time off to be with a family member who is on short-term rest and recuperation leave during deployment, you may ask the employee to provide a copy of the family member's Rest and Recuperation orders or other paperwork issued by the military indicating that the family member is on leave and the dates of that leave.

You don't need permission from the employee to verify the information in the certification. The form requires the employee to provide contact information for third parties with whom the employee will be meeting.

Authenticating or Clarifying Medical Certifications

Even after you receive a complete, sufficient medical certification, you may need to seek clarification or authentication from the health care provider. You may not ask for more information than the certification form requires, but you may ask for:

- clarification (to make sure you understand the health care provider's handwriting or the meaning of a response on the form), or
- authentication (that the health care provider verify that he or she provided or authorized the information on the form and signed it).

These procedures are available only for medical certifications: those for an employee's or family member's serious health condition, or for a family member's serious illness or injury entitling the employee to military caregiver leave.

However, you may seek clarification or authentication only after giving the employee an opportunity to cure any problems with the certification, as explained in "Incomplete or Insufficient Certifications," above. To seek clarification or authentication, someone from your company may contact the health care provider directly. Because the law protects the confidentiality of health-related information, you must follow these rules to make contact:

- You may only seek authentication or clarification, as defined above; you may not seek more information than the form requires.
- Only a health care provider, human resources professional, leave administrator, or management official may contact the health care provider. The employee's direct supervisor may not contact the health care provider.
- You must follow the requirements of the Health Insurance Portability and Accountability Act (HIPAA), which, among other things, may require the employee to provide a written authorization allowing his or her health care provider to discuss the employee's health information with a third party (including an employer requesting clarification of a certification). If the employee won't authorize the discussion, you may not contact the health care provider, but you may deny the employee's request for FMLA leave, if the certification is unclear. Ultimately, it's the employee's responsibility to clarify the certification, if necessary.

SEE AN EXPERT

Get some help with HIPAA requirements. One of the purposes of HIPAA is to protect the confidentiality of personal health information. The law imposes strict rules about any waiver of this right to confidentiality. For example, the employee's authorization must be in writing, describe the information that may be disclosed, and include an expiration date or event for which the authorization is valid. The regulatory provision allowing companies to make direct contact with a health care provider is relatively new, and there may be some kinks to work out. Our best advice is to talk to a lawyer to make sure your authorizations are legally valid and complete.

Second Opinions

What if an employee returns a complete and legible medical certification indicating that the employee or family member has a serious health condition, but you still have doubts? For example, the certification might say that the employee has a minor ailment (such as a cold or headache) or that the employee will need to be out of work for a long time for something that doesn't sound serious. In these situations, you have two options. You can accept the certification at face value and provide FMLA-protected leave, or you can require the employee to get a second opinion: another certification, from a health care provider of your choosing.

Second opinions are not allowed for qualifying exigency leave. They are also not allowed for military caregiver leave, unless the employee's certification was completed by someone other than a military health care provider.

> **CAUTION**
>
> **You can't use the "company doctor."** Although your company can choose the health care provider who provides the second opinion, you can't require the employee to see someone who is regularly employed by your company. This includes not only practitioners who are on the company payroll, but also practitioners whom your company regularly uses, unless access to health care in your company's area is extremely limited.

Your company must pay the costs of the second opinion, including the employee's or family member's reasonable travel expenses. You generally cannot require the employee or family member to travel beyond regular commuting distances, absent very unusual circumstances.

In some situations, the health care provider giving the second opinion will need to review medical information pertaining to the employee's or family member's serious health condition. If the employee or family member doesn't authorize his or her health care provider to release this information, and the second health care provider is unable to render a complete and sufficient second opinion as a result, you may deny the employee's leave request.

While the second opinion is pending, the employee is provisionally entitled to FMLA benefits. If the employee asks for a copy of the second opinion, you must generally provide it within five business days, absent extenuating circumstances.

> **SEE AN EXPERT**
>
> **If the second opinion contradicts the first, proceed with caution.** The FMLA gives you the right to get a third opinion if the first and second certifications differ (see "Third Opinions," below). Some courts have said that you must provide FMLA benefits unless you get this tie-breaking third opinion; others have said that you can deny benefits in reliance on the second opinion (although you might, of course, face a legal challenge from the employee, claiming that the first opinion was correct and that you improperly denied FMLA protections). Based on this conflict, the safest course of action is to go ahead with the third opinion. If you're considering denying FMLA benefits based on a second opinion, talk to an experienced employment attorney.

Third Opinions

If the first and second certifications contradict each other, you may ask the employee to get a third opinion, which will be binding on everyone. The provider who gives the third opinion must be agreed upon by the company and the employee, and both must act in good faith when choosing the provider. The penalty for failing to act in good faith is that the certification favoring the other party will be binding. For example, if you fail to act in good faith in choosing a provider, the initial certification—which presumably found that there was a serious health condition—rules. (Once you reach an agreement on who will provide the third opinion, put it in writing.) The employer must again pay the costs of this process, as well as travel costs. As with the second opinion, you must give the employee a copy of the third opinion, upon request, within five business days.

Recertifications

In some circumstances, you are allowed to ask an employee to provide a recertification of a serious health condition. (You may not request recertification of a qualifying exigency or of a serious illness or injury entitling the employee to military caregiver leave.) This process is intended to help employers fight abuse by employees, particularly employees who take leave periodically either because of a chronic condition that occasionally requires time off or because of a need for intermittent leave for medical appointments or other treatment.

You must give an employee at least 15 calendar days to return the recertification form (you can use the initial certification form for this purpose). You cannot request a second or third opinion for a recertification. How often you can request a recertification depends on the circumstances of the employee's leave.

TIP
You can ask for a new certification every year. You have the right to request an entirely new medical certification—not a recertification—every year, if the employee's or the family member's serious health condition lasts for more than a year (for example, if the condition is chronic or lifelong). Even if you already requested a certification or recertification, you can request a new certification after the employee's 12-month leave period expires. Unlike a recertification, you can get a second or third opinion on this new year certification.

The general rule is that you may request recertification only in connection with an absence and no more often than every 30 days. However, if the certification indicates that the serious health condition will last for more than 30 days, you must wait until the duration indicated on the original certification expires before requesting recertification. Except in all cases—including chronic conditions with no end date—you may request recertification every six months, in connection with an absence.

> **EXAMPLE:** Preston has asthma, for which he typically needs a couple of days of FMLA leave every month. His original certification indicates that the condition is chronic and is not expected to improve. You require Preston to submit a recertification every time he uses FMLA leave, as long as it's been at least 30 days since you last required recertification. Are you following the rules?
>
> No. Because Preston's condition is lifelong, you may not require recertification every 30 days. Unless one of the exceptions discussed below applies, you have the right to request recertification every six months and only in connection with an absence.

In some circumstances, you may require recertifications more often than every 30 days for short-term conditions, and more often than every six months for long-term conditions. You may request more frequent recertifications in any of the following situations:

- The employee requests an extension of leave.
- The circumstances described in the previous certification have changed significantly (for example, the employee has suffered complications or has been absent more often or for a longer period of time than was stated on the previous certification).
- The employer receives information that casts doubt on the employee's stated reason for the absence or the continuing validity of the certification.

> **EXAMPLE:** Brenda suffers from migraines. She has submitted a medical certification from her doctor, indicating that her migraines qualify as a chronic serious health condition. The certification also indicates that her migraines will cause her to miss several days of work each month, on average. Brenda has been taking about this much leave for the past six months.
>
> Brenda attends an after work "happy hour" event to send off a coworker who is leaving the company. After Brenda orders a glass of red wine, her friend John asks her, "What's going on? I've never seen you drink red wine before; I thought

it triggered your migraines." Brenda says, "I know! My doctor gave me this new medication that has totally changed my life! I've been eating chocolate, drinking red wine, and doing all kinds of things I never used to be able to do, and I haven't had a migraine for two months now."

Unbeknownst to Brenda, you—her manager—were standing behind her and overheard the conversation. The next day, you ask Brenda to recertify her health condition. You are well within your rights, as you have information that casts doubt on the continued validity of the certification.

 RELATED TOPIC

You can request a fitness-for-duty certification when an employee returns to work after leave for a serious health condition. The FMLA allows you to ask an employee to provide a statement from a health care provider, indicating that the employee is medically able to perform the job, before reinstating the employee. (For more information, see Chapter 11.)

Lessons from the *Real World*

Taking every Monday or Friday off might be enough to justify a recertification.

In response to a question from an employer, the Department of Labor (DOL) issued an Opinion Letter (an interpretation of the law) regarding recertifications based on suspected abuse. The employer asked whether a pattern of Friday or Monday absences might qualify as information that casts doubt on an employee's reasons for leave. The DOL agreed that it might, as long as there was no evidence of a medical reason for this pattern.

Many employers were heartened not only by this guidance, but also by the DOL's suggestion—now codified in the regulations—that the employer may present this information directly to the health care practitioner in seeking a recertification. The regulations now state that the employer "may provide the health care provider with a record of the employee's absence pattern and ask the health care provider if the serious health condition and need for leave is consistent with such a pattern."

29 C.F.R. § 825.308(e); Opinion Letter FMLA2004-2-A (May 25, 2004).

Common Mistakes Regarding Medical Certifications—And How to Avoid Them

Mistake 1: **Denying FMLA leave inappropriately—that is, when the employee is actually entitled to leave.**

Avoid this mistake by taking the following steps:

- Request a certification whenever an employee seeks leave for a serious health condition, military caregiver leave, or qualifying exigency leave. Do this as soon as possible, but within five business days, of the employee's request for leave. Don't make a decision without getting the information you need.
- Verify, authenticate, and clarify the certification as necessary.
- Get a second opinion if you doubt the employee's certification. Rather than disregarding a certification confirming a serious health condition, require the employee to get a second certification from a different health care practitioner.
- Get a third opinion—or talk to an attorney before taking action—if the first and second opinions conflict.

Mistake 2: **Violating an employee's (or family member's) medical privacy rights.**

Avoid this mistake by taking the following steps:

- Leave the diagnosis to the doctors. Rather than asking an employee for details about his or her medical condition, give the employee a certification form and have the health care practitioners give you only the information to which you are entitled.
- Check with a lawyer before choosing a medical certification form. Some states don't allow employers to request all of the information allowed by the FMLA (and included on the Department of Labor's optional medical certification form).
- Follow all the rules to talk directly to the employee's health care practitioner. Only certain company representatives may talk to the health care provider, and only then to clarify information on the form and only with the employee's permission.

- Keep separate, confidential files of medical records. Never put medical certifications and other health-related information in employees' personnel files.

Mistake 3: **Failing to give employees proper notice or enough time to get a certification.**

Avoid this mistake by taking the following steps:

- Use dated written requests for certifications that explain what employees must provide, the deadlines for getting it back to you, and the consequences of failing to return a certification. Unless you put it in writing, you won't have proof of when you requested the certification.

- Give employees at least 15 days to return a certification (or more time, if they have a plausible reason for missing the deadline). Don't try to shave a few days off, even for employees who are chronically absent or who should already know the rules.

- Work with employees to get the certification in rather than strictly enforcing the deadline. In the real world, courts often recognize that employees who are seriously ill or caring for a sick child or family member might reasonably need more time, especially because they have to rely on health care practitioners, who may be busy, out of town, or simply forget to complete the form.

- Let an employee know if a certification is incomplete or doesn't support the request for FMLA leave. If you don't tell an employee what's wrong with the form, you won't be able to rely on it as a valid reason to deny the employee's leave request.

Managers' Checklist: Certifications

☐ I requested a certification as soon as I learned that the employee was seeking leave for a potentially serious health condition, leave for a qualifying exigency, or military caregiver leave.

  ☐ I made the request in writing, dated and signed.

  ☐ The request included a deadline at least 15 days away and explained the consequences of failing to return the certification on time.

  ☐ I gave the employee a certification form.

  ☐ I did not request any information that goes beyond what's required by the form.

☐ I worked with the employee to get a complete certification.

  ☐ If the form was not returned on time, I contacted the employee immediately to find out why and explain the importance of getting the form in.

  ☐ If the form was returned incomplete or insufficient, I explained that to the employee in writing, told the employee what additional information was necessary to make the form complete and sufficient, and gave the employee at least seven days to cure the deficiency.

  ☐ If the form was in a foreign language, I asked the employee to provide a written translation.

☐ I followed the appropriate procedures to verify a qualifying exigency certification, if necessary.

  ☐ I contacted any third parties named in the certification to confirm that the employee is meeting with them and the purpose of the meeting.

  ☐ I contacted a representative of the Defense Department to confirm the family member's active duty or call to active duty.

  ☐ I asked for documentation if the employee is requesting time off for a family member's rest and recuperation leave.

  ☐ I did not request any additional information from the employee or anyone else regarding the certification.

Managers' Checklist: Certifications (continued)

☐ I followed the appropriate procedures to seek authentication or clarification of a medical certification, if necessary.

    ☐ I got written authorization from the employee for a company representative to contact the health care provider, if necessary.

    ☐ Only a health care provider, human resources professional, leave administrator, or management official contacted the health care provider—not the employee's direct supervisor.

    ☐ No one sought additional information from the health care provider, beyond authentication and clarification.

☐ I requested a second opinion if I had doubts about the initial medical certification.

    ☐ I sought a second opinion only of a certification of a serious health condition or military caregiver leave authorized by a health care provider outside of the military.

    ☐ I did not send the employee to a health care practitioner who is regularly employed by my company.

    ☐ While the second opinion was pending, I provided FMLA benefits to the employee.

    ☐ I provided a copy of the second opinion to the employee, within five days after receiving his or her request.

    ☐ Before acting on a second opinion that contradicts the first, I consulted with an attorney.

☐ I requested recertifications as appropriate.

    ☐ I requested recertification only every 30 days or when the employee's initial certification expired for short-term conditions, or every six months for long-term conditions, unless an exception allowed me to request one more often.

    ☐ I requested recertification whenever the employee's situation changed or I learned information that cast doubt on the employee's reasons for leave.

☐ I placed the medical certification(s) and any recertifications in confidential medical files, not the employee's regular personnel file.

Managing an Employee's Leave

Chapter Highlights

☆ You may postpone the start of an employee's leave if the need for leave was foreseeable and the employee could have provided you with 30 days' notice.

☆ Most employers cover an employee's workload during leave by asking coworkers to pick up the slack; other methods of handling work for an employee on leave include hiring temps, using consultants, outsourcing the work, or picking up some of the work yourself.

☆ You must continue an employee's group health benefits while the employee is on leave:
  • You may require the employee to pay his or her usual share of the premium, in one of several ways allowed by the FMLA.
  • If the employee is more than 30 days late in making premium payments, you may cut off insurance coverage, but only after providing written notice to the employee and at least 15 additional days to make up the payments.
  • Employees must make reasonable efforts to schedule foreseeable leave for planned medical treatment so it does not unduly disrupt your company's operations.

☆ You can temporarily transfer an employee on intermittent leave to another position, with equal benefits and pay, that better accommodates the need for leave.

☆ You may request periodic status reports from employees on FMLA leave regarding any changes in their planned return dates or their intent to return at all.

☆ You may discipline or even fire an employee who is on FMLA leave, as long as your reasons for doing so are entirely unrelated to the employee's leave. Before you do so, however, you should consult with a lawyer.

B y the time an employee actually starts using FMLA leave, you've already done quite a bit of work. You've dealt with coverage and eligibility requirements, handled paperwork and notices, and perhaps even had to do some math to figure out how many hours the employee has worked, how much leave the employee can take, and so on. At this point, you might be thinking that most of your work is done.

There are, however, a few more things on your FMLA to-do list. You'll need to provide continued health care benefits while employees are on leave, follow the rules for employees on intermittent leave, and make sure that you'll be ready to reinstate employees upon their return.

In addition to these legal requirements, a number of practical considerations come to the forefront when employees go out on leave. How can you make sure an employee's work gets done? How often should you communicate with an employee on leave to find out how things are going and when the employee intends to return to work? What can you do to ensure a smooth transition to and from leave? And can you ever discipline or replace an employee on FMLA leave? This chapter explains how to manage FMLA leave and provides practical strategies for minimizing disruptions to your company.

Scheduling Leave

When an employee requests time off, you should calendar the employee's leave. (Typically, you'll want to do this as you complete the employee's notice forms, covered in Chapter 8.) Mark the date when the employee plans to start leave, how long the employee expects to be gone, and when the employee intends to return. If the dates are uncertain—for example, the employee doesn't know exactly when she'll have to stop working before having a baby or how long a parent will take to recuperate from surgery—make your best guess based on what the employee tells you and the information in the certification, if applicable.

As you calendar the employee's leave, keep in mind the basic scheduling rules set out below. Now is the time to determine, for example, whether you have reason to postpone the start of the employee's leave or ask the employee to reschedule leave. If you decide not to allow the employee to take leave on the dates requested, you should tell the employee right away so he or she can make appropriate arrangements.

CAUTION

Raise scheduling issues in writing. If you decide to postpone or reschedule the employee's leave, let the employee know in writing when you provide the designation notice form. That form doesn't explicitly address this subject, but it does indicate the dates for which the employee requested leave. If you provide the notice form without telling the employee that you aren't granting leave for the exact dates the employee requested, the employee will be understandably confused and might make plans based on his or her original request. The best practice is to put your scheduling decision in writing and attach it to the notice form, then discuss it with the employee.

Postponing the Start of Leave

As explained in Chapter 8, employees must give 30 days' advance notice if they need leave for a foreseeable reason. Examples of foreseeable leave include time off for scheduled, nonemergency surgery; for the birth or adoption of a child; or to care for a family member who has treatment scheduled well in advance. (Remember, an employee who can't give 30 days' notice of foreseeable leave—for example, because the employee learned of the need for leave only a few weeks ahead of time—must give as much notice as is practicable under the circumstances.) If the employee fails to give this notice, you can delay the start of the employee's leave until 30 days have passed since the employee gave notice.

CAUTION

You can delay the start of an employee's leave only if you have informed the employee of the duty to provide the notice required under the FMLA. This information should be included in your company's written FMLA policy and in workplace FMLA posters, as explained in Chapter 2.

If an employee doesn't give 30 days' notice of foreseeable leave, you may ask the employee to explain why it was not practicable to do so. You should put your request in writing and ask the employee to write out his or her response.

You may not delay an employee's leave when the employee has given adequate notice under the FMLA rules covered in Chapter 8, even if the employee hasn't provided as much notice as your company usually requires.

For example, if your company requires employees to schedule planned absences three months in advance, you may not penalize an employee who gives the 30 days' notice required by the FMLA for missing your company's notice deadline. However, your company may require employees to comply with its other notice requirements—for example, that employees must contact a particular person or put their leave request in writing—unless unusual circumstances prevent the employee from doing so.

Of course, you shouldn't delay an employee's leave just because you can. You'll have to carefully weigh the facts to decide whether to exercise this right. The reason for caution here is simple: An employee whose leave is delayed may challenge your decision in court, especially if the employee is harmed by the delay. What's more, you will look like the bad guy to other employees who report to you. You will also have poisoned your relationship with the employee who needed leave earlier (and will return to work at some point).

Here are a few things to consider when deciding whether to postpone leave:

- **Why the employee needs leave.** If delaying FMLA leave could cause someone to suffer physical harm, you have good reason to be lenient. For example, if the employee or a family member requires surgery for a life-threatening condition, it's best to allow the employee to take scheduled leave, rather than insisting on a full notice period.

- **How difficult it would be for the employee to reschedule.** In some cases, an employee or family member can reschedule a medical procedure relatively easily, but other times, canceling could mean waiting months for another opportunity. Or, the employee might need leave for an event that can't be rescheduled, such as the birth of a child. The harder it is for the employee to postpone taking leave, the more likely you are to face problems if you insist on 30 days' notice.

- **Your company's needs.** If you really need 30 days' notice for business reasons—for example, because it will take that long to cover the employee's accounts or because your company's busiest season will be over by then—then it makes more sense to delay leave if the employee hasn't give sufficient notice.

- **The employee's reason for failing to give notice.** Remember, the employee has to give only as much notice as it practicable under the circumstances. If the employee had a plausible reason for not giving notice on time, it's best to grant leave without a delay.

EXAMPLE: On May 1, Cora tells you, her manager, that she needs to take several days off, starting May 10, to have surgery to remove a cancerous lump from her breast. Cora's surgeon is a renowned physician whose services are in high demand, and she only found out that she'd been scheduled (after a cancellation) on May 1, the day she notified you. Can you require Cora to delay her leave until June 1?

No. Although Cora knew that she would need time off at some point, she didn't know the exact date of her surgery until the day she gave notice. Under the FMLA, this constitutes as much notice as is practicable under the circumstances, so you cannot require her to delay her leave.

Now assume that Cora actually scheduled her surgery more than a month ago but didn't tell you about it until May 1. Should you require her to delay her leave? It's risky. Cora didn't give the required notice, but she needs surgery for a potentially life-threatening condition. If you require her to miss her scheduled appointment, she might have to wait a long time to get a new date. Although you have the right to require her to wait for 30 days, it doesn't seem like a good idea to exercise it here. If delay could lead to serious medical problems, it's probably best not to require it.

If Cora's surgery was for something less urgent—for example, to remove her tonsils—the balance would shift. You would be well within your rights to require a full 30 days' notice. A delay wouldn't cause Cora any harm, and she has no excuse for failing to give notice as required, so you are on safer ground if you require her to delay her leave.

If you decide, after considering all the facts and circumstances, that you will insist on 30 days' notice, put your decision in writing (including the earliest date the employee's leave can begin) and talk to the employee about it. Listen carefully to the employee's response; you may learn something that could change your mind. If so, simply provide a new designation notice form.

Rescheduling Leave

In addition to the 30-day notice requirement for foreseeable leave, there are a couple of additional timing issues to consider. They are:

- **One-year limit on parenting leave.** As explained in Chapter 5, new parents must conclude their parenting leave within one year after the child is born or placed with them. Review this requirement when you sit down with the employee to discuss his or her time off to make sure the employee understands it.

- **Scheduling foreseeable treatment to avoid undue disruption.** Employees are obligated to make reasonable efforts to schedule foreseeable leave for planned medical treatment so as not to unduly disrupt the employer's operations. This is true whether the leave will be taken intermittently or all at once. And, for all intermittent leave for a serious health condition or military caregiver leave, employees must work with you to come up with a schedule that meets the employee's needs without unduly disrupting company operations. This means you can ask the employee to reschedule planned treatment or to work around the company's needs. However, any changes must be approved by the employee's health care provider. If the health care provider insists that treatment must begin immediately, for example, you can't make the employee wait until your company's annual reports are filed. (See "Managing Intermittent Leave," below, for more information.)

Unforeseeable Leave

As explained in Chapter 8, an employee who needs leave for an unforeseeable reason—emergency surgery or premature labor, for example—need give only as much notice as is practicable under the circumstances. If the employee has a true emergency, you might receive notice only after the employee has already missed work. How can you work out scheduling issues in this situation?

The answer depends on the circumstances. If the employee needs leave for reasons other than his or her own serious health condition—for example, because the employee's family member has been in an accident or the employee's wife has delivered a baby prematurely or been called to active military duty—you should be able to spend a few minutes on the phone with the employee. You should ask how long the employee expects the situation to last; if the employee doesn't know, tell the employee that you'll call again in a few days to check in.

If the employee is unable to talk to you personally—for example, because the employee is in a coma, recovering from surgery, or simply too weak to attend to work details—talk to a close family member. Under the FMLA, you may talk to the employee's spokesperson (typically, an adult family member) if the employee is unable to give notice personally. In this situation, you should again ask about the condition and how long it's expected to last. If the family member doesn't know, ask to be kept in the loop and call back in a few days to follow up.

> ⓘ CAUTION
>
> **Compassion is the order of the day.** An employee who needs emergency leave is typically facing a very tough situation such as a sudden injury or illness or a difficult birth. Although it's important to fulfill your notice obligations, don't go overboard trying to get the employee to do the same. Be sensitive to the employee's situation, and do what you can to get the information you need without being demanding or intrusive.

Covering an Employee's Duties During Leave

As a manager, you're responsible not only for administering an employee's FMLA leave properly, but also for making sure the employee's work gets done. If you're wondering how other managers do it, here's the answer: According to a 2012 survey on the FMLA conducted by the Department of Labor, almost two-thirds of responding employers said that they covered the work of an employee on leave by assigning it to coworkers. Only 3.2% of employers reported hiring a temporary replacement to do the work.

One likely reason many employers simply redistribute the work of employees on leave is that employees tend to come back fairly quickly. The 2012 survey showed that almost half of all FMLA leaves lasted for ten days or less, the equivalent of a regular vacation.

As we all know, however, statistics give only a general picture. Every situation is different, and you'll have to consider all of the facts and circumstances when trying to figure out how to get the work done.

Available Options

There are a number of ways to get work done while an employee is on leave. In some cases, you'll be able to use just one of these strategies; other situations might call for a combination of approaches. Here are some commonly used options:

- **Rely on coworkers.** This strategy makes good sense, especially if other employees do similar work: The coworkers already know how to do the job. Your role is to figure out what changes might need to be made (if any) to allow the employee's coworkers to take on extra work, or how to divide the work amongst several employees. In some instances, you might even handle some higher-level work yourself, such as supervising employees or handling key transactions or relationships.

   EXAMPLE: Jody is a customer service representative in a call center staffed by 12 employees. All of them do the same job: answering phone calls from customers who have questions about the company's products, processing orders and returns on a same-day basis, and contacting customers who have purchased the company's products to assess their satisfaction with the experience.

   When Jody takes three weeks of FMLA leave, her manager, Leticia, realizes that it will take too long for a temporary replacement to learn the ropes. By the time a temp gets up to speed, Jody will be back at work. Instead, Leticia decides to ask Jody's coworkers to handle her calls. To make sure the workload doesn't get overwhelming, Leticia makes answering and returning customer calls the top priority and allows orders and returns to be put off until the following day, if necessary. Leticia also asks two of the company's summer interns to take over the customer satisfaction surveys until Jody returns from leave. By making these minor adjustments, Leticia ensures that her short-handed team will still be able to get its work done.

- **Hire a temporary replacement.** Whenever coworkers won't be able to take on the employee's job duties—maybe they're too busy or don't have the necessary skills—it's time to look outside the company. Just make sure that any temp you hire understands that the job is for a very limited time; otherwise, you might be faced with a legal claim when the time comes to let the temp go.

- **Hire a consultant.** If you need to replace someone who does highly creative or technical projects, consider hiring an outside consultant: an independent contractor who specializes in particular types of work. If the work is specialized and really can't wait, it might be worth the expense to hire a pro for specific tasks like rolling out a new computer system or designing new company branding.
- **Outsource the work.** It sometimes makes sense to hire an outside company to do an employee's work (for example, if no one in-house has the skills but an outside agency offers the same service).

> EXAMPLE: Sanjiv works in the bookkeeping department and spends a few days each month processing payroll. The rest of his time he collects accounts receivable. Sanjiv plans to take ten weeks of FMLA leave when his daughter is born. Although his coworkers can pick up his accounts receivable work, only his manager, Brenda, knows how to do the payroll. Unfortunately, Brenda will be preparing the company for an audit while Sanjiv is out and won't have any time to devote to handling the payroll.
>
> Brenda decides to use an outside payroll service while Sanjiv is out. It costs significantly less than hiring a replacement or training another employee to do the payroll. And, Brenda knows that the outside service knows how to handle deductions, withholdings, and other wage adjustments, which assures her that the company won't run afoul of wage and hour or tax laws while Sanjiv is away.

No matter which option(s) you choose, you'll probably have to undo any changes when the employee returns to work because you're required to reinstate the employee when his or her leave is over. (Chapter 11 explains this requirement in detail.) This is why it's important that you explain to the people who will do the employee's job, whether they are the employee's coworkers or outside temps or contractors, that the situation is temporary. You don't want replacements believing they've received a promotion or landed a permanent position with your company.

As you can see, there are many ways to get work done while an employee is on leave. What you should not do, however, is ask the employee to continue working while on leave. Although it's acceptable to check in briefly to get necessary information that only the employee has (such as how to contact a client or how a particular delivery is tracked), don't ask the employee to perform any actual work while on leave. Crossing this line can lead to a claim that you interfered with the employee's right to take FMLA leave.

Lessons from the *Real World*

Asking an employee to work while on leave violates the FMLA.

While Joan Smith-Schrenk was on FMLA leave, she alleged that her manager asked her to update case files, complete a safety review project, and personally deliver that project to the office. Smith-Schrenk estimated that she spent 20 to 40 hours working while she was on FMLA leave and that her manager's request interfered with her FMLA rights.

Her employer, Genon Energy Services, disputed her claims. The employer pointed out that Smith-Schrenk was allowed to take all of the FMLA leave she requested and was reinstated to her previous position when she returned from leave. Therefore, the company said, she couldn't point to any legal violation or any damages caused by having to work during her leave.

However, the Court disagreed with the employer. After reviewing a number of cases on the issue, the Court held that an employer can expect an employee to field minimal contacts during leave, such as an occasional brief phone call about the location of a file or the status of a project. However, asking an employee to actually perform work during leave crosses the line and interferes with the employee's right to time off. And, because the employee would be entitled to pay for any work performed while on unpaid leave, damages might be available for the violation. Therefore, the Court allowed Smith-Schrenk to take her FMLA violation claim to trial.

Smith-Schrenk v. Genon Energy Services, Civil Action H-13-2902 (S.D. Tex. 2015).

Talk to the Employee

Before you decide how to handle an employee's workload during leave, you should talk to the employee about it, if possible. Of course, if the employee takes leave for a medical emergency, you may not get this opportunity. You'll have to patch something together quickly until you get a chance to speak with the employee and figure out how long he or she will be gone.

The employee is your best source of information about exactly what he or she does every day, which job duties are top priorities, which coworkers might be able to step in and handle certain tasks, and so on. The employee also has a vested interest in making sure his or her work is handled properly during leave. After all, nobody wants to return from leave to find a pile of unfinished work, strained relationships with customers or clients, missed deadlines, and other problems. Employees who take pride in their work and value their place in the company will be eager to collaborate with you on a strategy for a smooth transition from work to leave and back again.

But you also have to proceed with caution when talking to an employee about handling his or her work. The FMLA prohibits you from interfering with an employee's right to take leave, which includes discouraging the employee from using the FMLA. If you pressure the employee not to take leave, imply that the employee's opportunities to advance might suffer if the employee takes leave, or require the employee to work when he or she is on leave, you could run into legal trouble.

> **EXAMPLE:** Luisa is a salesperson for an office supply company. She handles some of the company's largest accounts. Luisa is planning to take a full 12 weeks of FMLA leave when she has a baby. You meet with her to talk about handling her workload. You start the conversation like this: "You know, Luisa, our back-to-school business in August and September is huge, and you're planning to be out until September. If you could come back a few weeks early, we wouldn't have to assign your accounts to someone else. Of course, you can take a longer leave if you want, but I can't guarantee that you'll get those accounts back if we have to move them."
>
> Oops! You've basically said that you will punish Luisa for taking the full leave to which she's entitled. Here's a better way to start the discussion: "Congratulations, Luisa! I'm so excited for you. As you know, you'll be out during the biggest sales period of the year, so I want to get your ideas about how we should handle your accounts while you're gone, especially Office Club and Binders 'n' More. I really want to work with you to figure out how we can keep these customers happy, and keep our sales high, even though you won't be here. Do you think it makes sense to hire a temporary replacement, or can the other salespeople pick up the slack?"

Your conversation with the employee will depend on the facts, including what the employee does, how long the employee will be out, whether the employee supervises others, and so on. Here are some pointers that will help you in your conversation:

- **Always start by acknowledging the employee's situation.** Congratulate or offer sympathy to the employee as appropriate. Rushing straight into a discussion of work details appears insensitive to the employee's needs, and your conversation may be strained as a result.

- **Briefly state the facts.** Review what you know about the employee's job and requested leave to make sure you've got the details right. For example, you might say, "I'd like to get your feedback on how to cover your work while you're out and make sure your transition to leave and back to work is a smooth one. I understand you'll be out for five weeks and that one major project milestone will come up during that time. Is that right?"

- **Learn the priorities.** Ask what the employee has on his or her plate, focusing particularly on projects, deadlines, meetings, and deliverables that need to be handled while the employee is out. For example: "What are the most important things that we need to take care of while you're gone? What can wait until you return?"

- **Discuss options.** Ask whether the employee has any ideas or concerns about job coverage, such as which coworkers might be able to pick up the work, whether to hire a temp, or whether some matters would best be handled by you or another higher-up at the company. You might say, "When Jane took parental leave, I called on her two major accounts and the rest of the team divvied up the others. Do you think that approach will work for your leave? Are there any accounts that you think I should cover?"

- **Ask what to say.** Find out how the employee would like you to position his or her absence with third parties (vendors, clients, customers, and so on) and coworkers. Some employees want others to know what's going on, while others prefer to keep things private, and you should respect the employee's wishes. For example: "I'll tell the outside auditors that you'll be on leave for four weeks. I know some of your coworkers already know about your father's condition; would you prefer that I announce that you'll be taking leave to help care for him, or would you rather I simply say that you'll be out?"

- **Recap your strategy.** After you've talked through the options and developed a plan, review it with the employee. If either of you will have to gather more information before you can make a final decision, schedule another brief conversation. For example, you might say, "I'm going to ask Mark about his workload, and you're going to try to reschedule the in-house trainings until after you return from leave. Let's meet again on Thursday to see where we are. If everything works out, we'll plan to have Mark and Stacey cover your IT calls, and I'll free up some of their time by bringing in a part-time temp to handle the departmental paperwork."

Lessons from the *Real World*

Company that pressures employee to take fewer days off interferes with the employee's FMLA rights.

Vanessa McFadden was a legal secretary at a law firm when her husband was diagnosed with cancer. She asked for leave to take care of him and was granted some time off, but said she was misinformed about her FMLA rights and pressured not to take as much time off as she needed. She said that the human resources manager at the firm told her that missing work on days when her husband had medical appointments was going to be a problem. Because she felt that she had to report to work, McFadden arranged for her sister to care for her husband on those days and paid her for doing so.

The D.C. Court of Appeals found that McFadden had the right to go to trial on her claim that the law firm interfered with her FMLA rights. Based on the facts, the Court found that a jury could reasonably conclude that McFadden had to pay her sister to take care of her husband because the firm (and the HR manager, sued in her individual capacity) had led her to believe that she could not take time off to care for him herself.

McFadden v. Ballard Spahr Andrews Ingersoll, LLP, 611 F.3d 1 (D.C. Cir. 2010).

Handle Logistics

After you've developed a plan to cover the employee's work, it's time to execute it. If you'll need to hire a temp or consultant, make the necessary arrangements. If coworkers will be taking on part of the load, talk with them and find out whether they'll need additional resources or help. Tell the employee's outside contacts—such as clients, suppliers, and so on—that the employee will be out, and give them the name of someone else to call if they have any questions or concerns.

Continuing Employee Benefits During Leave

While an employee is on FMLA leave, you must continue the employee's coverage under your company's group health plan, just as if the employee did not take leave. If the employee usually has to contribute toward the premium, you may continue to require that contribution, but your company must continue to pay its share of the premium as well. Whether you have to provide other types of benefits during leave depends on your company's policies.

The employee is entitled to continue the same type of coverage and benefit levels as before the leave. For example, if the employee's family was covered, then the continuation must include family coverage. However, any changes to the benefits plan, new plans, premium increases, and so on still apply to the employee. And, employees on leave have the same right to change their coverage as they would have had if they were employed. So an employee on leave during an open enrollment period has the same right to change coverage as employees who are actually working during that period.

Employees do not have to continue their benefits during FMLA leave if they don't want to. However, because you must restore the employee's benefits when you reinstate the employee—and you must do so immediately, without any waiting period, physical examination, or other requalification procedure—you might have to continue the benefits and seek reimbursement later from the employee. (Chapter 11 covers benefits restoration when an employee returns to work.)

What Is a Group Health Plan?

A group health plan is any plan an employer creates, maintains, or contributes to, in order to to provide health care to employees, former employees, and their families. This includes self-insured plans, vision plans, dental coverage, and other health care plans, whether they are components of a single health care plan or administered separately.

A group health plan does not include health insurance programs under which employees purchase individual policies from insurers if all of the following are true:

- The employer makes no contribution.
- Employee participation is voluntary.
- The employer's role doesn't go beyond allowing the insurer to publicize its plan to employees, collecting premiums through payroll deductions, and sending them to the insurer.
- The employer doesn't receive any compensation or other benefit from the program, other than reasonable payment for the cost of collecting and remitting premiums.
- The employee's premium does not increase if the employment relationship ends.

Cafeteria Plans

Some companies provide benefits through a cafeteria plan: a benefit program through which employees choose from a menu of benefits, such as health coverage, life insurance, disability insurance, and so on. Employees are allotted a certain number of dollars or "points" to spend on the options; if they choose not to spend the entire amount, they can typically receive the remainder as compensation.

Employers must continue making cafeteria plan payments toward group health insurance premiums (including dental and vision benefits) while an employee is on FMLA leave. If other benefits—such as life insurance or child care coverage—are paid through a cafeteria plan, the employer is not required to continue the portion of the payment that goes toward these benefits, unless it does so for employees on other types of unpaid leave. (See "Other Types of Benefits," below, for more information.)

Flexible Spending Accounts

A flexible spending account (FSA) allows employees to set aside pretax income for medical expenses not paid by health insurance (such as co-payments, premiums, and expenses that are outside of the employer's plan) or for dependent care expenses. The employee determines how much to set aside each year (typically, through payroll deductions), within limits set by law.

FSAs are funded entirely by employees, so there aren't any employer contributions to be continued during FMLA leave. Employees on leave must be given three options for dealing with their FSAs:

- continue making payments as if they were still working
- continue their participation in the plan but stop making payments during leave, or
- stop participating in the plan while on leave.

If the employee either stops making payments or pulls out of the plan altogether during FMLA leave, the employee has a choice upon reinstatement: return to the previous coverage level or choose a prorated coverage amount that doesn't include payments for the time spent on leave.

> EXAMPLE: David has an FSA and decides to commit $1,200 to it for the year. His employer sets aside $50 from David's twice-monthly paychecks and deposits it in his FSA. David is out for two months on FMLA leave. He decides to continue his coverage but suspend his payments during that time.
>
> When he returns, David would have to make higher payments to set aside a total of $1,200. Because he missed $200 worth of payments while on leave and there are eight pay periods left in the year, he would have to have an additional $25 set aside each pay period, for a total pretax contribution of $75, if he wanted to set aside the whole $1,200. Alternatively, he could continue setting aside $50 per paycheck and reduce his total coverage for the year to $1,000.

Multiemployer Health Plans

A multiemployer health plan is a special type of health insurance coverage unique to unionized companies. At least two employers contribute to a multiemployer plan, which is maintained pursuant to one or more collective bargaining agreement(s) between unions and employers.

Employers that contribute to these plans must follow the same benefits continuation rules as other employers. For example, they cannot provide less coverage or charge the employee a higher premium to continue benefits than the employee would have had to pay if working. However, there are a couple of different rules for multiemployer plans:

- If the plan contains special provisions for maintaining coverage during FMLA leave (for example, through pooled contributions from all employers subject to the plan), the employer may follow those provisions rather than continuing to contribute the same amount as would have been due if the employee were continuously working.

- Employees who receive health care coverage through a multiemployer plan cannot be required to use "banked" hours during FMLA leave. Typically, an employee banks hours when he or she works more hours than are necessary to maintain eligibility for health care coverage; the employee can then use these banked hours to maintain eligibility when the employee's hours drop below the minimum threshold for eligibility. This provision relieves employees of the obligation to use banked hours to maintain eligibility during periods of FMLA leave.

Other Types of Benefits

For all other types of benefits, your company must follow its usual policies for employees on the same type of leave (that is, paid or unpaid). If your policies do not provide for other benefits to continue or accrue during leave, you do not have to continue them or allow them to accrue during FMLA leave. For example, if your company typically does not allow paid vacation leave to accrue while an employee is on unpaid leave, you do not have to allow it to accrue while the employee is on unpaid FMLA leave. The same is true of seniority and benefits based on seniority.

> ⓘ **CAUTION**
> **Apply paid leave policies if employees use paid time off for FMLA leave.** If an employee uses paid time off during FMLA leave, you must follow your company's policies for paid leave. For example, if you allow employees to continue to accrue seniority or sick and vacation leave while using paid time off, you must also allow them to accrue these benefits while using paid time off during FMLA leave.

You have no legal obligation to continue other insurance benefits—such as life or disability insurance—while an employee is on FMLA leave, unless you continue these benefits for other types of leave. But as a practical matter, you may need to continue these benefits to make sure you'll be able to restore the employee's benefits upon reinstatement. As you'll learn in Chapter 11, you must give a returning employee the same benefits, at the same levels, that the employee had before taking leave, and you cannot require the employee to requalify for benefits. If your insurance programs would require an employee who drops coverage and then picks it up again to requalify, you might have to keep the employee enrolled to avoid violating the FMLA. (If so, you can seek reimbursement for the employee's share of the premiums when the employee returns to work; see "Restoring Pay and Benefits" in Chapter 11.)

Premium Payments

The FMLA provides several ways to collect the employee's share of the premium for group health coverage. If the employee uses paid leave during FMLA leave, the employee's share must be collected as it ordinarily would be for any other type of paid leave (typically, through payroll deductions). If the employee uses unpaid FMLA leave, the employer may collect the premium in any of the following ways:

- The employee makes the payment at the same time it would ordinarily be due through payroll deduction. In other words, the employee would have to pay the premium every payday.

- The employee makes the payment at the same time it would be due if the employee were receiving continuing coverage through COBRA.
- The employee pays the premium in advance to a cafeteria plan (at the employee's option).
- The employee pays according to the same rules that apply to other employees on unpaid leave, as long as those rules don't require the employee to pay the premium before leave starts or require the employee to pay more than he or she would have to pay if not on leave.
- The employee pays in any manner agreed to by employer and employee. For example, you might agree that the employee can prepay the premiums by having a larger amount deducted each pay period prior to taking foreseeable leave.

Whichever method you choose, you must give the employee advance written notice of how and when the payment must be made and the consequences of failing to pay. You can provide this notice as part of the employee's rights and responsibilities notice, covered in Chapter 8.

If the employee's premium payment is more than 30 days late, you may terminate the employee's coverage. However, you must send the employee written notice of your intent to do so. The letter must state that the payment has not been received and that the employee's coverage will terminate if payment is not received by a certain date; this date must be at least 15 days after you send the letter.

POLICY ALERT
The date the employee's coverage officially terminates depends, in part, on your policies for other types of unpaid leave. If your company has an established policy that allows it to terminate coverage retroactively to the date of the missed payment, it may do so. If it does not have this type of policy, it may terminate coverage effective 30 days after the missed payment.

Here is a sample letter telling an employee that health insurance coverage will terminate unless payment is received; see Appendix C for a digital copy.

Sample Notice of Termination of Group Health Coverage

March 28, 2018

Corinne West

123 Main Street

San Francisco, CA 94910

Dear Corinne,

As I informed you by written notice when you first requested FMLA leave, you are required to pay your share of the premium for group health insurance. We agreed that you would pay these amounts by getting a check to me, in the amount of $36.45, on the 1st and 15th of every month. I have attached a copy of the written notice explaining this requirement, for your reference.

You submitted a check on February 15 and March 1. However, I did not receive a check from you on March 15. I am writing to inform you that we are going to terminate your health insurance coverage if we do not receive your March 15 payment by April 14, 2018. You must continue to make your other premium payments on time.

Please take care of this right away. If you have any questions, feel free to call me at 415-555-1212.

Sincerely,

Jim Ramey

Jim Ramey

HR Director

Although you have the legal right to terminate coverage for a late payment, you also have a legal obligation to restore the employee's health benefits when he or she returns to work. You cannot require the employee to reapply, take a physical exam, or otherwise requalify for benefits. This obligation applies even if you terminate coverage because the employee fails to pay the premium. As a practical matter, this means you may have to continue the employee's coverage and even pay the employee's share of the premium. If you find yourself in this situation, you can require the employee to reimburse you for his or her share once the employee returns to work; Chapter 11 explains how.

Managing Intermittent Leave

Intermittent or reduced-schedule leave poses some unique managerial challenges. You and the employee might not know how long the employee's need for leave will last, when the employee will have to take time off, or even whether the employee will show up for work the next day. This can present some challenges when you're trying to make sure that the work gets done.

Scheduling

Employees who need intermittent or reduced-schedule leave for a serious health condition or to act as a military caregiver must try to schedule leave in a way that does not disrupt your company's operations. If the employee knows he or she will need intermittent or reduced-schedule leave, the employee should give you a proposed schedule of leave and try to arrange the time off in a way that accommodates the company's needs. Of course, this will be easier when the employee needs leave for scheduled treatment rather than for episodic flare-ups of a serious health condition.

This doesn't mean that the company has the right to veto an employee's leave schedule, however. The employee's health care provider will ultimately decide whether treatment or leave can be rescheduled or not. If the health care provider won't approve a change, you may not insist on it.

> EXAMPLE: Marcos needs weekly physical therapy for neck injuries from a car accident. Marcos tells you that he needs to be out for two hours every week for at least 12 weeks. You and Marcos agree that he will try to schedule the therapy for the late afternoon, when plenty of his coworkers will be available to handle his workload.
>
> When Marcos calls to schedule his treatment, he learns that there are no available late afternoon slots for a couple of months. Marcos's doctor says that he must begin physical therapy immediately or risk permanent damage. In this situation, can you insist that Marcos wait for an afternoon appointment?
>
> No. Marcos's doctor has the last word, and treatment must start immediately. You should work with Marcos to figure out which of the available time slots would be least disruptive for the company.

When an employee needs leave for an episodic problem—such as migraines, asthma, or any other condition that comes on suddenly or waxes and wanes in intensity—it can be very difficult to manage the employee's time off. After all, the employee typically can't predict when the condition will flare up. If the condition is unpredictable, you cannot insist that the employee take leave only according to a set schedule. As long as the employee is otherwise entitled to leave and either is taking military caregiver leave or has (or is caring for someone who has) a serious health condition, the employee has the right to take unscheduled time off if it's medically necessary.

> **EXAMPLE:** Caroline suffers from Crohn's disease, a chronic condition that causes inflammation of the intestines. On occasion, the disease flares up and she has severe abdominal pain and vomiting that makes it impossible for her to work. If she qualifies for FMLA leave, Caroline is likely entitled to take intermittent leave when her condition incapacitates her, even if she can't give any notice or "schedule" this time off.

Transfers

If an employee has a foreseeable need for reduced-schedule or intermittent leave for planned medical treatment, or if your company agrees to allow intermittent or reduced-schedule parenting leave, you have a couple of other options. You may transfer the employee to another position that better accommodates the employee's leave schedule or change the employee's original position to better accommodate the employee's need for leave, as long as the employee still receives the same pay and benefits. If transferred to an alternative position, the employee must be qualified for the position.

The alternative position need not have the same job duties as the employee's original position. However, the company cannot transfer the employee to a less desirable position that could discourage the employee (or others) from taking leave. For example, a change that dramatically increases the employee's commute or moves the employee from the day shift to the night shift violates the FMLA. If the alternative position is a clear and obvious demotion, it won't fly.

Lessons from the *Real World*

An employee must make reasonable efforts to reschedule foreseeable intermittent leave that would result in understaffing.

Scott Kaylor was a CT technician at Fannin Regional Hospital. During his employment at the hospital, Kaylor saw his doctor regularly for treatment for a degenerative back disease.

On December 27, 1994, Kaylor was hospitalized for a flare-up of his back injury. He spent three weeks on FMLA leave, then returned to work. On January 31, Kaylor told his supervisor that he had an appointment with his doctor on February 3. This appointment was one of his regular treatments and had been scheduled before he was hospitalized. Kaylor's supervisor told him he could not take the day off because it would leave them short-staffed and asked him to reschedule the treatment.

After hearing from other employees that Kaylor planned to call in sick on February 3, his supervisor asked him whether he intended to show up. He said that he would come to work. On the 3rd, however, he called in sick, claiming to have a stomach virus. But he still went to his doctor's appointment for back treatment. The doctor said that Kaylor could have gone to work that day, and the doctor's notes didn't mention a stomach virus.

Kaylor was fired for abuse of sick leave. Kaylor sued, claiming that he had a legal right to take intermittent FMLA leave on February 3 and could not be fired for doing so. The court disagreed, finding that Kaylor had an obligation to make reasonable efforts to reschedule his leave after his supervisor told him that it would cause staffing problems. Because he didn't follow the rules for intermittent leave, Kaylor wasn't protected by the FMLA.

Kaylor v. Fannin Regional Hospital, 946 F.Supp. 988 (N.D. Ga. 1996).

EXAMPLE: Roger is a human resources manager for a large hotel chain. He reports to the company's headquarters but travels two or three days each week to conduct trainings for employees in other cities. Roger's doctor certifies that he will need to spend four hours per day caring for his son during a ten-week cancer treatment regimen.

The company needs to continue its trainings during Roger's leave, and Roger can no longer travel. The company would be within its rights to transfer Roger to a different position with the same pay and benefits. For example, it might require Roger to handle compensation and benefits issues, to coach other representatives so they can handle the out-of-town trainings, or to help the company revise its nationwide hiring standards, if Roger is qualified to do those tasks. However, if the company tried to transfer Roger to work at the front desk of one of its hotels or process reservations in a call center, that would violate the FMLA.

Once the employee's leave ends, you must return the employee to his or her original position or an equivalent one (see Chapter 11).

Tips to Prevent Abuse

Some managers worry that employees who qualify for intermittent leave will abuse that right to take time off whenever they want and that the company just has to sit back and take it. This isn't quite true, however. Although employees have a right to take intermittent leave if it's medically necessary or for a qualifying exigency, this doesn't mean that they are free to use that time off for any purpose. If you think an employee might be abusing intermittent leave—for example, by taking unscheduled intermittent leave only on Fridays or calling in sick whenever a major deadline is looming—here are a few things you can do:

- **Check the certification.** As explained in Chapter 9, you should always get a certification when an employee takes FMLA leave. On the form, the health care provider and/or employee must give certain facts about the need for leave. For example, the certification for qualifying exigency leave asks the employee to estimate a leave schedule, including the frequency and duration of appointments, meetings, and other events; the employee also must provide the names and contact information of those with whom the employee will meet. The medical certification forms ask the health care provider to give similar information, such as a treatment schedule, the frequency and duration of absences for appointments, and so on. If the employee's time off doesn't jibe with these predictions, you can seek recertification of a serious health condition (Chapter 8 explains how) or contact the third parties the employee names in a qualifying exigency certification to make sure those meetings are taking place as claimed.

- **Get a new certification if the employee's reason for leave changes.** For example, if an employee takes time off every week for scheduled treatment for an injury, then claims to need additional leave for another condition, require a certification of the new condition. This will help you pin down exactly what the employee needs and why.

- **Let the doctor review the employee's schedule for a serious health condition.** The FMLA regulations allow you to provide a copy of the employee's absence pattern to the health care provider when you request recertification of a serious health condition. You can ask the provider whether the serious health condition and the employee's need for leave is consistent with the pattern of absences. A doctor who sees that an employee is gaming the system—by always taking leave on Fridays, for example—may be willing to place some limits on the certification.

- **Require employees to adhere to a schedule for foreseeable intermittent leave.** If an employee needs intermittent leave only for scheduled treatment (not for a condition that might worsen suddenly), you can ask the employee to stick to the schedule. Of course, the employee's doctor might have to cancel every once in a while, but if the employee seems to be taking a lot of unscheduled time off, you should ask the employee what's going on and seek recertification.

- **Require employees to talk to a manager for every absence.** One of the toughest challenges that arises from intermittent leave is properly recording and designating the time off. It's especially difficult if an employee takes a lot of unscheduled time off in small increments. This is why it's a good idea to require employees using intermittent leave to call in and let a manager know why they're taking time off; the manager can then record the leave as FMLA leave or pass the message on to the person responsible for managing the FMLA in your organization. If the employee is unable to call in ahead of time for health reasons, make sure the employee provides notice as soon as possible.

In the past, there was some confusion over whether companies could enforce their own notice rules when employees use FMLA leave. However, the FMLA regulations now clearly state the following guidance for employers:

- **An employee who gives the amount of notice required by the FMLA is entitled to use FMLA leave.** As long as the employee gives 30 days' notice for foreseeable leave and as much notice as is practicable for unforeseeable leave, the employee is entitled to the protections of the FMLA.

- **You may require employees to follow your company's other notice procedures.** If your company requires employees to give written notice or call their supervisors for all absences, for example, you can require employees taking FMLA leave to do the same.

- **You may require employees to follow your regular procedures for using paid leave if the employee wants to substitute paid leave for FMLA leave.** As long as the employee gives the notice required by the FMLA, the employee is entitled to use unpaid FMLA leave. However, an employee who wants to use accrued paid leave during that time may be required to follow your usual procedures, even if they require more notice than the FMLA. For example, if your vacation policy requires employees to give six weeks' notice to use paid vacation, an employee who gives only 30 days' notice may not use paid vacation until six weeks have elapsed; however, the employee is still entitled to unpaid FMLA leave for that time off.

Requesting Status Reports

The FMLA gives employers the right to require an employee on leave to provide periodic reports on his or her status and intent to return to work. This rule serves a couple of purposes: For one, it helps employers manage the employee's workload and plan for a smooth reinstatement. As explained in Chapter 11, employers must reinstate employees immediately upon their return from leave, as long as employees provide at least two business days' notice of the intent to return. Knowing when the employee plans to return to work helps employers prepare for the transition.

For another, requiring status reports also gives an employer notice if the employee won't return to work. If the employee tells the employer, unequivocally, that he or she will not return to work, the employer can replace the employee permanently or make any other necessary changes. If the employee voluntarily chooses not to return—for example, to stay home with a healthy baby—then the employer can also discontinue the employee's health benefits and seek reimbursement for any premiums already paid. (These rules are explained in Chapter 11.)

If you require status reports, tell employees what you expect. Your request must be reasonable, considering the facts and circumstances of the employee's leave. If you ask for reports too frequently or request too much detail, especially of an employee who is struggling with a serious health condition, you could run into legal trouble. The Department of Labor has said that employers that take advantage of this limited right to communicate with employees on leave by making disruptive or burdensome requests could violate the law. At some point, an employer that is too persistent could appear to be punishing the employee for taking leave or trying to bully the employee to either return to work or forfeit his or her health benefits.

How often you should request a status report depends on how long the employee will be on leave and how definite the employee's return-to-work date is. If the employee will be on leave for 12 weeks and has a scheduled return-to-work date, you might ask for a status report once a month, then check in with the employee a week or two before the planned return date, to make sure that the employee is still coming back as scheduled. If the employee doesn't know how long he or she will need to be off, you might reasonably request more frequent status reports. And for a shorter leave, you might simply ask the employee to check in a week before returning, to make sure everything is still going according to plan.

You should ask for only two pieces of information in the status report: whether the employee still intends to return to work and, if so, when. Don't try to use a status report requirement to get medical information; that's governed by the recertification process explained in Chapter 9.

You can request that employees make status reports orally or in writing. These days, it may be easiest to have employees email you their status updates. But some employees may prefer to use the phone. If you allow oral status reports, however, you must document any changes to the employee's leave dates or intent to return to work. If the employee calls and tells you that he or she is no longer planning to come back, for example, you should put that in writing immediately. The best practice is to also send a confirming letter or email to the employee right away, to make sure you got it right.

Lessons from the *Real World*

Weekly phone calls are too frequent, but it doesn't matter unless it keeps the employee from exercising his or her FMLA rights.

Regina Terwilliger was employed as a housekeeper at Howard Memorial Hospital. She requested and was granted FMLA leave for necessary back surgery and recuperation afterwards. While she was out on leave, her supervisor called her every week to ask when she was returning to work. During one call, Terwilliger asked whether her job was in jeopardy; her supervisor replied that she should come back to work as soon as possible. Terwilliger returned to her job after 11 weeks of leave, not the 12 weeks she had planned to take. She sued for interference with her right to take FMLA leave.

The court issued two opinions in this case. In the first, it ruled for Terwilliger, finding that her supervisor's weekly phone calls discouraged her from exercising her FMLA rights. In a second opinion, however, the court changed its mind. Terwilliger's doctor released her to return to work after 11 weeks. Therefore, the court found, Terwilliger hadn't actually been denied any benefit to which she was entitled. As she no longer had a serious health condition at 11 weeks, she was no longer entitled to FMLA leave. Whether or not the supervisor's calls were appropriate, they didn't have the effect of denying any of her rights. (Had Terwilliger felt so pressured that she came back to work while she still had a serious health condition, however, the outcome would have been different.)

Terwilliger v. Howard Memorial Hospital, 770 F. Supp. 2d 980 (W.D. Ark. 2011).

Disciplining or Firing an Employee During Leave

You may fire or discipline an employee who is on FMLA leave, as long as your reasons are entirely unrelated to the employee's use of the FMLA. This is easier said than done, though, because it might be hard to prove that the employee's FMLA leave played no part in your decision. This is particularly true if you are disciplining or firing the employee for poor attendance. Even if you consider only absences that were not covered by the FMLA, the employee may claim to have been fired in retaliation for taking legally protected leave.

The best practice is to make absolutely sure that you'll be able to prove that you had independent reasons for acting. You'll be on safest legal ground if you initiated discipline or termination proceedings before you knew that the employee might need FMLA leave. That way, the employee will have a tough time showing any relationship between the leave and your decision.

If you are imposing discipline for excessive absenteeism, you must be very sure that you aren't counting any protected absences against the employee. The best way to protect yourself in this situation is to document every absence—particularly the employee's stated reason for missing work—and implement your company's disciplinary procedures for any unauthorized time off. That way, you'll have a detailed record to counter the employee's claim that you violated the FMLA.

> EXAMPLE: Paul has asthma, which occasionally flares up and renders him unable to work. In his medical certification, Paul's doctor estimated that Paul might have to miss a day of work or so per month, except in the Spring when allergens might cause him to miss as many as three or four days per month. In October, Paul calls in sick six times, missing four days for the flu and two more days for a stomach bug. This uses up his available sick days. In November, Paul called in sick eight times, claiming to have headaches, a cold, and another stomach bug. By the first week in December, when Paul has again called in sick three times for various ailments, you decide to fire him.
>
> When you meet with Paul to lower the boom, he tells you that he's pretty sure his cold and flu were asthma-related and that his headaches and stomach upset might have been caused by a new drug he's been trying to control his asthma. You decide to fire him anyway.

Whoops! Paul may or may not be telling the truth, but you could find it hard to justify his termination to a jury. The better course of action would be to talk to Paul after his first unexcused absence in November, asking him directly whether it's related to his asthma. If the answer is yes, you could ask for a recertification, based on the difference between his doctor's estimate of leave and Paul's leave usage. If the answer is no, you could initiate progressive discipline for any unexcused absences going forward. This gives you proof that you are not disciplining Paul for exercising his FMLA rights, and it puts Paul on notice that he will need to stick to the rules from now on.

Even if you have entirely legitimate reasons for disciplining or firing an employee, you might find yourself on the wrong end of a lawsuit if you take action as soon as the employee asks for FMLA leave. Perceptions matter to the employee, the lawyer(s) whom the employee consults about filing a lawsuit, and the judge and jury. If you act right after the employee requests leave, it's probably going to look like you acted because of the request, even if that's not the case. Although you might eventually win in court (if the jury believes your side of the story), you and your company will spend a lot of time and money getting to that victory. You should consult with a lawyer whenever you are considering disciplining or firing an employee who has recently requested or taken FMLA leave.

TIP

You might need to talk about reasonable accommodations. If an employee who is out for his or her own serious health condition expresses concerns about being able to do the job after returning from FMLA leave, consider the possibility that the employee might have a disability as defined by the Americans with Disabilities Act (ADA). If so, your company has a duty to begin a conversation about whether and how you can make it possible for the employee to perform the job by providing a reasonable accommodation. It's best to start talking about possible accommodations as soon as you learn that the employee might have a disability, to give you time to make any necessary adjustments before the employee is ready to return. (See Chapter 12 for more on the ADA.)

Lessons from the *Real World*

An employee can be fired for previous performance problems discovered during FMLA leave.

Candis Smith worked as an administrative secretary at the Memorial Foundation of Allen Hospital. She was responsible for sending a receipt and thank-you card to hospital donors. In December 1998, Robert Justis, the executive director of the foundation, told Smith that he had received complaints from donors who had not been acknowledged for their contributions. Smith told him that she would try to send out acknowledgments as soon as possible.

Smith took FMLA leave starting January 1, 1999, to adopt a child from Romania. She left a stack of donor receipts that had to be sent out and wrote a note asking another employee to type thank-you cards and mail them, along with the receipts, to donors. One week into Smith's leave, another employee found another pile of donor receipts in Smith's work area. There were approximately 400 receipts, for donations totaling more than $350,000, going back a couple of months. One of the receipts was for a gift of $136,000, from one of the donors who had complained about not receiving a receipt.

Justis and Richard Seidler, the CEO of the hospital, decided to terminate Smith's employment immediately. On January 14, when she returned from Romania, they called her in for a meeting and fired her for failing to send out the receipts.

Smith sued, claiming that she was fired illegally for taking FMLA leave. As evidence, she pointed out that she was fired just two weeks after starting her leave and that she was fired for problems that came to light only because she took leave. The court didn't buy these arguments. Instead, the court noted that Smith was fired shortly after she started her leave because the Foundation didn't know how serious the problem was until it discovered the unsent receipts, which put the Foundation in a difficult position with its donors. In light of these facts, the timing of the decision did not demonstrate that Smith was fired for taking leave.

Smith v. Allen Health Systems, Inc., 302 F.3d 827 (8th Cir. 2002).

Common Mistakes Regarding Managing Leave—And How to Avoid Them

Mistake 1: **Requiring employees to give more notice than the FMLA requires.**

Avoid this mistake by taking the following steps:

- Don't require an employee to give more notice than is practicable under the circumstances.
- Delay the start of an employee's leave only if you have the right—and a good reason—to do so. Consider asserting your rights only if the employee could have given 30 days' notice, delaying the employee's leave won't harm the employee, and your company really needs the employee at work in the next 30 days.
- Ask employees to give you written reasons why they were unable to give 30 days' notice of foreseeable leave.
- Require employees to follow your paid leave policies to substitute paid leave for unpaid FMLA leave, while recognizing that you can't deny them the right to take unpaid leave if they meet the FMLA's requirements.

Mistake 2: **Overloading coworkers when an employee takes FMLA leave.**

Avoid this mistake by taking the following steps:

- Plan ahead if you know an employee will need leave (to have a baby, for example). Talk to the employee and coworkers ahead of time about your plans for getting the work done.
- Cross-train your employees. It will be much easier for employees to cover each other's work if they already know how to do it.
- Get extra help, if necessary. You might need to bring in a temp or consultant to help you get the work done, especially when an employee takes an extended leave.
- Take on important tasks yourself. It doesn't help your company to have inexperienced folks handling major clients or projects. Make time in your schedule to handle these key tasks.

Mistake 3: **Mismanaging intermittent leave.**

Avoid this mistake by taking the following steps:

- Seek recertification of a serious health condition, if necessary. If an employee is taking leave beyond what the original anticipated, ask for another one.

- Make sure that every qualified absence is designated as FMLA leave. An employee who takes a lot of intermittent leave may also take time off for other reasons, such as vacation or minor illnesses. You need to know which absences count as FMLA leave, so ask these employees to talk to you or another manager whenever they need time off.

- Require employees to stick to their treatment schedules. If an employee needs intermittent leave for scheduled treatment, the certification should state when that treatment will be. You can ask the employee to reschedule, with the doctor's approval, to avoid undue disruption to the company's operations.

- Transfer the employee, if necessary. You are entitled to transfer the employee temporarily to a position that better accommodates his or her need for intermittent leave (except for a qualifying exigency). Just make sure that the transfer isn't a demotion in disguise.

Mistake 4: Firing or disciplining an employee for taking FMLA leave (or appearing to do so).

Avoid this mistake by taking the following steps:

- Consult with a lawyer every time. Because it's so easy to get in trouble here, you should always talk to a lawyer to make sure that you've made the right decision before taking action.

- Make sure you have a very compelling reason to fire the employee. Even if your company is an at-will employer (as most are), this isn't the time to exercise your right to fire without a very good reason.

- Fire only if you can prove that you would have taken the same action if the employee hadn't taken leave. This means, for example, being able to document that termination proceedings were in the works before the employee requested leave or that you discovered truly egregious problems that warrant immediate firing.

- Don't count FMLA absences against an employee with an attendance problem. You can't consider FMLA leave when deciding whether an employee has missed so much work that termination is warranted.

Managers' Checklist: Managing FMLA Leave

Scheduling:

☐ I calendared the start and end dates of the employee's leave, if I know them.

☐ If the employee did not give 30 days' notice of foreseeable leave, I asked the employee to give me a written statement of the reasons why such notice wasn't given.

☐ If the employee did not give 30 days' notice of foreseeable leave, I considered whether to require the employee to delay the start of his or her leave.

☐ If I didn't let the employee take leave on the date requested because the employee didn't provide enough notice, I put that decision in writing and gave it to the employee.

☐ If the employee is taking parenting leave, I made sure the employee's leave will be complete within one year of the child's arrival.

☐ If the employee's foreseeable leave will cause undue disruption to the company's operations, I asked the employee to try to reschedule (subject to the approval of his or her health care provider).

☐ If the employee had to take unforeseeable leave, I made initial contact with the employee or a family member to gather information and made plans to follow up in a few days.

Handling the Employee's Work:

☐ If the employee was available, I talked to the employee and came up with a plan to cover his or her job duties during leave.

☐ If the employee's coworkers will pick up some extra work, I made any changes necessary to ensure that they will not be stretched too thin.

☐ I determined which, if any, of the employee's responsibilities I will handle and made the necessary arrangements to do so.

☐ If we will bring on temporary help, I made the necessary arrangements to hire a temp.

☐ If we will be using an outside consultant or company, I took any steps necessary to start the process.

☐ I informed everyone who needs to know about these arrangements, such as my manager, the employee's coworkers, vendors, clients, and so on, after asking the employee about his or her preferred characterization of the leave.

Managers' Checklist: Managing FMLA Leave (continued)

Benefits:

☐ I made arrangements to continue the employee's group health benefits—including medical, dental, and vision coverage—during FMLA leave.

☐ I applied any benefits changes to the employee, just as if he or she were not on leave.

☐ If the employee chose not to continue benefits, I made sure that we can reinstate those benefits immediately, without any requalification requirements, when the employee returns to work; if not, I continued the employee's benefits, arranged to pay the employee's share of the premium, and sought reimbursement from the employee after his or her return to work.

☐ I collected the employee's share of the premium as permitted by the FMLA and provided written notice, in advance, of how and when to make these payments.

☐ Before terminating the employee's coverage for failing to pay the premiums, I sent the employee written notice, including the following information:

  ☐ The employee's payment hasn't been received.

  ☐ The company intends to terminate the employee's coverage if payment isn't received by a specified date, at least 15 days after the date I sent the letter.

☐ Before terminating the employee's coverage for failing to pay the premiums, I made sure we could reinstate the employee's coverage without any requalification requirements. Or, if not, I continued health care coverage for the employee and sought reimbursement.

☐ For the continuation of benefits other than health care during leave, I followed my company's usual policies for employees on paid or unpaid leave, depending on whether the employee is using paid leave during FMLA-qualified time off.

☐ Before discontinuing any life, disability, or other insurance benefits, I made sure that we could reinstate the employee's coverage without any requalification requirements; if not, I continued the employee's coverage, arranged to pay the employee's share of the premium, and sought reimbursement from the employee after his or her return to work.

Reinstatement

Chapter Highlights

☆ An employee returning from FMLA leave is entitled to reinstatement to his or her former position or an equivalent position, unless an exception applies.

☆ An equivalent position must be virtually identical to the employee's former position in pay, benefits, job duties, worksite, shift, schedule, and other job terms and conditions.

☆ The employee must be reinstated immediately upon returning from leave, as long as the employee gave at least two workdays' notice.

☆ You may require an employee returning from leave for a serious health condition to provide a fitness-for-duty certification from a health care provider.

☆ When you reinstate an employee, you must also restore the employee's pay and benefits, including any automatic raises that occurred during leave.

☆ Employees are entitled to the same insurance coverage benefits and may not be required to take a physical, wait for open enrollment, or otherwise requalify for coverage.

☆ You might not be required to reinstate an employee under the FMLA if any of the following are true:
  • The employee cannot perform the essential duties of the position (however, the Americans with Disabilities Act might require your company to make a reasonable accommodation).
  • The employee's job was eliminated through company restructuring or layoffs, and the employee would have lost the job even if he or she hadn't taken leave.
  • The employee was fired for reasons unrelated to taking FMLA leave (such as poor performance or misconduct).
  • The employee was hired for a limited term or project, which has ended.
  • The employee obtained FMLA leave fraudulently (for example, by submitting a forged or altered medical certification).
  • The employee stated an unequivocal intent not to return to work.
  • The employee is a key employee (among the highest-paid 10% of employees within 75 miles) and reinstatement would cause substantial and grievous economic injury to your company.

☆ If an employee chooses not to return to work following FMLA leave, you may recoup your company's costs to continue the employee's health care coverage, as well as amounts you paid to cover the employee's share of premiums to continue other benefits.

The FMLA provides employees with job-protected leave, which includes the legal right to be reinstated to the same or an equivalent position once leave ends, unless an exception applies. The right to reinstatement gives meaning to the right to take leave: It ensures that employees will have jobs to return to when their leave is over.

This chapter will help you manage an employee's return to work. It covers every aspect of reinstatement, including what position you must restore the employee to, deadlines for reinstatement, how to handle employee benefits when an employee returns to work, and exceptional circumstances when you might not be legally required to reinstate an employee. It also explains your company's rights if an employee cannot, or decides not to, return to work after using up his or her allotment of FMLA leave.

The Basic Reinstatement Right

An employee must be reinstated to his or her former position or an equivalent position upon returning from FMLA leave. Although there are a few situations when an employee's right to reinstatement is limited (see "When Reinstatement Might Not Be Required," below), these cases are the exception rather than the rule. The employee is entitled to be reinstated even if your company made changes to accommodate the employee's absence, such as replacing the employee or restructuring his or her job.

What Is an Equivalent Position?

Although you are legally required to reinstate an employee returning from FMLA leave, that doesn't mean the employee has a right to be put back in exactly the same position he or she held before taking time off. Employers may reinstate the employee to his or her former position or to an equivalent position. In practice, however, this doesn't give employers much leeway: The equivalent position must be virtually identical, in every important respect, to the employee's former position.

TIP

If the employee's position has changed substantially due to company restructuring, different rules apply. See "When Reinstatement Might Not Be Required," below, to find out what your obligations are.

An equivalent position is one with equivalent pay, benefits, and other terms and conditions of employment. Here are some of the things courts will look at when determining whether a position is equivalent to the employee's former job:

- **Pay.** An employee is entitled to receive his or her former salary or hourly compensation, as well as any opportunities to earn extra money (through overtime, a shift differential, or performance-based bonuses, for example) that were previously available. (For more information, including how to handle bonuses and raises, see "Restoring Pay and Benefits," below.)

- **Benefits.** The equivalent position must offer the same benefits, at the same levels, as the employee's previous job. (For more information, see "Restoring Pay and Benefits," below.)

- **Job duties and responsibilities.** An employee is entitled to "substantially similar" job duties and responsibilities. Minor alterations (such as a change in the employee's reporting structure or job title) are allowed, but make sure the employee's new position is just as desirable—and has the same status in the company—as the employee's former position. If the new position looks like a demotion, the company could find itself in legal trouble.

- **Shift and schedule.** Ordinarily, an employee is entitled to be returned to the same shift and to the same or an equivalent schedule.

- **Worksite.** An employee must be reinstated to the same worksite or one that is geographically proximate to the employee's old worksite. A job at a different worksite is not an equivalent position if it significantly increases the employee's commute in time, distance, or both.

CAUTION

The Americans with Disabilities Act may require you to return the employee to the same position. Under the ADA, a qualified employee with a disability is entitled to the same position with a reasonable accommodation, unless it would pose an undue hardship on the employer. If both the FMLA and the ADA apply, you may not be able to return the employee to an equivalent position. (See Chapter 12 for more details on the interaction between the FMLA and the ADA.)

Lessons from the *Real World*

Taking away an employee's responsibilities for work does not violate the FMLA's right to reinstatement.

Phyllis Smith was the Assistant Supervisor of School Accounts for the East Baton Rouge Parish School Board. She assisted school principals and staff with bookkeeping, which included travel to the parish's schools to provide bookkeeping training and support to school officials.

Smith took parental leave under the FMLA. When she returned to work, her job description was revised. She no longer traveled to assist school officials onsite; instead, she audited the schools' books from a central office location. Smith agreed that her pay was the same and that her job duties were largely similar. However, she filed a lawsuit claiming that her new job was not equivalent to her old position because of the elimination of her travel responsibilities.

The court disagreed. It found that she was doing essentially the same work for the same pay before and after she took time off. The court also decided that eliminating travel from her job duties was only a minimal, intangible change, not a significant enough difference to support a lawsuit.

Smith v. East Baton Rouge Parish School Board, 453 F.3d 650 (5th Cir. 2006).

The FMLA doesn't prevent you from giving a returning employee a promotion or some other additional benefit, as long as the employee wants it. Similarly, if the employee asks to be restored to a different position, you can grant the request. For example, if an employee returning from FMLA leave is planning to move soon and requests a transfer to a different facility, you may grant the request without running afoul of the law. If the employee feels pressured or coerced to take a different position, however, that could violate the law.

> **EXAMPLE:** Charlotte works as a sales associate in the juniors' section of a large department store. She receives a base salary plus commissions based on her sales. She takes FMLA leave to care for her husband while he undergoes treatment for leukemia. When she returns, her boss, David, tells her that he would like to promote her to a position in the home furnishings department. David explains that she'll receive the same base salary, plus the opportunity to earn much more in commissions, because furniture is more expensive than junior clothing and accessories.
>
> Charlotte thanks David but tells him she wants to return to the juniors department. She explains that she enjoys keeping up with fashions and trends and feels her sales record is driven by her interest in this market. She doesn't think she'd do very well selling furniture.
>
> David responds, "You know, Charlotte, opportunities for advancement don't come along here very often. I'm telling you that we need you in home furnishings. You're free to say 'No, I'll only work where I want to, not where the company needs me,' but I can't guarantee that there will be other opportunities down the road for someone who displays this kind of attitude." Charlotte decides that she'd better accept the move.
>
> Did David violate the FMLA? You bet. Although the company is free to restore Charlotte to a different position if she voluntarily agrees, it isn't free to pressure her or threaten her job opportunities if she doesn't accept the new position. Here, Charlotte wasn't free to make a voluntary decision: She was told that refusing the new position would affect her future opportunities. This violates her legal right to reinstatement.

Deadlines for Reinstatement

An employee is entitled to immediate reinstatement once he or she reports for duty. In some situations, you'll know well in advance exactly when an employee will return to work. For example, if you and the employee agreed that the employee would take six weeks of leave, and the employee's time off goes as expected, the employee will simply report back once his or her leave is over.

> EXAMPLE: Barbara is pregnant and requests time off. She decides to take the full 12 weeks of leave all at once. Her first day off work is Monday, June 1. She takes three weeks of leave for a serious health condition (pregnancy and childbirth), and the remaining nine weeks as parental leave. She returns to work on Monday, August 24. Her employer is legally obligated to reinstate her to her former position (or an equivalent one) that same day.

Sometimes, however, an employee's return to work is delayed or accelerated. Typically, this happens when the employee's or family member's serious health condition takes an unexpected turn. Even in this situation, you must reinstate the employee immediately upon his or her return to work. However, you may require the employee to give you at least two business days' notice of the date he or she plans to come back. If the employee just shows up unexpectedly at work, and you are unable to reinstate the employee immediately, consider that your notice and reinstate the employee within two workdays.

> EXAMPLE: Calvin requests FMLA leave to care for his father, who needs hip replacement surgery. Because the doctor predicts recovery will take a couple months, Calvin requests eight weeks of FMLA leave. Instead, Calvin's father recovers in five weeks. Calvin lets his manager know that he will return to work right away. If the company can reinstate Calvin immediately, it should. If not, then Calvin is entitled to reinstatement within two workdays.

TIP

Ask the employee to keep you in the loop. You have the right to ask for periodic updates on the employee's plans to return to work. (Chapter 10 explains how.)

Lessons from the *Real World*

A company must reinstate an employee within two workdays or face the consequences.

Lori Hoge worked at a Honda production plant. Honda assigned her to a "door line" position, which accommodated her work restrictions based on a back injury.

On May 11, 2000, Hoge began taking FMLA leave for planned abdominal surgery. She reported for work on June 27. She said this was the agreed-upon date for her return to work; Honda said that it didn't expect her to return until sometime in July. Honda also told her it did not have an available position that accommodated her work restrictions because of changes to its manufacturing process. On July 31, 2000, she was reinstated on a part-time basis to a position on the engine line, and she didn't receive a full-time position until September 18.

Hoge sued Honda for failing to reinstate her when she was ready to return to work. Honda argued that it was entitled to take a "reasonable" amount of time to find an appropriate job, both because it didn't know when Hoge was returning to work and because her former position had changed.

The court sided with Hoge. The FMLA says employees are entitled to reinstatement upon their return to work, not within a reasonable time after they return. If Honda didn't know that Hoge was returning to work on June 27, it was entitled to take two days—the amount of notice Hoge should have given—to reinstate her to an equivalent, full-time position. Because Honda took several months to fully reinstate Hoge, it lost the case.

Hoge v. Honda of America, 384 F.3d 238 (6th Cir. 2004).

Fitness-for-Duty Certifications

If an employee takes leave for his or her own serious health condition, you may require the employee to provide a fitness-for-duty certification: a signed statement from a health care provider indicating that the employee is able to return to work. However, you may require this certification only if your company has a consistently applied practice or policy of requiring employees to provide a fitness-for-duty statement. The company need not require every employee to provide a fitness-for-duty certification, but it must require all similarly situated employees (that is, employees in that position and/or with that serious health condition) to provide one. For example, a company might require all employees in positions that require manual labor to provide such a certification following time off for an injury of any kind.

> **POLICY ALERT**
> **Include fitness-for-duty certification requirements in your written policies.** If your company has a uniform policy or practice of requiring certifications from similarly situated employees, it must include this information in its employee handbook or any other written material it provides to employees about the FMLA. (See Appendix B for more information on company policies that affect your rights or obligations under the FMLA.)

Contents of the Certification

A fitness-for-duty certification is a written statement, signed by the employee's health care provider (see Chapter 4 for information on who qualifies as a health care provider), that the employee is able to resume work following an FMLA leave. The employer may request certification only for the serious health condition that necessitated FMLA leave, not for any other illness or impairment.

You may require that the employee's certification specifically address the employee's ability to perform the essential functions of the job. To impose this requirement, you must give the employee a list of the essential job functions by the time you give the designation notice, and the designation notice must indicate that the fitness-for-duty certification will have to address the employee's ability to perform those functions. (See Chapter 8 for more on the designation notice.)

> **RESOURCE**
> **Need to know more about essential job functions?** You'll find lots of information on identifying job functions, determining which of them are essential, and writing them in a clear, descriptive manner in *The Job Description Handbook*, by Margie Mader-Clark (Nolo).

You may follow the procedures described in Chapter 9 to authenticate or clarify a fitness-for-duty clarification. However, you may request clarification or authentication only regarding the serious health condition for which the employee took leave. Unlike with a regular certification, you may not request a second or third opinion with a fitness-for-duty certification.

Notice and Deadlines

If you require fitness-for-duty certifications from employees returning from leave, you must include that requirement in the rights and responsibilities notice you give to each employee who requests leave. (See Chapter 8 for more information on this notice.)

You may postpone an employee's return to work until you receive the fitness-for-duty certification. You may contact the employee's health care provider to clarify the certification, but you may not delay the employee's reinstatement while waiting for a response.

Special Rules for Intermittent and Reduced-Schedule Leave

Generally, you may not require an employee to submit a fitness-for-duty certification each time the employee returns from using intermittent leave. However, you may request a fitness-for-duty certification once every 30 days if you have reasonable safety concerns regarding the employee's ability to perform his or her duties, based on the serious health condition for which the employee took leave. Reasonable safety concerns are defined in the regulations as a reasonable belief of significant risk of harm to the employee or others, considering the nature, severity, and likelihood of the potential harm.

If you are going to rely on this exception, you must tell the employee, when you issue the designation notice, that the employee will be required to submit a fitness-for-duty certification for each subsequent use of intermittent leave, unless the employee has submitted one within the past 30 days. (Your company can choose a longer interval; however, 30 days is the shortest period of time you can use.) You may not fire the employee while waiting for the certification.

EXAMPLE: John has epilepsy, for which he occasionally uses FMLA leave. Lately, his seizure activity has increased, leading his doctor to change his medication to one with side effects of dizziness, weakness, and drowsiness. John's work as a carpenter requires him to use power tools, climb ladders, and perform other activities that could pose significant risks to himself and others were he to have a seizure or suffer some of the side effects of his medication while working. John's company asks him to submit a fitness-for-duty certification every 30 days, in connection with his intermittent leave. Once John's doctor indicates that his condition and medications have stabilized, the company plans to lift the fitness-for-duty requirement.

Restoring Pay and Benefits

When you reinstate an employee, you must also restore the employee's pay and benefits. The requirements for restoring benefits depend on the type of benefit and your company's policies.

Pay

Whether you reinstate an employee to his or her former position or to an equivalent one, you must restore all components of the employee's pay including base wage or salary, plus the same opportunities to earn bonuses, a shift differential, overtime, commissions, and other extra compensation that he or she enjoyed before taking leave.

TIP
You can restart an exempt employee's pay midweek. An exempt employee (who is paid on a salary basis and is not entitled to earn overtime) is usually entitled to a full salary for any week in which he or she does any work. FMLA leave is an exception to this rule. If an exempt employee returns to work midweek, you can pay a prorated share of the employee's weekly salary. For example, an employee who returns to work on Wednesday morning is entitled to three-fifths of his or her usual weekly salary. (29 C.F.R. § 541.602.)

Raises

A returning employee is also entitled to any automatic raises that took place while the employee was out on leave. So if your company provides an annual cost-of-living raise to all employees, you must provide that same raise to an employee returning from FMLA leave.

If the raise is not automatic but is instead based on the employee's performance or seniority, the rules depend on your company's policies and practices. Generally, you must treat employees on FMLA leave just as your company treats employees who take unpaid leave for any other reason. If unpaid leave doesn't count toward an employee's seniority for purposes of awarding seniority-based raises, for example, then you don't have to count FMLA leave toward an employee's seniority.

> CAUTION
>
> **Employees substituting paid time off are not on "unpaid" leave.** As explained in Chapter 8, in certain circumstances an employee (either voluntarily or per company requirements) substitutes accrued paid time off for unpaid FMLA leave. If an employee is using paid time off during FMLA leave, you must treat that employee just like any other employee who is taking paid time off. Often, this means that at least certain benefits (for example, vacation or sick days) continue to accrue.

Bonuses

Your company's employees may be eligible to earn bonuses for certain behavior or actions, such as productivity, attendance, performance, safety, or customer service. If a bonus or other discretionary payment is based on achieving a certain goal, such as reaching a specific sales target, and an employee doesn't meet the goal because of FMLA leave, you don't have to provide the bonus unless you provide it to employees who miss the goal because of leave that doesn't qualify for FMLA protection. In other words, you can't treat employees who take FMLA leave worse than employees who take other types of leave.

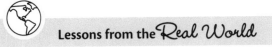

Lessons from the *Real World*

An employer may prorate a production bonus to account for FMLA leave.

Robert Sommer worked as a financial administrator for The Vanguard Group. Sommer took eight weeks of FMLA leave, from December 7, 2000 to February 4, 2001.

Vanguard had a partnership plan that paid employees an annual bonus based on company performance that year. Each employee's bonus factored in the employee's position, how long the employee had worked for the company, and how many hours the employee worked during the year. Employees who worked fewer than 1,950 hours during the year received a prorated bonus; hours spent on unpaid leave didn't count as hours worked.

Vanguard gave Sommer a prorated partnership plan bonus for 2001 because his FMLA leave brought his total hours worked for the year below the 1,950-hour threshold. Sommer received $1,788.23 less than he would have gotten had he worked the requisite number of hours.

Sommer sued Vanguard, arguing that it unfairly penalized him for taking FMLA leave by reducing his bonus. The court disagreed with Sommer's argument. It found that the partnership plan bonuses were productivity bonuses and that hours worked provided the basis for measuring productivity. Because the bonus was performance based, the company could legally provide a lesser bonus to recognize the time he was out on FMLA leave.

Sommer v. Vanguard Group, 461 F.3d 397 (3rd Cir. 2006).

EXAMPLE: FunCo offers employees an incentive for perfect attendance. Employees who have no absences for an entire year receive $1,500. Kara has no absences until November, when she takes two weeks of FMLA leave to care for her son while he recovers from mononucleosis. Kara then returns to work and has no more absences for the rest of the year. FunCo may deny Kara the perfect attendance bonus, as long as it also denies a bonus to employees who miss work for other reasons. If FunCo allowed employees to take two weeks of vacation in a year without jeopardizing their attendance bonus, it would have to give the bonus to Kara as well.

Benefits

You must restore an employee's benefits when the employee returns from leave, subject to any changes in benefit levels that took place while the employee was on leave and affected the whole work force. For example, if a company offers life insurance to its employees and increases the benefit from $30,000 to $35,000 while an employee is on leave, that employee is also entitled to the increased benefit amount.

The specific rules for restoring benefits depend on the type of benefit.

Insurance Coverage

An employee is entitled to restored insurance benefits, including life insurance, disability insurance, health benefits, and so on. Employees may not be required to requalify for benefits, wait for an "open enrollment" period, undergo a physical examination, be subjected to new preexisting conditions limitations or exclusions, or serve a waiting period.

As explained in Chapter 10, you must continue the employee's health insurance coverage while he or she is on leave, though you may also require the employee to pay any portion of the premium for which he or she is usually responsible. While your company can cut off an employee's health care benefits if the employee is more than 30 days late paying his or her share of the premium, those benefits must be restored, at the same level, when the employee returns from leave. An employee who chooses not to continue benefits during leave is also entitled to restoration.

To comply with this rule, your company may have to keep an employee enrolled in certain benefit programs during the employee's leave, even if the employee chose not to continue that coverage or failed to pay the required premium amount while on leave.

If your company is required to maintain insurance coverage during an employee's leave in order to restore benefits, you may seek reimbursement after the employee returns from FMLA leave. This rule applies to health insurance coverage and to other types of insurance benefits, such as life insurance. However, you may recover only the employee's share of the premium, not the company's share. If an employee doesn't return from leave, you may be able to recover your company's share of health insurance premiums in some circumstances; see "When You Can Seek Reimbursement for Benefits," below.

> EXAMPLE: Fatima takes 10 weeks of FMLA leave to care for her terminally ill father. Her health insurance costs her $150 every two weeks, which her employer normally deducts from her paycheck. Her employer chips in the same amount every two weeks for her health insurance. Her employer also offers disability insurance to employees. This benefit doesn't cost employees anything, although the company pays about $75 every two weeks per employee to provide it.
>
> Fatima doesn't pay any of her health insurance premiums while on leave, but her employer continues to pay them for her, so it can reinstate her insurance when she returns. Her employer also keeps paying for her life insurance so that it can restore her benefits upon her return. When Fatima returns to work, her employer seeks reimbursement to the tune of $1,875 for all of its payments during her leave.
>
> Whoops! Although Fatima's employer is entitled to seek reimbursement for her usual share of the health insurance premium, it cannot seek reimbursement for the company's share, nor for the life insurance that Fatima typically doesn't pay for. The most the employer can ask Fatima to repay is $750, the amount she should have paid while on leave.

If there are changes to a benefit plan while the employee is on leave, these changes apply to the employee as well. If, for example, premiums increase, coverage changes, or a new benefit becomes available, the employee must be treated as if he or she had been working continuously.

If a benefit is available only to employees who work a minimum number of hours each year, hours spent on FMLA leave do not count as hours worked. This means that, as a practical matter, an employee may be ineligible to receive certain benefits because the employee took FMLA leave.

Retirement Benefits

Just like other benefits, retirement benefits must be restored at the same level when an employee returns from leave. A few special rules apply to these benefits:

- FMLA leave cannot be treated as a "break in service" for purposes of pensions and other retirement benefit plans.

- If a retirement benefit requires an employee to be employed on a particular date to be credited with a year of service for vesting, contributions, or participating in the plan, an employee who is on FMLA leave is considered to be employed during that time.
- FMLA leave does not have to be counted as time in service or hours worked for purposes of vesting, accrual of benefits, or eligibility.

EXAMPLE: Hal began working at Jefferson's Tool and Die on January 1, 2016. The company allows an employee who has worked at least one year and is employed as of January 1 to participate in the 401(k) plan for the coming year. When Hal becomes eligible, he contributes monthly. The company matches his contributions up to $3,000 a year. Hal is always fully vested in his own contributions to the account; the company's contributions vest over three years, one-third each year.

Hal takes FMLA leave for all of December 2017 and January 2018 to bond with his new daughter. While Hal is on FMLA leave, his 401(k) account must be treated as if he is still working. The company may not close his account or otherwise treat his time off as a break in service. The company must also treat him as if he were employed on January 1 for purposes of participating in the program for the coming year. However, Hal's time off does not have to be counted toward the three-year vesting period. In other words, Hal might have to wait an additional two months to vest employer contributions that had already been made when he took leave.

Other Benefits

Many companies allow employees to accrue certain benefits, such as sick leave, vacation days, or other paid time off. Employees on FMLA leave are entitled to earn these benefits only if employees on other types of unpaid leave are. However, an employer may not take away benefits the employee has already earned: If the employee had accrued paid time off before taking FMLA leave and did not substitute that time for FMLA leave, that accrued paid leave must be available upon returning from FMLA leave.

The same rules apply to seniority. The company does not have to count FMLA leave toward an employee's seniority unless it counts other types of unpaid leave. However, the employee is entitled to the same seniority upon reinstatement that he or she had when starting leave.

When Reinstatement Might Not Be Required

There are several circumstances in which an employee might not be entitled to reinstatement after taking FMLA leave. Reinstatement may be denied if:

- The employee would have lost the job even if he or she hadn't taken FMLA leave.
- The employee can't perform an essential function of the job.
- The employee takes FMLA leave fraudulently.
- The employee fits within the "key employee" exception, which gives employers the right to deny reinstatement to certain highly paid employees, if returning them to work would cause substantial harm to the company.

Employee Would Have Lost the Job Regardless of Leave

An employee has no greater right to reinstatement than he or she would have had if not for taking leave. If the employee would have lost the job even if still employed, the FMLA does not guarantee reinstatement.

Restructuring and Layoffs

If the employee's job has been eliminated, the employee is not entitled to reinstatement. For example, let's say the company outsourced the work of the employee's department or closed the facility where the employee worked. In this situation, the employee would have lost his or her job whether the employee took FMLA leave or not, and the employee has no right to be reinstated.

However, this rule applies only if the restructuring is unrelated to the employee's leave. Changes made to accommodate the employee's leave—such as hiring a temporary replacement or shifting some job responsibilities around—don't relieve the company of its obligation to reinstate the employee. And, if the company made structural changes because it wanted to avoid reinstating an employee who took leave, that would violate the FMLA's prohibition against retaliation.

> **EXAMPLE 1:** Alexander takes FMLA leave to bond with his newborn son. While on leave, his company implements layoffs. The 50 employees with the least seniority lose their jobs, and Alexander is one of them. Alexander has no right to reinstatement.

EXAMPLE 2: Now assume that Alexander's company didn't have major layoffs. Alexander's manager, Maya, is upset about his leave. Maya doesn't think Alexander should use the full 12 weeks of FMLA leave. After all, his wife doesn't work, and she can stay home with the baby. Maya decides to eliminate Alexander's position so she doesn't have to reinstate him. She has already redistributed his work while he is on leave; she figures she'll just wait a while, then hire someone under a new job title to pick up the slack.

Maya's actions violate the FMLA. The only reason Alexander has no job to return to is because Maya wanted to punish him for exercising his legal right to take FMLA leave. What's more, Maya's sexist reasoning could leave her company open to a discrimination lawsuit.

Termination for Cause

As explained in Chapter 10, you may fire an employee who is on FMLA leave only for reasons entirely unrelated to the employee's use of the FMLA. If you have sufficient, independent grounds to terminate employment, you do not have to reinstate the employee. In this situation, as when the employee's job is eliminated in a layoff or restructuring, the employee would have lost the job whether or not he or she took FMLA leave.

CAUTION

Don't rely on the right to fire at will. Most employees work at will, which means that they can be fired at any time, for any reason that isn't illegal. But you should not exercise this right when firing an employee on FMLA leave. To successfully defend against an employee lawsuit (an all-too-common scenario when an employee is fired while on leave), you'll have to prove that your reasons for firing the employee were not related to the employee's use of the FMLA. As a practical matter, this means you must have a different reason for firing the employee, one that is compelling enough to convince a jury that your actions were justified.

You may also discipline an employee who takes FMLA leave, but only for independent reasons. If your discipline will make the employee's position less than equivalent (for example, the employee will be demoted, will have more onerous reporting requirements, or will lose some independence and job perks), that's okay, even though it would normally violate reinstatement requirements.

SEE AN EXPERT
Always get legal advice before firing or disciplining an employee on leave. As explained in Chapter 10, even though you believe you have entirely independent and sound reasons for firing an employee on FMLA leave, chances are very good that the employee will see things differently. This is the most likely basis of an FMLA lawsuit, so it's a good idea to talk to a lawyer before you take any action.

Temporary Employment

If the employee was hired for a set period of time only (for example, for two years), and that time runs out while the employee is on leave, the employee isn't entitled to reinstatement. Similarly, if the employee was hired to work on a discrete project and that project is completed while the employee is on leave, the employee isn't entitled to reinstatement. In both of these situations, employment would have been terminated even if the employee hadn't taken leave.

Employee Announces Intent Not to Return

If an employee states that he or she will not return from leave (in other words, the employee quits), your company is no longer obligated to continue the employee's health benefits or reinstate the employee. However, the employee must give clear and unequivocal notice of the intent not to return to work. If, for example, the employee says, "I'm afraid I might not be able to come back" or "I'm not sure we can afford to pay for day care," that's not good enough.

When you hear that an employee won't be returning from work, you should confirm it with the employee in writing. (See "Requesting Status Reports," in Chapter 10, for more information.)

Employee Cannot Perform an Essential Job Function

An employee who can't perform the job's essential functions once his or her leave runs out has no right to reinstatement under the FMLA. The FMLA provides only for reinstatement to the same or a similar position: It doesn't require an employer to provide a different position that the employee might be able to do. Therefore, if the employee can no longer do the job—even if that inability is due to the serious health condition for which the employee took leave—there is no right to job restoration under the FMLA.

> ### You Must Allow the Employee to Requalify for the Position
>
> Sometimes, an employee is physically able to do the job but is no longer qualified for the position as a result of taking leave. For example, the employee may have been unable to complete a necessary course, fulfill a certification requirement, or meet a service standard (such as a minimum number of hours in training). In these situations, you must give the employee a reasonable opportunity to fulfill any necessary qualifications after returning to work.

That's not the end of the story, however. If the employee has a disability as defined by the Americans with Disabilities Act (ADA), your company might be obligated to provide a reasonable accommodation: a change to the workplace or job that will allow the employee to do the essential functions of the position. In this situation, you would no longer have a reinstatement obligation under the FMLA, but you might have a legal duty to return the employee to a modified position under the ADA. (Chapter 12 explains the ADA in more detail.)

You might also have an obligation to give the employee more time off. Extended leave might qualify as a reasonable accommodation under the ADA, if it allows the employee to do the job upon return. If the employee is receiving workers' compensation, state law might also require you to hold the employee's job for a longer period of time. Although the employee has no further rights under the FMLA—and, therefore, has no valid legal claim against your company for failure to reinstate—the employee might still have claims under these other laws. (See Chapter 12 for more information.)

Fraud

If an employee obtains FMLA leave through fraud, the company is not obligated to reinstate the employee. This sometimes occurs when the employee submits false documents (such as a fake or altered medical certification) to get FMLA leave. In some cases, companies find out about the fraud only accidentally, when another employee happens to see the leave-taking employee engaged in activities that seem incompatible with the reason for leave.

Dealing With Employee Moonlighting

Some managers assume that an employee who works another job while on FMLA leave is necessarily committing fraud against the company. After all, an employee who has the time and ability to work should be working at your company, not taking leave. Right?

Not necessarily. It depends on the job requirements of each position. An employee who can't do physical labor for your company might be able to do paperwork for a different employer or for a spouse's business, for example.

According to the Department of Labor, you may terminate an employee who moonlights in either of these two situations:

- Your company has a uniformly applied policy prohibiting all employees, on any kind of leave, from working another job. An employee who moonlights while on FMLA leave has violated company policy, and you may deny reinstatement on that basis. (Note that some states, such as California, don't allow employers to impose an absolute ban on moonlighting; this is an area where you'll need to check with an employment attorney to make sure you're within your rights.)
- The employee's activities while on leave demonstrate that the employee fraudulently took FMLA leave. For example, an employee who is seen rock climbing, cleaning the gutters, or performing manual labor for another employer when he or she claims to be in traction or in another state caring for a parent, can be denied reinstatement.

POLICY ALERT

Prohibit moonlighting by employees on leave. You can avoid having employees continue to receive health benefits—and perhaps even receive paid time off, if they substitute paid leave for FMLA leave—while working for another company by adopting a strict policy that prohibits moonlighting while on leave, if your state allows it. (See Appendix B for more information on policies that affect FMLA rights and obligations.)

Lessons from the *Real World*

Employee may be fired based on employer's honest suspicion—supported by surveillance—that she was abusing leave.

Diana Vail worked the night shift for Raybestos Products Company, a manufacturer of car parts. Vail suffered from migraines and took intermittent FMLA leave when she was unable to work due to a migraine. Vail's absences picked up markedly in the summer of 2005; from May to September, she took 33 days of leave. Raybestos suspected she might be abusing leave because it knew she worked part time for her husband's lawn-mowing business during the day, and she tended to take time off during the weeks when his serivces were in high demand.

Raybestos hired an off-duty police sergeant to conduct surveillance of Vail. Vail took FMLA leave due to a change in her medication one evening; the next morning, she spent the day mowing lawns. That evening, she again called in sick, saying she was getting a migraine. Raybestos fired her for abusing FMLA leave.

Vail sued, claiming that her termination violated the FMLA. The court disagreed, however. It found that the employer had an honest suspicion, based on the surveillance and the pattern of Vail's absences, that she was abusing her leave. The court indicated that, although hiring someone to conduct surveillance "may not be preferred employer behavior," the information revealed by the surveillance allowed the company to fire her without violating the FMLA.

Vail v. Raybestos Products Co., 533 F.3d 904 (7th Cir. 2008).

Key Employees

Your company has a legal right to deny reinstatement to certain highly paid employees (called "key employees") if returning them to work would cause the company substantial and grievous economic injury.

Who Is a Key Employee

A key employee is a salaried employee who is among the highest-paid 10% of the company's employees within 75 miles of the employee's worksite. Here's what these terms mean:

- **Salaried employee.** The definition of a salaried employee comes from the Fair Labor Standards Act (FLSA). A salaried employee earns the same amount each week, regardless of how many hours the employee works or the quality or quantity of work performed. To be salaried, the employee must earn at least $455 per week.

- **Highest-paid 10%.** To find out whether an employee is in the highest-paid 10% of the workforce, divide the employee's year-to-date compensation by the total number of weeks worked in the year, including any weeks during which the employee took paid leave. You must include wages, premium pay, incentive pay, and bonuses. You don't have to include any amount that will be determined only in the future (such as the value of company stock options awarded during the year).

- **Company employees within 75 miles of the employee's worksite.** In determining which employees work within 75 miles, you should use the same rules used to determine an employee's eligibility for FMLA leave, explained in Chapter 3. Count all employees, whether they are eligible for FMLA leave or not.

You must determine whether someone is a key employee as of the date he or she requests leave.

Initial Notice to Key Employee

If you believe that you might deny reinstatement to a key employee, you must notify the employee, in writing, that he or she qualifies as a key employee and might not be reinstated if the company determines that reinstatement will cause the company substantial and grievous economic injury. You must provide this information with the rights and responsibilities notice, discussed in Chapter 8. If you need some time to determine whether the employee is a key employee, you must give this notice as soon as is practicable. If you don't, you must reinstate the employee no matter what damage it causes your company.

Notice of Determination of Substantial and Grievous Economic Injury

In addition to the above requirements, you can deny reinstatement to an employee only if reinstatement would cause your company substantial and grievous economic injury. The FMLA and its regulations don't provide much guidance on what constitutes a substantial and grievous economic injury. Perhaps because few employers rely on this exception to deny reinstatement, there have been very few court cases on the issue. A few things are clear:

- The injury must stem from reinstatement, not from the employee's absence.
- You don't have to show that the whole company will go under.
- You must show more than minor inconvenience or "undue hardship," as defined by the Americans with Disabilities Act.

Once you determine that substantial and grievous injury will result from reinstating the employee, you must tell the employee in writing. This second notice must include all of the following:

- a determination that reinstating the employee will cause substantial and grievous economic injury to the company
- the reasons for that determination
- a statement that the company may not deny FMLA leave to the employee
- a statement that the company intends to deny reinstatement to the employee once his or her FMLA leave is finished, and
- if the employee is already on leave, a deadline for the employee to return to work to avoid being denied reinstatement. You must give the employee a reasonable amount of time to return, considering the circumstances.

If you have already determined, when you give the employee his or her rights and responsibilities notice, that reinstating the employee will cause substantial and grievous economic injury, you can use that notice to provide this information. However, you will have to add more details than the form allows space for, so you'll have to attach an additional document. We have included a sample "Notice to Key Employee of Substantial and Grievous Economic Injury" below (see Appendix C for an electronic copy).

Lessons from the *Real World*

Failure to give key employee second notice—and a date by which the employee can return to work—violates the FMLA.

Elizabeth Neel worked for Mid-Atlantic of Fairfield as a licensed nursing home administrator. She requested FMLA leave after suffering neck injuries in a car accident. Her request was approved, and Mid-Atlantic informed her, in the rights and responsibilities notice, that she was a key employee to whom job restoration "may be denied." The company also checked the box indicating that "We have determined that restoring you to employment at the conclusion of FMLA leave will cause substantial and grievous economic harm to us."

Neel notified Mid-Atlantic that her physician had released her to return to work in a few weeks. After receiving this notice, Mid-Atlantic sent Neel a certified letter, stating that the company had found a replacement for her who would be starting work soon. When Neel informed the company of her firm return-to-work date, Mid-Atlantic responded that her position had been filled and that she was considered separated from the company.

The court found that Mid-Atlantic had not met its obligations under the key employee exception. Although it had warned Neel that she might be denied restoration, it failed to send the required second notice, explaining the basis for its decision that reinstating her would cause economic injury and giving her a date by which she could return to work. The court held that this "deprived her of an opportunity to weigh whether taking FMLA leave was in her best interest." Because Mid-Atlantic didn't give Neel the required information, it wasn't entitled to rely on the key employee exception. Therefore, its decision to terminate her employment and hire a replacement violated the FMLA.

Neel v. Mid-Atlantic of Fairfield, 778 F.Supp.2d 593 (D. Md. 2011).

Even if you intend to deny reinstatement, you must continue the employee's health benefits while the employee is on FMLA leave. The employee's FMLA rights continue unless and until the employee gives unequivocal notice that he or she doesn't intend to return to work or you actually deny the employee reinstatement at the conclusion of his or her FMLA leave. Also, you will not be able to recover your company's share of health care premiums paid while the key employee was on leave.

Notice to Key Employee of Substantial and Grievous Economic Injury

To: Carlos Sandoval

As indicated by written notice dated <u>January 22, 2018</u>, you are a key employee of this company. This means that you can be denied reinstatement following FMLA leave if such reinstatement would cause substantial and grievous economic injury to the company.

We have determined that reinstating you would cause substantial and grievous economic injury to the company, because <u>we have been unable to find a temporary replacement who is qualified to take over your responsibilities as Chief Financial Officer. To complete all of our annual financial filings by the end of March, we will have to hire a permanent replacement and commit substantial resources to bringing that person up to speed quickly. The company cannot afford to pay both you and your replacement to do this work, and we have no alternative positions available.</u>

We cannot deny you the right to take FMLA leave, or discontinue your health benefits, based on this determination. However, we intend to deny you reinstatement once your leave is finished.

If you wish to avoid these consequences, you must return to work no later than <u>March 1, 2018. This is the latest possible date that will enable us to operate without hiring a replacement and give you enough time to complete the annual reports. If you do not return to work by March 1, 2018,</u> we intend to replace you and deny you reinstatement.

Please contact me immediately if you have any questions.

Sincerely,

Carol Singh

Director of Human Resources

Dated: February 20, 2018

Handling a Key Employee's Request for Reinstatement

Even if you notify a key employee that he or she will be denied reinstatement and the employee doesn't return to work, the employee still has a right to request reinstatement after using FMLA leave. If the employee makes this request, you must redetermine, based on the facts available to you at that time, whether reinstatement would cause substantial and grievous economic injury.

If you conclude that such injury would result from reinstating the employee, you must notify the employee of this conclusion in writing. (You can modify the sample form above for this purpose.) If you reach a different conclusion—that is, you decide that the company won't suffer such an injury—then you must reinstate the employee according to the usual rules.

> **EXAMPLE:** Let's consider Carlos, the employee who received the sample notice of substantial and grievous economic injury, above. When Carol sent this notice, she had determined that reinstatement would cause such an injury. If Carlos doesn't return to work by the deadline Carol imposed, but instead requests reinstatement when his leave ends, Carol must again determine whether reinstating him would injure the company.
>
> If the company already hired a permanent replacement and paying both Carlos and the replacement would significantly harm the company's finances, Carol could justifiably conclude that she doesn't have to reinstate Carlos. On the other hand, if Carol were unable to find a replacement, and the company received extensions on its filing deadlines, reinstating Carlos might not cause such an injury. In fact, it might be exactly what the company needs. In this situation, Carol may not refuse to reinstate Carlos. Instead, she must reinstate him according to the rules explained in "The Basic Reinstatement Right," above.

When Employees Don't Return From Leave

When an employee is unable to, or decides not to, come back to work after taking FMLA leave, your company might be able to recover at least some of the money it spent to continue the employee's benefits.

When You Can Seek Reimbursement for Benefits

The company has a right to reimbursement only if the employee chose not to return to work. The purpose of this rule is to avoid heaping more problems on employees who are already losing their jobs due to circumstances out of their control.

You cannot recover any money spent on benefits continuation if the employee can't return due to:

- **The continuation of the serious health condition, illness, or injury for which the employee took leave.** This applies whether the employee is too ill to return to work or the employee's family member continues to require care after the employee's FMLA leave ends.

- **Other circumstances beyond the employee's control.** This exception applies if an employee cannot return to work for other reasons, such as: The employee needs time off to care for new child with a serious health condition; the employee's spouse is transferred to a location more than 75 miles away from the employee's worksite; the employee is needed to care for a relative who has a serious health condition but doesn't qualify as a family member under the FMLA; the employee is not reinstated due to the "key employee" exception (see above); or the employee is laid off while on leave. This exception doesn't apply if the employee chooses to stay home with a new child who is healthy or to stay with a parent who no longer has a serious health condition.

TIP

Request a certification for continuing health conditions. If an employee can't return to work because of a continuing serious health condition, or serious illness or injury of a servicemember, you are legally entitled to ask the employee to provide a medical certification. It's a good idea to request this form whenever an employee claims that a serious health condition prevents his or her return to work; otherwise, you might be giving up your right to reimbursement unnecessarily. The employee must return the form within 30 days after you request it. If the employee doesn't return the form on time, or the form indicates that the employee or family member no longer has a serious health condition, you may seek reimbursement.

You can't seek reimbursement if an employee returns to work. An employee who comes back for at least 30 days has returned to work, even if the employee later quits. Similarly, an employee who goes directly from FMLA leave to retirement or retires within 30 days after reinstatement is considered to have returned to work.

What Your Company Can Recover

If the employee doesn't return to work and neither of the exceptions described above applies, your company may recover the following amounts:

- **Health insurance costs.** The company may seek reimbursement for its share of the premium of the employee's health benefits. If the employee failed to pay his or her own share while on leave, the company may seek reimbursement for that as well. Self-insured employers can recover what the employee would have had to pay to continue health insurance benefits under the Consolidated Omnibus Budget Reconciliation Act (COBRA), which allows employees to continue their health insurance benefits for a period of time, at their own expense, after leaving a job. Although employers are allowed to charge employees an additional 2% under COBRA to cover the administrative expenses of continuing benefits, you cannot recover this additional amount under the FMLA.

! CAUTION
Your company can't recover its own premiums if the employee is on paid leave. As explained in Chapter 8, sometimes employees may—voluntarily or by company requirement—substitute accrued paid leave, such as sick or vacation time, for FMLA leave. If an employee does this and does not return to work, your company may not recover its share of the premium for health benefits while the employee was on paid leave.

- **The employee's share of premiums for other benefits.** If you continue any other benefits while an employee is on leave, like life or disability insurance, you may seek reimbursement of the employee's share of the premium only, not for your company's share. (As explained above, your company might choose to do this to make sure that it will be able to reinstate these benefits when the employee returns.)

How to Seek Reimbursement

The best way to start is simply to ask the employee to repay the money. If that doesn't work, your company can collect the employee's debt through deductions from amounts still owed to the employee (such as commissions, unpaid wages, or unpaid accrued vacation time), if allowed by law, or in the worst case, through a lawsuit. However, your company's right to seek reimbursement does not give it the right to cut the employee off entirely. For example, your company is still obligated to pay any claims the employee incurred while on FMLA leave (if it is self-insured) or to provide continuing coverage under COBRA.

CAUTION

Some states restrict deductions from employee paychecks. Talk to a lawyer before you start deducting the cost of providing benefits from compensation your company owes the employee.

State law may also require you to get an employee's written consent before taking a deduction to repay money the employee owes the company. If your company operates in a state that imposes this type of requirement, get the employee's written consent *before* the employee starts FMLA leave. Include a deduction authorization form in your standard FMLA paperwork, and ask the employee to sign it. Experience shows that it's much easier to get this type of consent up front, before the employee owes you any money.

Common Mistakes Regarding Reinstatement— And How to Avoid Them

Mistake 1: Failing to reinstate employees on time.

Avoid this mistake by taking the following steps:

- Check in with employees who are on leave. Ask employees to update you periodically on their plans to return to work. (See Chapter 10.)
- Keep track of employees on leave. Remember, you'll have to save an equivalent spot somewhere for returning employees. You can't wait until they're ready to come back to start looking for one.

Mistake 2: Mishandling benefits when an employee returns.

Avoid this mistake by taking the following steps:

- Don't require employees to requalify, reapply, or wait to restart their benefits. Remember, you can't make returning employees do anything in order to get their benefits back.
- Maintain employee benefits during leave, if necessary to ensure immediate reinstatement. Even if the employee chooses not to continue disability or life insurance while on leave, you may have to so you can reinstate it.
- Seek reimbursement when legally entitled to it. If you continued benefits at your own expense, you can recoup the employee's share of the premium once the employee returns from leave.

Mistake 3: Mishandling reinstatement of key employees.

Avoid this mistake by taking the following steps:

- Properly identify key employees in the first place. If more than 10% of your workforce are key employees, you didn't get it right.
- Provide all necessary notices. If you're going to refuse to reinstate a key employee, you must provide two written notices (and perhaps a third, if the employee requests reinstatement when the leave is over).
- Allow leave and continue benefits. You can't simply fire a key employee who requests FMLA leave. While a key employee is on leave, he or she is still employed by your company, and you have to allow leave (including substitution of paid leave) and continue the employee's health insurance coverage.

Managers' Checklist: Reinstating an Employee

If the Employee Was Reinstated:

☐ I reinstated the employee to the position he or she held prior to taking leave or to an equivalent position.

    ☐ The position has the same base pay, and the same opportunities to earn extra pay, as the former position.

    ☐ The position offers the same benefits, at the same levels, that the employee used to receive.

    ☐ The position has the same or substantially similar job duties as the employee's former job.

    ☐ The position has the same or a substantially similar shift or schedule as the employee worked before taking leave.

    ☐ The position is at the same worksite, or one that is geographically proximate to, where the employee worked before taking leave.

☐ I reinstated the employee immediately upon his or her return from leave or within two working days of receiving notice of intent to return to work from the employee.

☐ I restored the employee's pay, including base pay, opportunities to earn extra pay, and any across-the-board raises (such as cost-of-living increases) that became effective during the employee's leave.

☐ I restored the employee's benefits, including any across-the-board changes that took effect during the employee's leave.

    ☐ I did not require the employee to requalify for benefits, take a physical exam, wait a certain period of time, or do anything else to receive benefits.

    ☐ I did not count the employee's FMLA leave as a break in service for purposes of our pension plan.

    ☐ I counted the employee as "employed" while on leave if our pension plan requires employees to be employed on a particular date for purposes of contributions, eligibility, or vesting.

    ☐ I restored the employee's seniority-based benefits.

    ☐ If our company's policies allow employees to accrue seniority-based benefits while on unpaid leave, I added these accrued benefits to the employee's total.

Managers' Checklist: Reinstating an Employee (continued)

- ☐ I required the employee to provide a fitness-for-duty certification, but only if all of the following are true:
  - ☐ I gave the employee notice that a certification would be required.
  - ☐ Company policy requires it for all similarly situated employees.
  - ☐ I gave the employee a list of the essential job functions, if the fitness-for-duty certification must address the employee's ability to perform them.

If the Employee Was Not Reinstated:

- ☐ I did not reinstate the employee because one of the following occurred:
  - ☐ The employee was unable to perform an essential function of the position.
    - ☐ I researched our company's obligations under the Americans with Disabilities Act and/or workers' compensation law.
  - ☐ The employee's position was eliminated, for reasons unrelated to his or her FMLA leave.
  - ☐ The employee was fired for reasons unrelated to his or her FMLA leave.
    - ☐ If the employee was fired for attendance problems, I made sure that the employee's FMLA leave was not counted against him or her.
    - ☐ I talked to a lawyer to make sure that we are on legally safe ground in taking this action.
  - ☐ The employee's job or work was temporary and has been completed.
  - ☐ The employee committed fraud in obtaining FMLA leave.
    - ☐ If the employee was not reinstated solely because he or she worked another job while on FMLA leave, I made sure our company policies prohibit moonlighting.
  - ☐ The employee gave unequivocal notice that he or she did not intend to return from FMLA leave and confirmed this in writing.

Managers' Checklist: Reinstating an Employee (continued)

- ☐ The employee is a key employee, and reinstating him or her would cause our company substantial and grievous economic injury.
  - ☐ The employee is among the highest-paid 10% of employees within a 75-mile radius.
  - ☐ I notified the employee, when he or she requested leave or shortly thereafter, of this key employee status.
  - ☐ I notified the employee when the company determined that reinstatement would cause substantial and grievous economic injury, stated the reasons for this determination, and gave the employee a reasonable time frame to return to work.
  - ☐ If the employee requested reinstatement at the end of leave, I reevaluated whether reinstating him or her would cause substantial and grievous economic injury and notified the employee of my conclusions.

✓ Managers' Checklist: If an Employee Doesn't Return From Leave

☐ I determined why the employee did not come back to work.

☐ If the employee did not return to work because of the continuation of a serious health condition, illness, or injury:

   ☐ I asked the employee to provide a medical certification.

   ☐ I did not seek reimbursement for premiums the company paid to continue the employee's health insurance.

☐ I did not seek reimbursement for health insurance premiums if the employee could not return to work for reasons beyond the employee's control.

☐ If the employee's failure to return from leave was voluntary, I determined what amount (if any) we can recover from the employee for what we spent on benefit premiums while the employee was on leave.

   ☐ I included in this amount our company's share of the premium for health insurance continuation during the employee's leave.

   ☐ If the employee did not pay his or her share of the premium for health insurance, I included any part of the employee's share that we paid during the employee's leave.

   ☐ If we continued any other insurance benefits (such as life or disability coverage), I included any amounts we paid toward the employee's share of the premium during the employee's leave.

   ☐ I did not include the company's share of the premium for any other insurance benefits.

☐ Regardless of whether or not we are entitled to seek reimbursement from the employee, I offered the employee continued health care coverage under COBRA and, if we are self-insured, paid any claims the employee incurred while on FMLA leave.

☐ Before seeking reimbursement by deducting from money we still owe the employee, I made sure that this is allowed by state law.

How Other Laws Affect FMLA Leave

Chapter Highlights

☆ An employee covered by the FMLA and other employment laws is entitled to every protection of every applicable law. If the laws call for different approaches to the same situation, you must apply whichever law is more beneficial to the employee.

☆ An employee who has a serious health condition under the FMLA may also have a disability under the Americans with Disabilities Act (ADA).

- Only qualified employees with disabilities—those who can perform the essential functions of the job, with or without a reasonable accommodation— are protected by the ADA.

- Employers must provide reasonable accommodations to allow employees with disabilities to do their jobs. This may include more time off than the FMLA requires, changes to the job, or a transfer to another position.

☆ An employee who does not return to work at the end of FMLA leave may be entitled to continuing health benefits pursuant to the Consolidated Omnibus Budget Reconciliation Act (COBRA).

☆ Federal antidiscrimination laws prohibit employers from discriminating based on race, color, national origin, religion, sex (including pregnancy), age, or genetic information in any aspect of employment, including providing leave.

☆ Time an employee spends on leave to serve in the armed forces counts as time worked when determining the employee's eligibility for FMLA leave. State laws also give employees the right to take time off for a variety of reasons, including family and medical leave, military family leave, adoption, and pregnancy.

- Some of these laws cover smaller employers, have more lenient eligibility require-ments for employees, allow longer periods of leave, allow leave to care for a broader range of family members, or allow leave for different purposes from the FMLA.

- If an employee takes leave that is covered by both the FMLA and a state law, that leave counts against the employee's entitlement pursuant to both laws.

- If an employee takes leave that is covered by the FMLA or the state law but not both, the employee may be entitled to more than 12 weeks of total leave.

☆ An employee whose serious medical condition comes from a workplace injury or illness is probably also entitled to workers' compensation benefits; an employee who is out on leave for a workers' comp injury or illness almost always has a serious health condition covered by the FMLA.

- An employee who is on FMLA leave does not have to accept a "light duty" position; however, an employee who rejects such a position may no longer be entitled to workers' comp benefits.

- Most state workers' compensation laws do not require employers to hold an employee's job for the duration of his or her workers' comp leave; this might come into play if an employee uses up his or her FMLA leave and still needs time off.

The FMLA is not the only law that might protect an employee who needs time off for family or medical reasons. Depending on the employee's condition and/or situation, other federal laws may also apply. For example, other laws may protect the employee from disability discrimination or provide for continued health insurance. And that's not all: State laws that provide for family and medical leave, pregnancy disability leave, workers' compensation, or temporary disability insurance might also come into play.

Sometimes, these laws cover the same territory as the FMLA. How do you know which to follow? The basic rule when employment laws overlap is this: The employee is entitled to every benefit available under every law that applies. If the FMLA and another law both cover the employee's situation, the employee is entitled to the protections of both laws. If both laws apply and provide different rights, the employee is entitled to the protections that are most beneficial in the circumstances.

This chapter explains how to apply this rule when more than one law protects an employee who takes family and medical leave. This is a topic that many managers dread, and it can be a bit daunting. But, understanding the purpose and requirements of each law will help you figure out what to do.

TIP

Consider each law separately. The easiest way to make sure you meet all of your legal obligations when laws overlap is to think of each law as a separate protection. Run through the laws that might apply, think about what each requires or prohibits, then make sure you offer or provide those protections to the employee. See "Do Other Laws Apply?" at the end of this chapter for assistance.

Federal Laws

A handful of federal laws other than the FMLA might protect an employee who takes family or medical leave. These laws, which are covered in detail below, include:

- the Americans with Disabilities Act (ADA), which protects disabled employees from discrimination and requires employers to make reasonable accommodations to allow employees with disabilities to do their jobs

- the Consolidated Omnibus Budget Reconciliation Act (COBRA), which requires employers to provide continued health insurance to employees and former employees
- Title VII of the Civil Rights Act, which prohibits discrimination on the basis of race, national origin, sex (including pregnancy), and religion, and
- the Uniformed Services Employment and Reemployment Rights Act (USERRA), which requires employers to provide certain rights and benefits to employees who take military leave.

Americans with Disabilities Act (ADA)

If an employee's serious health condition under the FMLA also qualifies as a disability under the ADA, both laws apply. Here, we explain some basic ADA concepts and how the ADA and FMLA might overlap.

TIP
The ADA and FMLA have different purposes. Although the ADA and FMLA both are intended (in part, at least) to help employees with physical or mental ailments, they have different goals. The goal of the ADA is to bring qualified workers with disabilities into the workforce—and keep them there—by requiring employers to make reasonable changes to allow them to do their jobs. The goal of the FMLA's medical leave provision, on the other hand, is to allow workers who are unable to do their jobs to take time off for family or health reasons.

ADA Basics

The Americans with Disabilities Act (ADA) prohibits employers with 15 or more employees from discriminating against employees with disabilities who can perform the job's essential functions with or without a reasonable accommodation. An employee has a disability for purposes of the ADA if the employee:

- has a long-term physical or mental impairment that substantially limits a major bodily function or a major life activity, such as the ability to walk, talk, see, hear, breathe, reason, work, or take care of oneself

- has a history of such an impairment (for example, the employee suffered cancer or depression in the past), or
- is perceived by the employer as having a disability. This sometimes comes up when an employee has an obvious impairment (such as a limp or speech impediment) that is not actually disabling.

> ## CAUTION
> **A temporary or short-term condition might qualify as a disability, depending on how it affects the employee.** A garden-variety cold or the flu is not a disability, for example. However, if one of these minor ailments turns into pneumonia, that might be disabling. Similarly, normal pregnancy is not a disability under the ADA, but serious complications of pregnancy—such as gestational diabetes or preeclampsia—could be disabilities, depending on how they affect the employee. Even though these conditions are, by definition, temporary, they can substantially limit major life activities while active.

Employers are required to make reasonable accommodations to allow employees with disabilities to do their jobs. A reasonable accommodation is assistance (technological or otherwise) or a change to the workplace or job that allows the employee to perform its essential functions: the job's most fundamental tasks. Examples include providing voice-recognition software for an employee with carpal tunnel syndrome; altering the height of a desk for an employee in a wheelchair; providing a distraction-free environment for an employee with attention deficit disorder; or allowing a diabetic employee to take more frequent breaks to eat and drink, take medication, or test blood sugar levels.

Under the ADA, an employer does not have to provide a reasonable accommodation if doing so would create an undue hardship. Whether an accommodation creates an undue hardship depends on a number of factors, including:

- the nature and cost of the accommodation
- the size and financial resources of the business and the facility where the employee works
- the structure of the business, and
- the effect the accommodation would have on the business.

An accommodation that would be extremely costly (for example, adapting technical equipment that would eat up months' worth of company profits) or would change the character of the business (for example, installing bright lighting in a previously dimly lit, romantic restaurant) could create an undue hardship.

Rules for Handling Medical Records

Under the FMLA, employee medical records must be handled confidentially, kept in secured files (separate from personnel files), and released only to limited people in limited circumstances. These rules also apply to medical records covered by the ADA. (You can find a description of these rules in Chapter 13.)

Overlap Between the FMLA and the ADA

The FMLA and the ADA overlap only if an employee has both a serious health condition under the FMLA and a disability under the ADA. Although many ailments—such as cancer, multiple sclerosis, HIV/AIDS, stroke, and diabetes—likely qualify under both laws, some do not. For example, an employee who is pregnant without serious complications or has a broken bone is covered by the FMLA but not the ADA. An employee who is blind or hard of hearing and can perform the job's essential functions with an accommodation has a disability but perhaps not a serious health condition requiring time off.

An employee who is protected by both the FMLA and the ADA is entitled to the rights provided by both laws: up to 12 weeks of job-protected leave with benefits continuation under the FMLA, and a reasonable accommodation to enable the employee to perform the job's essential functions under the ADA. If the laws allow different rights in the same situation, the employee is entitled to whichever provides the greater benefit.

EXAMPLE: Sam uses a wheelchair due to a back injury that left him paralyzed from the waist down. He needs to have surgery related to his condition and expects to be out of work for two months. Because you know Sam has a disability, you consider whether he is entitled to two months off as a reasonable accommodation. Sam's job is to maintain, update, and troubleshoot the company's website. No one else knows how to do this work and, because the website is relatively new, it requires a lot of work to keep it running smoothly. You decide that it would be an undue hardship to give Sam two months off, and you tell him that the company will have to replace him.

Although you might have been right under the ADA, you were wrong under the FMLA. Sam's disability almost certainly qualifies as a serious health condition, for which he is entitled to FMLA leave (assuming he is otherwise eligible). The FMLA doesn't include an undue hardship defense: An eligible employee can't be denied leave because it would place too much of a burden on the company (unless the employee qualifies as a "key employee," as explained in Chapter 11). You must give Sam his time off and figure out some way to get the work done in his absence.

There are several situations in which the FMLA and ADA are most likely to overlap: when an employee requests a modified schedule, when an employee requests (or an employer proposes) modified job duties, and when an employee is unable to return to work after FMLA leave.

TIP

Count disability leave as FMLA leave. If an employee is covered by both the ADA and the FMLA, make sure you count any time off the employee takes due to his or her disability as FMLA leave, too. And, remember to give all notices and paperwork required by the FMLA.

Schedule Changes

An employee can take FMLA leave intermittently or on a reduced schedule, and this might also be a reasonable accommodation for an employee's disability under the ADA. If the employee is protected by both laws, the FMLA provides the greater benefit, because employees are entitled to job protection and benefits continuation during intermittent or reduced-schedule leave. And, even if an employer transfers an employee to a different position that better accommodates the need for leave, that position must have the same pay and benefits as the employee's original position. The ADA allows a transfer as a reasonable accommodation (if the employee can't be accommodated in his or her former position), but doesn't give the employee the right to the same pay and benefits, nor to benefits continuation.

> **EXAMPLE:** Najeet is scheduled to begin a ten-week round of chemotherapy and radiation treatment for cancer and needs time off work. She asks to work 20 hours a week for the duration of her treatment. You tell Najeet that you are happy to grant her request as a reasonable accommodation for her disability but remind her that the company provides health benefits only to employees who work at least 30 hours a week. You offer her COBRA coverage, for which she would have to pay the entire premium, until she is able to once again meet the minimum hours requirement.
>
> Uh-oh! In this situation, the FMLA provides a greater benefit, and Najeet is entitled to its protections. She can take the time off she needs for treatment with continued health insurance benefits, regardless of the company's policy on eligibility for coverage. Under the FMLA, Najeet has to pay only her usual share of the premium (if any), not the whole thing.

Job Modifications

The FMLA does not entitle an employee to a different job or to any changes in his or her current job. Instead, the FMLA provides for reinstatement, once leave is over, to the same or an equivalent position: a position that is "virtually identical" to the employee's former position. In contrast, the ADA may entitle an employee to job modifications or even to a different position in the company as a reasonable accommodation. Here are a couple of ways this issue might play out when an employee has both a disability and a serious health condition:

- **The employee asks for changes to the job.** You must consider whether the requested changes constitute a reasonable accommodation and whether providing them would be an undue hardship. If the accommodation won't work, you must work with the employee to come up with a different accommodation. If you and the employee conclude that time off might reasonably accommodate the employee's disability, your obligations under the FMLA kick in.

EXAMPLE: Carmen is a dispatcher for a delivery company. She works from 6 a.m. until noon. When she arrives, she reviews the schedule to see which deliveries must be made that day, assigns deliveries to drivers, and arranges for the items to be loaded on the trucks. By about 10 a.m., all of the trucks have left the warehouse. Carmen spends the rest of her day processing paperwork from the morning deliveries.

Carmen is diagnosed with depression, for which her doctor prescribes medication that makes her groggy and disoriented in the morning. Carmen asks if she can change her schedule to arrive at work at 10 a.m. and work until 4 p.m. The FMLA doesn't apply, because she isn't asking for time off. You consider it as a request for a reasonable accommodation, and you deny it as an undue hardship. The essential duties of Carmen's job require her to be there in the early morning. There wouldn't be anything for her to do later in the day. You research whether there are other positions in the company that Carmen might be suited for, but there are no positions for which she is qualified.

You and Carmen talk through some alternatives, none of which will work. Carmen says, "My doctor said that this side effect might go away after I've been taking the drug for a month or so. Some of his other patients have had that happen." You ask Carmen whether she wants to take some time off work and see whether she feels well enough in the mornings to resume her job. You explain her right to leave under the FMLA, and she decides to use it.

- **You offer a light-duty position.** If an employee requests time off for a serious health condition/disability, some employers respond by offering a light-duty position (often, one that doesn't require lifting or other physically strenuous activities). If the employee wants to keep working and accepts the position, that's fine. If, however, the employee is covered by the FMLA, he or she does not have to take the position, and you must inform the employee of his or her FMLA rights. The employee can choose to take FMLA leave rather than working a light-duty assignment, as long as the employee is eligible.

Lessons from the *Real World*

When an employee's depression causes poor attendance, she isn't protected by the ADA but might be entitled to FMLA leave.

Theresa Spangler worked in the Demand Services Department of the Federal Home Loan Bank of Des Moines. After she was diagnosed with dysthemia (a form of depression), she began having attendance problems. Over the years, she took two leaves of absence for treatment and missed several days of work due to her depression.

After being warned, being put on probation, and facing customer complaints about her absences, Spangler was eventually fired for excessive absenteeism when she called in saying she would be out for "depression, again." She sued the bank for violating the ADA and the FMLA.

The court found that Spangler had no claim under the ADA because she could not prove that she could perform the job's essential functions with or without accommodation. One of Spangler's job duties was to make sure member banks had adequate daily cash, and the court found that regular attendance was therefore an essential function of her job.

The court also found, however, that Spangler might have a valid FMLA claim. Unlike the ADA, which protects employees who can do the job but might need an accommodation, the FMLA protects employees who cannot perform the job's essential functions, at least for a limited time. When Spangler called in and said she would miss work for depression, the company should have treated it as a request for FMLA leave.

Spangler v. Federal Home Loan Bank of Des Moines, 278 F.3d 847 (8th Cir. 2002).

Reinstatement

Once an employee's FMLA-protected leave runs out, the company must reinstate the employee to the same or an equivalent position. If the employee is not able to return to work or perform the essential duties of his or her position, the company's FMLA obligations end. However, if the employee is also covered by the ADA, the company must provide a reasonable accommodation, unless it creates an undue hardship. This means that the company might have to provide additional leave (see below), make changes to the employee's position to allow the employee to do the job, or even transfer the employee to a different position. And, the ADA requires the company to return the employee to the same job with a reasonable accommodation—not an equivalent one—unless doing so would be an undue hardship. Therefore, if an employee's leave qualifies under both laws, you might not be able to reinstate the employee to an equivalent position.

More Leave as a Reasonable Accommodation

What are your legal obligations toward an employee whose FMLA leave has run out but is unable to return to work? Under the FMLA, you have no further duty. You must reinstate the employee, but only if the employee can perform the essential functions of the job.

Under the ADA, however, the answer is much less clear. The Equal Employment Opportunity Commission (EEOC), the federal agency that enforces the ADA, has said that employers might need to provide more leave than required by the FMLA as a reasonable accommodation for a disabled employee who cannot yet return to work. As long as such leave doesn't pose an undue hardship for the employer, the employer might need to provide it. However, some courts have ruled against this interpretation, finding that an employee who needs lengthy time off is, by definition, an employee who cannot perform the essential functions of the job with or without an accommodation—and, therefore, is not protected by the ADA.

Because of this conflict, you should talk to a lawyer before making a decision not to provide additional leave to an employee who has exhausted FMLA leave but is still unable to return to work. Here are a few things to keep in mind in this situation:

- **The nature of the job.** If regular attendance is an essential function of the job (as it often is), some courts have found that an employee who needs a significant amount of time off is not a qualified employee with a disability. Therefore, the employee is not protected by the ADA or entitled to a reasonable accommodation.

- **How much (and what type of) leave the employee needs.** Many courts have found that an employer is not required to provide open-ended leave as a reasonable accommodation. Courts are more likely, on the other hand, to see a finite, short period of leave as a reasonable accommodation. If an employee can return to work two weeks after his or her FMLA leave has run out, for example, a court is more likely to find that the employee is entitled to this time off. Similarly, if the employee needs a few hours off every week but is otherwise able to work, a court is more likely to find in the employee's favor. In this instance, the employee's time off allows the employee to do the job, which is the nature of a reasonable accommodation.

- **How much time off the employer provides in other circumstances.** If an employer allows extended leaves for other purposes, it will be hard-pressed to claim that letting an employee with a disability take extended leave is an undue hardship. Treating employees differently because they have disabilities is the essence of disability discrimination.

> **RESOURCE**
>
> **For more information on the ADA.** The EEOC has a number of helpful resources available on its website, including a fact sheet on how the ADA interacts with the FMLA. You can find these resources at www.eeoc.gov. An excellent resource on reasonable accommodations is the Job Accommodation Network (JAN), at askjan.org.

Consolidated Omnibus Budget Reconciliation Act (COBRA)

COBRA allows employees, former employees, and their families to receive continuing coverage under an employer's group health plan after experiencing a "qualifying event": an event that would end coverage under ordinary circumstances, such as a layoff or reduction in hours. Employees and their families typically have to pay for this continued coverage, but they pay the employer-negotiated group rate, which is often less expensive than an individual rate. This right to continued coverage lasts for 18 to 36 months, depending on the type of qualifying event. COBRA applies to employers with 20 or more employees.

Often, COBRA and the FMLA don't overlap at all. Taking FMLA leave doesn't count as a qualifying event under COBRA, because employers are legally obligated to continue the employee's group health benefits during leave (as explained in Chapter 10). In a few situations, however, an employee who takes FMLA leave might be entitled to COBRA protection:

- **The employee can't return to work after FMLA leave.** If an employee is unable to come back to work when FMLA leave runs out, the employee is entitled to continued health care coverage under COBRA. The qualifying event occurs on the last day of the employee's FMLA leave. Similarly, if an employee passes away while on FMLA leave, and the employee's family is covered by your company's group health plan, the employee's death is the qualifying event that entitles his or her family members to the protections of COBRA.

- **The employee chooses not to return to work.** As explained in Chapter 10, an employer's obligation to provide continued health benefits ends if the employee provides unequivocal notice of his or her intent not to return to work. But the employee can continue coverage under COBRA. The qualifying event in this situation occurs on the date the employee gives such notice.

- **The employee returns to work with a schedule or position that is not entitled to benefits.** Many companies provide group health benefits only to certain employees (typically, those who work a minimum number of hours per week). If an employee takes FMLA leave and chooses to return to a part-time position, the employee might no longer be entitled to benefits. The qualifying event here, for COBRA purposes, occurs on the last day of the employee's leave.

These rules apply even if the employee failed to pay his or her portion of the premium while on leave or the employee refused coverage during FMLA leave. Neither situation deprives the employee of the right to coverage.

RESOURCE

Need more information on COBRA? You can find detailed information on COBRA's requirements, including the paperwork and notices your company must provide to an employee who is entitled to continuing coverage, in *The Essential Guide to Federal Employment Laws,* by Lisa Guerin and Sachi Barriero (Nolo).

Title VII of the Civil Rights Act

Title VII prohibits employers with 15 or more employees from discriminating on the basis of race, color, religion, sex (including pregnancy), and national origin. Title VII applies to every aspect of the employment relationship, including hiring, compensation, benefits, and termination. It also prohibits harassment on the basis of any of the characteristics listed above.

There are a few ways Title VII might overlap with the FMLA. Because Title VII prohibits employers from discriminating in the provision of benefits, an employer might violate Title VII by administering requests for FMLA leave in a discriminatory way. For example, if you routinely allow white employees to take foreseeable leave on short notice while requiring nonwhite employees to provide 30 days' notice, that would violate Title VII. In this type of situation, the employer is using the FMLA as a vehicle for discrimination.

Overlap may also occur when an employee takes FMLA leave for pregnancy and childbirth. Courts have interpreted Title VII's prohibition against pregnancy discrimination to require employers to treat pregnant employees just as they treat other workers who are temporarily disabled by other conditions. This means that you cannot treat employees who take FMLA leave for pregnancy any differently from other employees who use the FMLA. It also means that you might have to provide time off to a pregnant employee who isn't eligible for FMLA leave (because, for example, she hasn't worked enough hours in the past year) if you provide such time off to employees with other types of short-term disabilities.

Parenting and caretaking leave are another potential source of overlap. This issue typically arises when a male employee wants to take parental leave or leave to care for a seriously ill or injured family member. Even in this day and age, some employers still expect women to be the primary parents and caretakers. However, denying a man FMLA leave based on these expectations doesn't just violate the FMLA; it's also gender discrimination, prohibited by Title VII.

EXAMPLE: Connor is an employee at your company. He and his wife, who does volunteer work for a local nonprofit, have a young son who has leukemia. Connor asks to work a reduced schedule while his son undergoes treatment that is expected to leave him fatigued, ill, and unable to care for himself. You respond: "Connor, I'm so sorry to hear about your son, but isn't your wife available to take care of him? We could really use you around here, and if she puts her volunteer work on hold, your family won't lose part of your salary. I'm sure he'll want his mother at a time like this."

Oops. It's not an employer's right to tell employees how to manage their private lives—including which parent should be the primary caretaker, whose job is more important to the family, and so on. If you denied FMLA leave to Connor because you think his wife should take care of their son, your company might well face a lawsuit for violating both the FMLA and Title VII's prohibition on sex discrimination.

Uniformed Services Employment and Reemployment Rights Act (USERRA)

USERRA provides a number of employment-related rights to employees who take time off to serve in the Armed Forces. Such employees may not be discriminated against based on their service. They are also entitled to reinstatement and benefits restoration upon returning from leaves of up to five years, and they may not be fired, except for cause, for up to a year after they return from service.

> **TIP**
>
> **Your state may have a similar law.** Many states have laws prohibiting discrimination against, or providing employment-related rights to, individuals serving in the Armed Forces or state militias. These laws can overlap with the FMLA the same way Title VII and USERRA do, and their protections could be even broader. To find out more about the laws in your state, talk to an experienced lawyer.

USERRA and the FMLA overlap only when determining an employee's eligibility for FMLA leave. As explained in Chapter 3, an employee must have worked for the employer for at least one year and worked at least 1,250 hours during the previous year, to qualify for FMLA leave. You must count time the employee spends on leave for military service as time worked when determining eligibility for FMLA leave. When calculating the employee's hours, you can use the employee's schedule prior to taking military leave.

EXAMPLE 1: For eight months, George, a member of the Army Reserve, works full time (40 hours a week) in your company's IT department. He is called for service and takes six months of military leave, then returns to work. After he has been back for a month, George requests FMLA leave to care for his seriously ill wife. Is he eligible for leave?

Yes. You must count the six months George spent on leave as hours worked. This means that George has "worked" 15 months for your company and 2,080 hours (40 hours a week times 52 weeks) in the last year. He is eligible for FMLA leave.

EXAMPLE 2: Now assume that George works a part-time schedule, 20 hours per week. Is he still eligible for FMLA leave?

No. Although George still gets credit for 15 months of work for your company, he hasn't "worked" enough hours in the last year. You must credit George with an entire year of work at his previous schedule—20 hours per week. That means George gets credit for only 1,040 hours (20 hours a week times 52 weeks), which falls short of the threshold for FMLA coverage.

State Laws

In addition to the federal laws described above, there are state laws that might overlap with the FMLA as well. This section describes the types of state laws that might come into play as you administer the FMLA:

- state family and medical leave laws
- workers' compensation statutes, and
- temporary disability or family leave insurance programs.

State Family and Medical Leave Laws

A number of states have adopted their own laws that allow employees to take time off for family and/or medical reasons. These laws fall into a handful of categories:

- comprehensive family and medical leave laws similar to the FMLA that may provide additional protections or apply to more employees
- military family leave laws, which allow employees to take time off when certain family members are called to serve in the military

- pregnancy disability leave laws, which allow female employees to take time off for conditions related to pregnancy and childbirth
- adoption leave laws, which generally require employers to make the same parental leave available to adoptive parents that they make available to biological parents
- small necessities laws, which provide time off for employees to attend a child's school conferences or other school activities or to take a relative to routine medical and dental visits
- domestic violence leave laws, which require employers to allow employees to take leave to seek medical care, attend legal proceedings or therapy appointments, or otherwise deal with domestic violence issues, and
- paid sick leave laws, which require employers to provide a certain amount of sick time, with pay, to employees.

CAUTION

Your state may require you to offer other types of leave. In this section (and in Appendix A), we discuss only those state laws that might overlap with, or provide leave similar to, the FMLA. We do not cover the many other types of leave laws states have adopted, such as laws requiring leave for voting, military service, jury duty, or donating blood or bone marrow. To find out more about your state's leave laws beyond the realm of family and medical leave, contact your state labor department. (You'll find contact information in Appendix A.)

Each of these categories is explained more fully below. Appendix A provides basic information on each state's family and medical leave laws, including which employers are covered, what the eligibility requirements are, and so on.

TIP

Remember to designate FMLA leave. If any time an employee takes off pursuant to a state law also qualifies as FMLA leave, designate it as such and provide the required notices (explained in Chapter 8). If you don't, the employee may be entitled to additional leave.

Comprehensive Family and Medical Leave Laws

About a dozen states currently have laws that require employers to provide family and medical leave. These laws are quite similar to the FMLA, in that they typically provide a certain number of weeks of parenting, caretaking, or medical leave to eligible employees. However, these laws differ from the FMLA in the following important ways:

- **Some apply to smaller employers.** For example, Vermont employers must provide parental leave if they have at least ten employees, and they must provide leave to care for a seriously ill family member if they have at least 15 employees. In such a state, smaller employers may be covered only by the state law, not the FMLA.

- **Some cover more family members.** In California, for example, an employee may take leave to care for a domestic partner with a serious health condition. When an employee takes leave to care for a family member who is not covered by the FMLA, it doesn't count as FMLA leave. This means, for example, that an employee in California could take 12 weeks (the state law maximum) of family leave to care for a seriously ill domestic partner and still have 12 weeks of FMLA leave left to use.

- **Some may allow longer periods of leave.** In Connecticut, for example, employees are entitled to 16 weeks of family and medical leave in a two-year period. If an employee needs 16 weeks at once, this provides more leave than the FMLA requires.

Whether leave taken pursuant to one of these state laws counts as FMLA leave depends on whether both laws apply. When an employee takes leave for a reason that's covered by state law but not by the FMLA (for example, to care for a grandparent, in Hawaii), the FMLA doesn't apply, and the employee's leave doesn't use up any of his or her FMLA entitlement. If, however, the employee's leave is covered by both laws (for example, that Hawaiian employee takes leave to care for a parent), the time counts against both the employee's FMLA and state leave entitlements.

If your company does business in a state with a comprehensive family and medical leave statute, keep these tips in mind:

- **Start by figuring out which laws apply.** If the employee's leave is covered only by your state's law, you don't have to deal with the FMLA at all, and vice versa.
- **If both laws apply, the leaves run concurrently.** If an employee takes leave for a reason covered by both the FMLA and your state's law, the employee uses up both types of leave at once. If the employee uses all leave provided by state law while on FMLA leave, no additional leave is available, even for reasons covered only by state law.
- **If only one law applies, the employee will be able to "stack" leave.** If an employee's time off counts only under one law and not the other, the employee will still have leave available. This means that the employee could take significantly more than 12 weeks of leave in a 12-month period, if the employee is eligible.

> **EXAMPLE:** Oregon's family and medical leave law allows eligible employees to take up to 12 weeks of leave per year for various reasons, including caring for a family member with a serious health condition. The definition of "family member" includes a parent-in-law. If an employee in Oregon took 12 weeks of leave to care for a child with a serious health condition, that leave would use up both the employee's FMLA and state leave entitlements, and no leave would be available for the rest of the year. If, on the other hand, the employee first took 12 weeks of leave to care for his or her mother-in-law, that leave would count against the state leave entitlement only. The employee would still have 12 weeks of FMLA leave to use in the same year, assuming the employee meets the FMLA's eligibility requirements.

Military Family Leave

In recent years, some states have passed laws that require employers to give some time off to employees with family members serving in the military. Some of these laws apply only to certain family members (for example, spouses), and most apply whether the family member is subject to a federal or state call to active duty. Typically, these laws provide only a small amount of leave.

These laws may overlap with qualifying exigency or military caregiver leave under the FMLA. For example, Minnesota allows certain family members to take one day off to attend military events. If the employee is the parent, spouse, or child of the servicemember, that leave would also count as qualifying exigency leave. If the employee is the servicemember's grandparent or sibling, however, the leave would be covered by state law only. Similarly, some state laws allow employees to take leave during a family member's deployment, but don't limit the circumstances under which the employee may take leave. In these states, an employee who uses leave for a family member and a reason that qualifies under the FMLA would be using both types of leave; however, if the employee took time off that didn't fall into any of the qualifying exigency categories, that time would count only against the employee's state law entitlement.

Pregnancy Disability Leave

Some states require employers to provide time off for pregnancy disability: the length of time when a woman is temporarily disabled by pregnancy and childbirth. Typically, these laws don't provide for a set amount of time off per year or per pregnancy. Instead, they require employers to provide either a "reasonable" amount of leave or leave for the period of disability, often with a maximum time limit. For example, Louisiana requires employers to allow a "reasonable period" of leave for pregnancy disability; the statute goes on to say that this period shouldn't exceed six weeks for a normal childbirth but might be as long as four months for a complicated childbirth, depending on the circumstances.

Because pregnancy is a serious health condition under the FMLA, leave an employee takes under a state pregnancy disability leave law typically runs concurrently with FMLA leave. If your state's law provides for more than 12 weeks of pregnancy disability leave, the first 12 weeks will use up the employee's FMLA allotment. Although the employee may be entitled to take more time off, the employee won't necessarily be entitled to continued health insurance if the state law doesn't require it.

CAUTION

You might need to provide reasonable accommodations for pregnant employees. Recently, a number of states have amended their laws on pregnancy discrimination to add a requirement that employers reasonably accommodate the work restrictions of a pregnant employee. For example, you might have to provide light-duty work, relieve an employee of certain physical job duties (such as heavy lifting), give an employee a stool so she can sit while working, transfer an employee to a job that is less physically demanding, or change an employee's work schedule to accommodate morning sickness. Depending on your state's law, you might also have to allow an employee to take some leave. Like the ADA, these laws may provide different rights than the FMLA—essentially, the right to remain at work with changes to the job, rather than the right to time off. As always, the employee is entitled to all protections available, under both state and federal law.

Adoption Leave Laws

A handful of states require employers to offer the same leave to adoptive parents as to biological parents. Generally, these laws don't require an employer to offer parental leave. However, those employers that choose to offer some form of parental leave must make it equally available to adoptive parents. A couple of these states set an age limit: For example, New York employers that provide parental leave must allow adoptive parents to use it, but only if they are adopting a child who is no older than preschool age or, if disabled, no older than 18.

The FMLA provides leave for adoption, so any time an employee takes off pursuant to one of these state laws would also count as FMLA leave (and you should designate it as such).

Small Necessities Laws

Some states require employers to allow time off for various family needs, such as attending a child's school functions, taking a child to routine dental or medical appointments, or helping with elder care. These laws have come to be known as "small necessities" laws, to recognize needs that don't take up much time but are important to employees. Here are a few examples:

- In Illinois, employees can take up to eight hours off in any school year—not to exceed four hours in a single day—to attend a child's school conferences or classroom activities, if those activities can't be scheduled during nonwork hours.
- In Washington, DC, employees can take up to 24 hours off per year to attend a child's school-related events, including parent-teacher association meetings, student performances, teacher conferences, and sporting events, as long as the child actually participates and is not just a spectator.
- In Vermont, employees can take a total of 24 hours of leave per year for school activities; to attend or accompany a child, parent, spouse, or parent-in-law to routine medical or dental appointments or other appointments for professional services; or to respond to a medical emergency involving the employee's child, parent, spouse, or parent-in-law.

Many of these laws apply to situations not covered by the FMLA (such as school conferences or routine doctor's appointments). In this situation, the leave provided by a small necessities law would be in addition to FMLA leave, and the two laws wouldn't overlap. However, there are limited situations in which the FMLA might also apply. For example, if your company does business in Vermont, and a parent takes small necessities leave to respond to a child's medical emergency, that might also qualify as FMLA leave (depending on whether the child has a serious health condition).

Domestic Violence Leave Laws

Some states allow employees to take time off for issues relating to domestic violence. In Colorado, for example, employees can take up to three days of leave to seek a restraining order, obtain medical care or counseling, relocate, or seek legal assistance. These laws usually apply to employees who need to help a family member, such as a child, who has been a victim of domestic violence, as well.

Whether leave taken under one of these statutes qualifies as FMLA leave depends on whether the employee has a serious health condition or is caring for a family member with a serious health condition. An employee who takes time off to appear in court to testify against her abuser might not qualify for FMLA leave; an employee who is hospitalized following a violent incident probably does. When an employee takes domestic violence leave, you should find out whether a serious health condition is present. If so, you should designate the leave accordingly.

Paid Sick Leave Laws

In 2011, Connecticut became the first state to require employers to provide paid sick leave to eligible employees. Since then, a number of other states have joined the trend. As we go to press, eight states and the District of Columbia require employers to offer at least a few days of paid sick leave each year, and many other states are considering enacting similar laws.

Each state has its own rules, but these laws typically allow employees to accrue paid sick leave at a certain rate (for example, one hour for every 30 hours worked), which they may then use when they are ill. These laws often allow employees to use their paid sick time to care for an ill family member or for reasons relating to domestic violence, as well. State laws requiring paid sick leave are covered in Appendix A, along with other state family and medical leave laws.

This is a fast-growing trend, and one sure to affect many employers. In 2017, for example, the large law firm Littler Mendelson asked employers what types of state and local laws had recently been enacted that impacted their business. The most popular answer—given by almost 60% of respondents—was paid leave laws. This is an area where the law is changing quickly, and requirements are brand new. If you have to change your paid leave policies as a result of a new state or local law, it's wise to get some legal help to make sure you've covered all of your bases.

Putting It All Together

Now that we've reviewed the most common types of state laws that provide leave for family and medical reasons, it's time to see how they might work with the FMLA when an employee needs time off. Here are a few examples that will help you see how the process works.

> **EXAMPLE 1:** Joan works for a company in California. She and her domestic partner, Betty, are expecting a baby in a couple of months; Joan is carrying the baby. Joan's doctor puts her on bed rest for the last four weeks of her pregnancy. Joan also wants to take some parental leave after the baby is born. What are her leave rights?

Under California law, Joan can take up to four months of pregnancy disability leave, taken concurrently with her 12 weeks of FMLA leave (as leave for a serious health condition). However, she gets an additional 12 weeks of parental leave under the California Family Rights Act (CFRA), which doesn't cover pregnancy disability. If Joan is disabled for the last four weeks of her pregnancy and another four weeks after the baby is born, she has used up eight weeks of FMLA leave. However, she is still entitled to 12 weeks of CFRA leave, which she can use for any purpose covered by that law—including time to bond with her child. This means Joan can take 24 weeks off in one block and still be entitled to job reinstatement (12 weeks of FMLA and pregnancy disability leave, plus 12 more weeks of CFRA leave). In fact, if she is disabled by pregnancy and childbirth for the full four months, she can take up to seven months of job-protected leave before returning to work (four months of pregnancy disability leave, the first 12 weeks of which are also FMLA leave, plus 12 more weeks of CFRA leave).

If Carla has accrued time off under California's paid sick leave law, she can use that to get paid during her pregnancy disability leave too.

EXAMPLE 2: Carla works for a company in Hawaii. Carla's boyfriend batters her son, who is hospitalized for his injuries. Under Hawaii law, Carla is entitled to up to 30 days of unpaid leave per year to deal with domestic violence issues. Hawaii also has a comprehensive family and medical leave law, which allows employees to take up to four weeks off per year to care for a family member with a serious health condition. What are Carla's leave rights?

If Carla takes three weeks off to care for her son, that time counts against her state family and medical leave entitlement, her FMLA entitlement, and her domestic violence leave entitlement. Carla may use her remaining domestic violence leave to relocate her family and seek a restraining order against her boyfriend. However, because that leave is not protected by either the FMLA or Hawaii's leave law, Carla is still entitled to one week of state family leave and nine weeks of FMLA leave in the same 12-month period.

EXAMPLE 3: David, a single father of three children, works for a company in Vermont. Vermont law allows him to take up to 24 hours of leave per year to participate in a child's school activities, take family members to routine medical or dental appointments, or respond to a family member's medical emergency. Vermont also has a comprehensive family and medical leave law that provides up to 12 weeks of leave in a year for the same reasons covered by the FMLA. What are David's leave rights?

If David uses his 24 hours of leave to attend parent-teacher conferences and take his children to regular medical and dental checkups, he still has 12 weeks of FMLA leave and state family and medical leave left to use. Because school activities and routine appointments are not covered by those laws, this time off doesn't count against his state or federal family and medical leave entitlement.

David can also use his accrued paid sick leave to get paid for some of this time off: Vermont's paid sick leave law covers not only time off for the employee's own illness, but also time spent caring for family members, taking family members to certain medical and professional appointments, and caring for family members when the school or other place where they usually spend the day is closed for public health or safety reasons.

EXAMPLE 4: Maek works for a company in Rhode Island. He has cerebral palsy and needs time off work occasionally for reasons related to his condition. Rhode Island law allows employees to take up to 13 weeks off every two calendar years for family and medical reasons, including the employee's own serious health condition. What are Maek's leave rights?

If Maek needs 13 weeks off in one year, the first 12 weeks use up his FMLA entitlement for that year; the final week is covered under state law only. Maek is not entitled to any additional state leave for the rest of that year or the following calendar year. However, Maek does have an additional 12 weeks of FMLA leave to use in the following year (when that leave year starts depends on how the company calculates its 12-month FMLA period; see Chapter 7). Maek's condition may also qualify as a disability under the ADA, in which case he may be entitled to additional time off as a reasonable accommodation. And, Maek may be entitled to pay for some of his time, under the state's paid sick leave law.

Workers' Compensation

Most employers in nearly all states are required to carry workers' compensation insurance (workers' comp), which covers medical bills and pays partial wage replacement to employees who are unable to work due to a work-related injury or illness. Typically, state law provides that an employee's injury or illness is covered by workers' comp if it is related to work, whether it occurs at the workplace during normal work hours or not. For example, injuries are typically covered if they happen during a workshift, while the employee is running a work errand, while the employee is traveling for business, or while the employee is attending a required work function (such as a company picnic or team-building event).

If an employee's serious health condition is due to a work-related injury or illness, both the FMLA and workers' comp might apply. In this situation, the employee would be entitled to up to 12 weeks of unpaid, job-protected leave under the FMLA, and to partial wage replacement, medical bill coverage, and perhaps some retraining or occupational therapy under workers' comp.

TIP

An employee who is out on workers' comp leave probably has a serious health condition under the FMLA. Under the laws of many states, an employee becomes entitled to temporary disability benefits under workers' comp only after being out of work for a specified waiting period (typically, at least three days). And, an employee seeking workers' comp benefits is usually being treated by a doctor. This adds up to incapacity of more than three days with continuing treatment by a health care provider: a serious health condition. The upshot for managers is this: Whenever an employee is out of work and receiving workers' comp benefits, you should designate that time as FMLA leave.

Workers' Comp Medical Inquiries

As explained in Chapter 9, employers have limited rights to request medical information under the FMLA. The employer may require the employee to submit a medical certification from a health care provider, giving some basic facts about the serious health condition that necessitates leave. However, the employer may not request additional information. Although the employer can, with the employee's consent, contact the employee's health care provider, this is only for the limited purpose of clarifying and authenticating the information on the medical certification form.

The workers' compensation statutes of most states allow quite a bit more contact between employers and health care providers. If an employee is on FMLA leave for a workers' comp injury, and the state's workers' comp law allows direct contact between the employer and the employee's health care provider, the FMLA doesn't prohibit that contact. In other words, the employer can still communicate with the health care provider in any way the workers' comp statute allows, as long as that communication relates to the employee's workers' comp injury.

Workers' comp is, of course, a very detailed and complicated system, which varies greatly from state to state. Our purpose here is not to explain your obligations under workers' comp law, but to highlight the areas where your obligations under the FMLA and workers' comp are most likely to overlap: light-duty assignments and reinstatement.

Light Duty

Under the FMLA, an employee with a serious health condition is entitled to leave for up to 12 weeks, until he or she is once again able to do the original job or one that is nearly identical to it. The employee doesn't have to come back early to a different position or "light duty" work, even if he or she is capable of lesser tasks or responsibilities.

Workers' comp is different. If the company offers a light-duty position that the employee is medically able to perform, the employee typically has to accept that position or lose his or her benefits under workers' comp. This is true even if the employee is on FMLA-protected leave.

An employee who decides to accept a light-duty position rather than remain on FMLA leave doesn't give up the right to be reinstated to his or her former position. However, the employee's right to reinstatement lasts only until the end of the 12-month FMLA leave year; if the employee is still unable to perform his or her old job by that time, the employee no longer has a right to return to it.

Reinstatement

Unlike the FMLA, workers' comp laws often don't place a time limit on how long an employee may be off before returning to work. But they typically don't give an employee the right to be reinstated, either. Although employers may not fire or discipline employees for making a worker's comp claim, most states do not explicitly prohibit an employer from firing an employee who is out with a workers' comp injury (for example, because the employer has to fill the position and cannot wait any longer for the employee to recuperate). Some states do require reinstatement, however; check with a lawyer to find out how your state deals with this issue.

An employee who is out with a workers' comp injury that is also a serious health condition under the FMLA is still entitled to only 12 weeks of job-protected leave. The fact that the employee has a workers' comp injury does not extend this protection. If the employee is unable to return to work after 12 weeks, the laws of some states allow the employer to terminate employment, unless the employee has a disability that requires reasonable accommodation (see "Americans with Disabilities Act (ADA)," above).

CAUTION

Talk to a lawyer before you fire someone with a workers' comp claim. Although the laws of your state may allow you to fire someone who is out on workers' comp leave (after the employee's FMLA leave entitlement has run out), that doesn't mean it's a good idea. Whenever you fire an employee who has exercised a legal right, you risk a retaliation lawsuit. Before you fire someone who is using workers' comp, consult with an experienced employment attorney.

State Disability Insurance and Paid Family Leave Programs

A handful of states (California, Hawaii, New Jersey, New York, and Rhode Island) have temporary disability insurance programs that provide partial wage replacement (typically funded by payroll deductions) to workers who are temporarily unable to do their jobs due to disability. California, New Jersey, New York, and Rhode Island also have paid family leave programs, which provide partial wage replacement to workers who need time off for parenting leave or to care for a seriously ill family member. (In 2020, paid family leave programs will go into effect in Washington and the District of Columbia.)

An employee who has a serious health condition, has a family member with a serious health condition, or takes time off to bond with a new child may be entitled to payment from one of these programs, depending on the state's eligibility requirements. However, not all of these laws give employees any substantive rights to a particular amount of time off or to job protection. Instead, some simply provide pay to employees who are otherwise entitled to time off, whether pursuant to the FMLA or some other law.

Common Mistakes Regarding Other Laws and Benefits—And How to Avoid Them

Mistake 1: Confusing the ADA's requirements with the FMLA's.

Avoid this mistake by taking the following steps:

- Figure out which law applies. An employee with a serious health condition doesn't always have a disability, and vice versa. If only one law applies, you don't have to comply with the other.

- Apply the most beneficial provisions to each situation. If both laws apply, the employee is entitled to the maximum protections available. This may depend on what the employee wants. If, for example, an employee qualifies for FMLA leave but wants to work with a reasonable accommodation, you must provide the accommodation. Conversely, if the employee could work with a reasonable accommodation but wants to take FMLA leave, you must provide leave.

- Remember that undue hardship doesn't apply to the FMLA. This is a common source of confusion: Although the ADA doesn't require an employer to provide a reasonable accommodation if it poses an undue hardship, no such defense applies to FMLA leave. The employer must provide the leave, no matter how difficult it might be. (The employer might not have to reinstate "key employees" if that would cause grievous economic harm to the company, however; see Chapter 11.)

- Consider additional time off or job modifications for employees who can't return to their old jobs. Although the FMLA entitles an employee to return to his or her former position (or an equivalent one) after using up leave, the ADA might entitle the employee to additional protections, such as more leave or changes to the job, as a reasonable accommodation for the disability. If it appears that an employee won't be able to return to work after completing FMLA leave, it's time to start thinking about reasonable accommodations.

Mistake 2: Forgetting to designate leave taken concurrently under the FMLA and other statutes as FMLA leave.

Avoid this mistake by taking the following steps:

- Always consider the FMLA when an employee takes time off for his or her own illness or injury. Some companies outsource their workers' compensation claims handling, then neglect to designate this time off as FMLA leave. Or, if an employee has had an obvious disability (for example, having to use a wheelchair) from his or her first day of work, you might be so accustomed to following the ADA that you forget to consider the FMLA when the employee needs leave.
- Think "FMLA" when an employee uses state temporary disability insurance programs. Any time for which the employee is reimbursed by one of these programs (in the states that have them) is almost always FMLA leave.
- Designate parenting leave—whether taken pursuant to state law, company policy, or otherwise—as FMLA leave. Parenting leave is FMLA leave, plain and simple.

Mistake 3: **Getting confused as to whether state leave laws apply.**

Avoid this mistake by taking the following steps:

- Many states have different standards than the FMLA. Whenever you're faced with a leave situation, start by determining which laws cover your company, the employee, and the reason for leave.
- Count leave only against the law that covers it. Sounds simple enough, but many managers have mistakenly counted state leave against an employee's FMLA entitlement when the reason for leave isn't covered by the FMLA. For example, if your state allows employees to take time off to care for grandparents, domestic partners, or in-laws, that time off cannot count against the employee's FMLA leave entitlement because the FMLA doesn't allow leave for those reasons.
- Pay careful attention to record keeping. If your company is subject to both the FMLA and a state leave law, you must designate leave under every law that applies and keep careful track of the employee's leave usage under each law. If an employee's leave is covered by one law and not the other, for example, you'll have to keep records of that fact so you and the employee know how much leave is still available for what purposes.

Do Other Laws Apply?

Americans with Disabilities Act (ADA)

Applies if:

- Employer has at least 15 employees.
- Employee has a disability: a physical or mental impairment that substantially limits one or more major life activities.
- Employee can perform the job's essential functions, with or without a reasonable accommodation.

Overlaps with the FMLA if:

- Employee has a serious health condition that also qualifies as a disability.

If the ADA and the FMLA both apply:

- Employee may be entitled to a reasonable accommodation instead of, or upon returning from, leave.
- Employee is entitled to take FMLA leave, if eligible, rather than accept a reasonable accommodation "light duty" position.
- Employee may be entitled to more leave than the FMLA requires as a reasonable accommodation.

Consolidated Omnibus Budget Reconciliation Act (COBRA)

Applies if:

- Employer has at least 20 employees.
- Employee receives benefits from employer's group health plan.
- Employee has a qualifying event that would otherwise end health coverage.

Overlaps with the FMLA if:

- Employee does not return from FMLA leave for any reason.
- Employee returns from FMLA leave to a position that does not offer health benefits.

If COBRA and the FMLA both apply:

- Employee (and/or employee's dependents, if covered by employer's group health plan) may receive continued benefits for 18 to 36 months, but must pay the entire premium.

Do Other Laws Apply? (continued)

Title VII

Applies if:

- Employer has at least 15 employees.

Overlaps with the FMLA if:

- Employer makes FMLA decisions on the basis of race, religion, or other protected characteristics.
- Employer treats men and women differently in administering the FMLA.
- Employer treats pregnancy leave different than other types of FMLA leave.

Uniformed Services Employment and Reemployment Rights Act (USERRA)

Applies if:

- Employee takes leave to serve in the Armed Forces.

If USERRA and the FMLA both apply:

- Time the employee spends on military leave protected by USERRA counts as months and hours worked for the employer, for purposes of calculating employee's eligibility for FMLA leave.

State Family and Medical Leave Laws

Apply if:

- Employer meets the coverage requirements of the state law: Some apply to smaller employers than the FMLA.
- Employee meets the eligibility requirements of the state law: Some require less time-in-service for eligibility.
- Employee is taking leave for a reason covered by the state law: Some allow leave for a wider variety of family members or for different conditions from the FMLA.

Overlap with the FMLA if:

- Employer is covered by both laws, employee is eligible for leave under both laws, and employee is taking leave for a reason covered by both laws.

If a state family and medical leave law and the FMLA both apply:

- Time the employee takes off counts against the employee's leave entitlement under both laws.

Do Other Laws Apply? (continued)

State Workers' Compensation Laws

Apply if:

- Employer is required to carry workers' compensation coverage (almost all are).
- Employee suffers a work-related injury or illness.

Overlap with the FMLA if:

- Employee's work-related injury or illness is also a serious health condition.

If a state worker's compensation law and the FMLA both apply:

- Employee cannot be required to accept a light-duty position; however, employee's workers' compensation benefits may cease if the employee chooses not to work light duty.
- Employee who cannot return from work after FMLA leave may still have some reinstatement rights under the state workers' compensation law.

State Temporary Disability Insurance and Paid Family Leave Programs

Apply if:

- Employee works in California, Hawaii, New Jersey, New York, or Rhode Island—and beginning in 2020, Washington or the District of Columbia.
- Employer is covered by the program, and employee is eligible for benefits from the program.
- Employee is temporarily unable to work due to disability or takes leave for parenting or to care for a seriously ill family member.

Overlap with the FMLA if:

- Employee's temporary disability is also a serious health condition under the FMLA.
- Employee is taking parenting leave or leave to care for a seriously ill family member that is also covered by the FMLA.

Do Other Laws Apply? (continued)

If a state temporary disability insurance program and the FMLA both apply:

- Time for which the employee is on leave and receiving compensation from the insurance program counts against the employee's FMLA leave entitlement.
- Employee may not be able to fully substitute paid leave, and employer may not be able to require employee to substitute paid leave, for time during which the employee is receiving compensation from the state program. However, employer and employee may agree that employee can use enough paid leave to bring the employee's total compensation to his or her usual salary. (See Chapter 8.)

Record-Keeping Requirements

Chapter Highlights

☆ Keep all FMLA documents and forms organized and readily accessible, for at least three years.

☆ Keeping accurate, organized records will help you:
- track employee hours for FMLA eligibility determinations
- track employee leave time taken and still available
- remember the dates that employees will return to work after leave
- remember when to request recertification of an employee on leave (see Chapter 8)
- show others (including the U.S. Department of Labor) that you have complied with the FMLA
- justify FMLA designations or other decisions, and
- protect confidential medical records.

☆ The three types of records you need to keep under the FMLA are:
- company-wide FMLA data
- individual employee FMLA records, and
- confidential medical records.

By now, you probably realize that you have to handle a lot of paperwork under the FMLA, what with notices, forms, and so on. While it may seem like a lot to keep track of, it's necessary to keep accurate records of employee FMLA eligibility, leave taken, and available leave time. You also need to keep the documents that employees taking FMLA leave are required to give you. Keeping all of these documents together in an organized, easily retrievable manner will make your job much easier as you manage FMLA leave and will help you stay out of legal trouble, too.

In this chapter, we explain what documents you need to maintain and provide some suggestions for the best way to keep them. Good document control will ensure that you meet all your obligations under the FMLA. It will also make it easier to respond if an employee ever challenges leave decisions or if a governmental agency conducts an investigation, as you will be able to quickly pull all of the documents showing that you followed the law.

Why You Should Keep Records

If your company is covered by the FMLA, the law requires you to "make, keep, and preserve" detailed records of FMLA leaves taken by employees, including copies of all notices given to, and received from, employees taking leave. Good organization of records is not just the law—it is also a good business practice. Thorough, accurate records help you keep track of how much leave each employee has taken or is eligible for, return dates for employees on leave, and other important information.

Keeping accurate records will also help you avoid expensive and time-consuming legal battles. You may have to show certain documents to the employee, his or her spokesperson, or even to the Department of Labor (DOL) if the agency decides to examine your company's FMLA practices. And, if any employee challenges your company's FMLA practices, you may have to gather certain documents to show that you provided adequate notices, denied leave based on adequate documentation, or treated the employee consistently with company policy and past practice. By putting all such records in separate files for each employee, you will be able to pull the exact document you need in any of these situations.

While the FMLA doesn't insist on a particular form or order for keeping the records, whatever form they are in must be clear and identifiable by date or pay period. They must be kept for at least three years and readily available for inspection, copying, and transcription by the DOL upon request. Records kept on a computer system must be available for transcription or copying upon request by the DOL as well.

> **TIP**
> **Do a regular checkup.** Keeping orderly FMLA records doesn't do you much good if the information is out of date or otherwise inaccurate. Be sure to periodically update the records so that they reflect recent leave taken by an employee, any changes in employee hours or FMLA status, or any other new data. A good way to do this is to review and update the files at the time of six-month or annual employee reviews.

Keeping Track of Company Workforce FMLA Data

If your company is covered by the FMLA, but none of its employees are eligible for FMLA leave (because, for example, none of them work within a 75-mile radius of 50 employees), you only need to keep basic payroll data, including:

- payroll records showing that your company is covered by the FMLA
- documents describing employee benefits (whether kept in hard copy or electronic form), and
- documents describing your company's paid and unpaid leave policies (whether kept in hard copy or electronic form).

Keep all of these company workforce records together for easy review. These records can be kept in your company's usual human resources area. The manager in charge of FMLA compliance should be tasked with controlling, updating, and maintaining these records.

Individual Employee Records

If your company has employees who are eligible for FMLA leave, you also need to keep records relating to those employees. These records include:

- basic payroll and identifying data for each employee, including:
  - name and address
  - occupation
  - rate of pay and terms of compensation
  - daily and weekly hours worked per pay period
  - additions to or deductions from wages, and
  - total compensation paid
- charts showing the dates FMLA leave is taken by each eligible employee (for example, from time records or requests for leave)
- charts of FMLA leave time available to each employee
- for FMLA leave of less than a full day, records of the hours of leave taken
- copies of notices of the need for FMLA leave given by each employee, if in writing
- copies of all general, eligibility, rights and responsibilities, and designation notices given by your company to each employee taking FMLA leave
- records confirming a family relationship, for employees who take leave for parenting or caring for a family member with a serious health condition
- copies of all certification forms for qualifying exigency leave
- records of premium payments for employee benefits
- subsequent notices issued to any employee on leave informing the employee of a change in FMLA information
- status reports received from employees on leave
- records of any dispute between an eligible employee and your company regarding designation of leave as FMLA leave, including:
  - any written statement of the reasons for designation from either your company or the employee
  - any written statements of the reasons for the disagreement from either your company or the employee, and
  - a written statement of how the dispute was resolved
- initial notice to a key employee that he or she might not be reinstated
- final notice to a key employee that reinstatement is denied
- notes, memos, letters, emails, or other documents that refer to the reason for any decision to grant or deny FMLA leave, including designation decisions, and
- confirmation that an employee has elected not to return from leave.

These records should be organized by employee but kept in a file separate and apart from the employee's regular personnel file. Each employee's FMLA file can be kept next to his or her personnel file. The manager in charge of FMLA compliance should oversee the control, updates, and maintenance of these files, with the assistance of each employee's immediate supervisor.

If your company is a joint employer with another company (see Chapter 2), your record-keeping duties depend on whether your company is the primary or secondary employer. As a primary employer, you must keep all of the records listed above. As a secondary employer, you must keep only the basic payroll data listed above.

If your company isn't required to keep overtime or minimum wage records for its FMLA-eligible employees (for example, because thay are exempt employees), you don't have to keep records of actual hours worked, provided that both of the following are true:

- Your company treats any employee employed for at least 12 months as eligible for FMLA leave.
- Your company reaches written agreement with any employee taking intermittent or reduced-schedule leave as to the employee's normal schedule or average hours worked each week.

TIP
For the sake of accuracy and convenience, your company should keep records of hours worked by all employees. This will make it easier for you to track employee FMLA eligibility, intermittent and reduced-schedule leave taken, and FMLA leave available.

Special rules apply to airline flight crew employees. In addition to keeping records of hours scheduled for airline flight crew employees, airline employers must maintain records that establish the applicable monthly guarantee for each category of employee covered by the guarantee. These records include relevant collective bargaining agreements or employer policies that establish the monthly guarantee.

Medical Records

When an employee requests FMLA leave for the employee's own serious medical condition, a family member's serious health condition, or a family member's military service-connected serious illness or injury, the employee has to give you certain documents containing medical information upon request. These medical records or any other documents containing medical information must be treated as confidential and kept in files separate and apart from your company's usual personnel files. Such records include:

- medical certifications
- recertifications
- medical histories of employees or their family members created for FMLA purposes
- fitness-for-duty certifications received from the employee when returning from FMLA leave, and
- second and third opinions you requested to verify a medical need for leave.

And, if the ADA also applies, you must keep the medical records in conformance with ADA confidentiality requirements. Under both the FMLA and the ADA, your company can disclose medical information only in the following circumstances:

- You can inform supervisors and managers of necessary restrictions on an employee's work or duties and any necessary accommodations.
- You can inform first aid and safety personnel if the employee's physical or medical condition might require emergency treatment.
- You must provide the information to government officials upon request.

(42 U.S.C. § 12112(d)(3); 29 C.F.R. § 1630.14(c).)

> **EXAMPLE:** Your employee, Cara, has disclosed to you that she is HIV positive and needs to take intermittent leave to attend medical appointments. One of your company's managers later asks you if you have noticed that Cara seems thin and listless. You tell the manager privately that Cara is ill but "doesn't have full-blown AIDS," so you hope she will be able to get treatment for her condition. You figure that a fellow manager who has expressed concern for an employee may be told about the employee's condition, as long as it is done privately. Have you acted lawfully?

Unfortunately, no. Cara's diagnosis is confidential medical information. You cannot disclose confidential medical information just because a manager is genuinely concerned, unless the manager needs to know because of restrictions on the employee's ability to work or the manager is a first aid provider at the worksite and the employee's condition may require emergency care.

CAUTION

The ADA's confidentiality rule applies to employee medical records even if the employee is not disabled. All employee medical records should be treated as confidential, regardless of whether or not the employee has a disability as defined by the ADA (see Chapter 12).

The confidentiality of employee medical records is also protected by the Health Insurance Portability and Accountability Act (HIPAA). (42 U.S.C. § 1320d and following.) In general, HIPAA bars an employer from discussing an employee's medical condition with the employee's health care provider unless the employee has consented to the discussion. There are exceptions to this general rule when health care is provided to the employee at the employer's request (for example, where the health care provider is retained by the employer in connection with the employer's medical benefits for employees).

You may need to ask for certain medical information covered by HIPAA in order to determine if a leave request is FMLA qualified. You can ask the employee to complete an incomplete medical certification or for a second opinion from a health care provider, and you may contact the health care provider in certain circumstances. (See Chapter 9 for a full discussion of how you can legally verify the medical reason for the leave.)

The Department of Labor regulations require your company to comply with the Genetic Information Nondiscrimination Act (GINA). Under GINA, all employers must treat any records that contain "family medical history" or "genetic information" as confidential, including records related to FMLA leave. An employer is allowed to disclose employee and/or family member genetic information in a manner that is consistent with the requirements of the FMLA.

RESOURCE
Learn more about GINA. GINA prohibits employers with 15 or more employees from discriminating against employees and applicants on the basis of genetic information. You can find a discussion of GINA and how to avoid violating the genetic discrimination law in *The Essential Guide to Handling Workplace Harassment & Discrimination,* by Deborah C. England (Nolo).

TIP
Add GINA language to FMLA certification forms. When requesting FMLA medical certifications or fitness-for-duty certifications for employees requesting or taking FMLA leave, your company has an obligation under GINA to instruct health care providers not to collect or provide any genetic information belonging to the employee or the employee's family member. To make sure you fulfill this requirement, add language to your company's medical and fitness-for-duty certification forms to include this instruction to health care providers. If you're using the DOL forms, they already contain the required GINA language.

SEE AN EXPERT
Get some record-keeping help. Consult an attorney with expertise in the ADA, HIPAA, and state medical records confidentiality laws to find out how you must handle employee medical records under these laws, as well as under the FMLA.

Review by the Department of Labor (DOL)

Another important reason to keep accurate records of FMLA leaves is because you may have to show these records to the DOL. You don't have to submit records to the DOL unless the DOL requests them. The DOL can ask to examine your company's FMLA records only once in a 12-month period, unless it suspects that the company may have violated the FMLA. DOL investigations occur in two circumstances:

- **Employee complaints.** Most frequently, DOL investigations are triggered by employee complaints, which the agency keeps confidential. The DOL won't tell you the name of the complaining employee, the nature of the complaint, or even if a complaint was made.

- **Industry investigations.** The DOL also selects certain types of businesses or industries to investigate because the agency believes they have a high rate of FMLA violations (for example, in industries that employ a high percentage of employees who don't speak English or have a lot of younger workers).

In a typical investigation, the DOL will do the following:

- **Examine the records listed above.** Even if investigating just a single complaint, the DOL may look at all your records. It may also take notes about, make transcriptions of, or make photocopies of the documents reviewed.

- **Interview certain employees.** Usually, these interviews will happen on company premises, but not always. The purpose of these interviews will be to verify the information in the records you presented and to confirm employees' particular hours.

- **Meet with your company representative.** The DOL will meet with someone with authority to make decisions and commit your company to corrective actions (for example, your FMLA compliance manager, if that person has such authority, or a company officer) if a violation is found.

Your company may (and probably should) be represented by an attorney during the investigation. And, after a finding is made, your company has the opportunity to present additional facts to the DOL for consideration. The DOL won't reveal information from your company's records to any unauthorized person.

Now You're Ready!

Congratulations! You've educated yourself on what the FMLA requires of your company and what it offers your employees. You have all of the tools you need to assess, administer, and track FMLA leave requests and time off, including forms, charts, posters, and sample policies. Now you and your employees can move forward together with the goal of keeping your workplace family friendly, healthy, and operating smoothly.

Common Mistakes Regarding Record Keeping—And How to Avoid Them

Mistake 1: **Losing track of the amount of FMLA-protected leave time an employee has available.**

Avoid this mistake by taking the following steps:

- Keep the payroll and leave records listed in this chapter organized and readily accessible.
- Consult those records whenever an employee requests FMLA leave.
- Update the information in the records periodically (for example, at the time of each employee's annual review).

Mistake 2: **Granting (or denying) an employee's requests for intermittent leave because you have lost track of how much leave the employee has already taken and when.**

Avoid this mistake by taking the following steps:

- Keep hourly or daily payroll and leave records for employees taking intermittent or reduced-schedule leave, depending on how the leave time is taken.
- Keep an updated intermittent or reduced-schedule leave chart for each employee taking such leave, including a running total of leave time taken and when (see Appendix C for a sample).

Mistake 3: **Improperly disclosing confidential employee medical information.**

Avoid this mistake by taking the following steps:

- Keep each employee's medical information in a separate file (not in the employee's personnel or FMLA file).
- Reveal medical information only when allowed by the law.

Managers' Checklist: Record Keeping

☐ I have collected all FMLA forms and documents for the employee and have put the documents into a file separate from the employee's personnel file, including:

  ☐ payroll records (showing FMLA eligibility or noneligibility)

  ☐ charts showing FMLA leave time taken and FMLA leave time available

  ☐ general, eligibility, rights and responsibilities, and designation notices provided to the employee

  ☐ notices and other documents provided by the employee, and

  ☐ periodic reports of employee status while on leave.

☐ I have kept a chart showing the running total in hours or days (depending on how the leave was taken) of intermittent or reduced-schedule FMLA leave time taken by the employee taking such leave.

☐ I have kept all employee (or employee family member) medical information in separate files.

☐ I have treated medical records and the information in them as confidential, barring others from gaining access to them except supervisors and managers to provide necessary accommodations or first aid personnel if a condition might require emergency medical treatment.

State Laws and Departments of Labor

This appendix summarizes basic information about each state's family and medical leave laws. We have included only laws that apply to private employers; laws that apply to government employers are not listed here. If your state is not included, it has no applicable leave laws as of 2017.

We have not included all state leave laws, only those that provide for family and medical leave. For example, we have not included state laws that require employers to give leave for military service, jury duty, or voting. We also have not included city laws, which might provide additional rights.

A number of states have laws that require employers to make reasonable accommodations for an employee's disability. As explained in Chapter 12, a reasonable accommodation could potentially include providing time off beyond what the FMLA or your state's family leave law explicitly requires. These disability laws are not included in the pages that follow. Similarly, almost half of the states require employers to provide reasonable accommodations for pregnant employees. These laws are included below only if they specifically mention time off as a possible accommodation.

The following categories of laws are included (each is explained in more detail in Chapter 12):

- **Family and medical leave laws.** These laws provide leave similar to the FMLA, such as leave for the employee's own serious health condition, leave to care for a seriously ill family member, and parental leave.
- **Paid sick leave laws.** These laws require employers to provide a set amount of paid sick time, which the employee can use for his or her own illness or other medical needs, or to care for a family member who is ill.
- **Military family leave laws.** These laws allow employees to take time off when certain family members are called to serve in the military.
- **Pregnancy disability leave laws.** These laws provide leave when a woman is disabled by pregnancy, childbirth, and related conditions.
- **Adoption leave laws.** These laws provide leave for adoption, generally by requiring employers who offer leave for childbirth to make the same leave available to adoptive parents.
- **Small necessities laws.** These laws provide leave for activities relating to a child's school and/or to take a child or elderly relative to routine medical and dental appointments.

- **Domestic violence leave laws.** These laws provide leave for an employee who has been, or whose family member has been, a victim of domestic violence.
- **Temporary disability insurance laws.** These laws provide partial wage replacement, often from a state fund to which employers and employees contribute, during the time when an employee is temporarily unable to work due to disability (including pregnancy).
- **Paid family leave laws.** These laws provide partial wage replacement— again, often from a state fund to which employers and employees contribute—to employees who take time off to spend with a new child or care for an ailing family member.

We provide some basic information on each law, including which employers are covered, which employees are eligible for leave, how much leave must be provided, and for what purposes. Unless otherwise stated, all leave is unpaid. We have not included every detail about every law including what constitutes a "serious health condition" under a state's rules, what a medical certification must include, whether employers have posting or record-keeping requirements, and so on. To find out more about your state's laws, including information on recently passed laws, contact your state's department of labor (contact information is at the end of this appendix). If you have any questions about how the FMLA interacts with your state's laws, consult with an experienced employment lawyer.

Arizona

Paid Sick Leave (Ariz. Rev. Stat. § 23-371 and following)

Covered Employers: All employers.

Eligible Employees: All employees.

Reasons for Leave: Employees may use paid sick leave:

- for the diagnosis, treatment, or care of a mental or physical illness, injury, or health condition of the employee or a family member
- for preventive care of the employee or a family member
- when the employee's place of business or the employee's child's school has been closed for a public health emergency, or when the employee or the employee's family member has been exposed to a communicable disease such that the person's presence in the community may jeopardize the health of others, or
- for specified purposes if the employee or a family member is a victim of sexual violence, domestic violence, abuse, or stalking.

Amount of Leave: Employees accrue one hour of paid sick leave for every 30 hours worked, up to 40 hours of paid leave each year for employers with 15 or more employees, or up to 24 hours of paid leave each year for employers with fewer than 15 employees. Employees hired after July 1, 2017 may be required to wait 90 days after hire to begin using accrued paid sick leave.

Family Members: Parents, children, spouse, grandparents, and siblings; domestic partner; spouse's or domestic partner's parents, children, grandparents, and siblings; any other person related by blood or affinity, whose relationship to the employee is equivalent to a family relationship.

California

Family and Medical Leave (Cal. Gov't. Code §§ 12945.2 and 12945.6)

Covered Employers: Employers with at least 20 employees for leave for the birth, adoption, or foster placement of a child; employers with at least 50 employees for all other types of leave.

Eligible Employees: Employees who have worked for at least one year and at least 1,250 hours in the 12 months preceding leave.

Reasons for Leave: For the birth, adoption, or foster placement of a child; for the employee's own serious health condition; or to care for a family member with a serious health condition. Disability for pregnancy, childbirth, and related conditions is not covered by this law. If both parents work for the same employer, they may be limited to a total of 12 weeks of leave for the birth, adoption, or foster placement of a child.

Amount of Leave: 12 weeks in a 12-month period.

Family Members: Same as FMLA, plus domestic partners and children of domestic partners.

Drug and Alcohol Rehabilitation Leave (Cal. Labor Code §§ 1025 to 1028)

Covered Employers: Employers with at least 25 employees.

Eligible Employees: All employees of covered employers.

Reasons for Leave: Employers must allow employees to take leave to voluntarily enter a drug or alcohol rehabilitation program as a reasonable accommodation, unless it would create an undue hardship.

Paid Sick Leave (Cal. Lab. Code §§ 245 to 249)

Covered Employers: All employers.

Eligible Employees: Employees who have worked at least 30 days in a year since beginning employment. Employees may begin using paid sick leave after 90 days of employment.

Reasons for Leave: Employees may use paid sick leave:
- for preventive care for the employee or a family member
- for the diagnosis, treatment, or care of an existing health condition of the employee or a family member, or
- for specified purposes if the employee is a victim of domestic violence, stalking, or sexual assault.

Amount of Leave: Employees accrue one hour of paid sick leave for every 30 hours worked, subject to a cap of 48 hours. Employers may limit the amount of leave an employee may use in one year to 24 hours.

Family Members: Parents, children, spouse, registered domestic partner, grandparents, grandchildren, and siblings.

Military Family Leave (Cal. Mil. & Vets. Code § 395.10)

Covered Employers: Employers with at least 25 employees.

Eligible Employees: Employees who work an average of 20 or more hours per week.

Reasons for Leave: While a spouse is on leave from deployment during a period of military conflict; the spouse must be a member of the National Guard or Reserves who has been deployed during a period of military conflict, or a member of the U.S. Armed Forces who has been deployed during a period of military conflict to an area that the president has designated as a combat theater or combat zone.

Amount of Leave: Up to ten days of unpaid leave in a qualified leave period (the time during which the spouse is on leave from deployment during a period of military conflict).

Pregnancy Disability Leave (Cal. Govt. Code § 12945)

Covered Employers: Employers with at least five employees.

Eligible Employees: All employees of covered employers.

Reasons for Leave: Disability relating to pregnancy, childbirth, or related conditions.

Amount of Leave: A reasonable period, not to exceed four months.

Small Necessities Law (Cal. Lab. Code § 230.8)

Covered Employers: Employers with at least 25 employees.

Eligible Employees: All employees of covered employers.

Reasons for Leave: To participate in activities at the child's school or day care.

Amount of Leave: Employees receive 40 hours of unpaid leave in any 12-month period, not to exceed eight hours in a single month. If both parents work for the same employer, employer may prohibit them from using this leave at the same time.

Domestic Violence Leave (Cal. Lab. Code §§ 230 and 230.1)

Covered Employers: All employers, for leave to obtain a restraining order; employers with at least 25 employees for a broader set of reasons.

Eligible Employees: Any employee who is the victim of sexual assault, stalking, or domestic violence.

Reasons for Leave

- **All Employers:** For the employee to obtain a restraining order or seek other judicial relief for the employee or his or her child.
- **Employers With 25 Employees:** For the employee to:
  - seek medical treatment
  - obtain services from a rape crisis center or domestic violence shelter or program
  - get counseling, or
  - engage in safety planning and/or relocate.

Amount of Leave: None stated. The law does not create a right to additional time off beyond what the FMLA provides for absences also covered by that law.

Temporary Disability Insurance

California has a state temporary disability insurance program, funded by withholdings from employees' paychecks. Eligible employees who are unable to work due to a temporarily disability (including pregnancy) can receive 60% or 70% of their usual wages, depending on their earnings. For more information, go to the state's website, www.edd.ca.gov/Disability.

Paid Family Leave

California's temporary disability insurance program also funds paid family leave. Eligible employees may collect the same benefits available for a temporary disability for up to six weeks in order to care for a seriously ill parent, spouse, domestic partner, or child, or to bond with a new child. For more information, go to the state's website, www.edd.ca.gov/Disability.

Colorado

Family and Medical Leave (Col. Rev. Stat. § 8-13.3-203)

Covered Employers: Employers covered by the FMLA.

Eligible Employees: Employees who are eligible under the FMLA.

Reasons for Leave: To care for a domestic partner or a partner in a civil union who has a serious health condition.

Amount of Leave: Same as allowed by the FMLA.

Family Members: Domestic partners or partners in a civil union. Same-sex spouses who were legally married in a state that recognizes same-sex marriage qualify as partners in a civil union under Colorado law.

Domestic Violence Leave (Col. Rev. Stat. § 24-34-402.7)

Covered Employers: Employers with at least 50 employees.

Eligible Employees: Employees who have worked at least 12 months and have been the victim of domestic violence, sexual assault, domestic abuse, or stalking.

Reasons for Leave: For the employee to:

- seek medical treatment or counseling for the employee or his or her children
- seek a civil protection order
- seek new housing or make an existing home secure, or
- seek legal assistance or attend court-related proceedings.

Amount of Leave: Three days in a 12-month period.

Adoption Leave (Col. Rev. Stat. § 19-5-211)

Covered Employers: All employers.

Eligible Employees: All employees.

Leave Provided: Employer that provides parental leave following the birth of a biological child must make the same amount of leave available to adoptive parents. This requirement does not apply to stepparent adoptions.

Connecticut

Paid Sick Leave for Service Workers (Conn. Gen. Stat. §§ 31-57r and following)

Covered Employers: Employers with at least 50 employees.

Eligible Employees: All service workers employed by covered employers. Service workers include nurses, restaurant and hotel staff, security guards, retail clerks, and many other job classifications, as listed in the law.

Reasons for Leave: Employees may use paid sick leave:
- for preventive medical care or for their own injury, illness, or health condition
- for the preventive medical care or the injury, illness, or health condition of a spouse or child, or
- to handle matters arising from domestic violence or sexual assault, including medical care, counseling, relocating, obtaining services from a victims' services group, or attending legal proceedings.

Amount of Leave: Employees are entitled to accrue one hour of paid sick leave for every 40 hours worked, up to 40 hours of paid sick leave per year.

Family and Medical Leave (Conn. Gen. Stat. §§ 31-51kk to 31-51qq)

Covered Employers: Employers with at least 75 employees, to be determined annually on October 1.

Eligible Employees: Employees who have worked for at least one year and at least 1,000 hours in the 12 months preceding leave.

Reasons for Leave: For the birth, adoption, or foster placement of a child; for the employee's own serious health condition; to care for a family member with a serious health condition; to handle certain qualifying exigencies (as defined in the FMLA) arising from a family member's military duty; or for organ or bone marrow donation.

Amount of Leave: 16 weeks in any 24-month period. The 24-month period begins on the first day of an employee's leave. Spouses who work for the same employer are entitled to a total of 16 weeks for the birth, adoption, or foster placement of a child and to care for a parent with a serious health condition.

Family Members: Same as FMLA, plus parents-in-law, domestic partners, and domestic partners' children.

Military Family Leave (Conn. Gen. Stat. § 31-51ll)

Covered Employers: Employers with at least 75 employees.

Eligible Employees: Employees who have worked for at least one year and at least 1,000 hours in the 12 months preceding leave.

Reasons for Leave: To care for a spouse, child, parent, or next of kin who is a current member of the Armed Forces and incurred a serious illness or injury in the line of duty.

Amount of Leave: 26 weeks in a single 12-month period. Like the FMLA, state law provides a per-servicemember, per-injury leave entitlement.

Pregnancy Disability Leave (Conn. Gen. Stat. § 46a-60(a)(7))

Covered Employers: Employers with at least three employees.

Eligible Employees: All employees of covered employers.

Reasons for Leave: Disability relating to pregnancy, childbirth, or related conditions.

Amount of Leave: A "reasonable" leave of absence.

Reinstatement: Employee is entitled to be restored to the same or an equivalent position, unless the employer's circumstances have changed such that this would be impossible or unreasonable.

Domestic Violence Leave (Conn. Gen. Stat. § 31-51ss)

Covered Employers: Employers with at least three employees.

Eligible Employees: All employees of covered employers.

Reasons for Leave: Employees who are victims of family violence may take leave to:
- seek medical care or psychological or other counseling
- obtain services from a victim assistance organization
- relocate, or
- participate in civil or criminal proceedings.

Amount of Leave: Up to 12 days of unpaid leave per calendar year. Employees may also use accrued paid leave during this time off, including compensatory time, vacation time, personal days, and so on.

District of Columbia

Family and Medical Leave (D.C. Code §§ 32-501 and following)

Covered Employers: Employers with at least 20 employees.

Eligible Employees: Employees who have worked for at least one year and at least 1,000 hours in the previous 12 months.

Reasons for Leave

- **Family Leave:** For the birth, adoption, or foster placement of a child; for the permanent placement of a child for whom the employee permanently assumes and discharges parental responsibility; or to care for a family member with a serious health condition.
- **Medical Leave:** For the employee's own serious health condition.

Amount of Leave: Sixteen weeks of family leave plus 16 weeks of medical leave in any 24-month period. Leave for birth, adoption, or placement of a child must be taken within 12 months of child's arrival. If two family members work for the same employer, they can be limited to a total of 16 weeks of family leave and can take no more than four weeks of such leave at the same time.

Family Members: Same as FMLA, plus anyone related by blood, custody, or marriage, and anyone sharing the employee's residence with whom the employee has a committed relationship.

Paid Sick, Family, and Domestic Violence Leave (D.C. Code §§ 32-531.01 and following)

Covered Employers: All, but leave depends on size.

Eligible Employees: All employees of covered employers. (Special rules apply to tipped employees of restaurants and bars.) Leave begins to accrue from the start of employment, but employees may not use leave for the first 90 days of employment.

Reasons for Leave: For the employee's or family member's physical or mental illness, injury, or medical condition; for the employee's or family member's medical care, diagnosis, or preventive medical care; for employee or family member who is a victim of stalking, domestic violence, or abuse to get medical attention, utilize services, seek counseling, relocate, take legal action, or take steps to enhance health and safety.

Amount of Leave:

- For employers with 100 or more employees, employees are entitled to accrue one hour of paid leave for every 37 hours worked, up to seven days of leave per year. Employers may cap employee use of leave at 56 hours per year.

- For employers with 25 to 99 employees, employees are entitled to accrue one hour of paid leave for every 43 hours worked, up to five days of leave per year. Employers may cap employee use of leave at 40 hours per year.

- For employers with fewer than 25 employees, employees are entitled to accrue one hour of paid leave for every 87 hours worked, up to three days of leave per year. Employers may cap employee use of leave at 24 hours per year.

Family Members: Same as the FMLA plus domestic partners, parents-in-law, grandchildren, children's spouses, siblings, siblings' spouses, a child who lives with the employee and whom the employee has responsibility for, and a person with whom the employee shares a mutual residence and committed relationship.

Small Necessities Law (D.C. Code §§ 32-521.01 and following)

Covered Employers: All employers.

Eligible Employees: All employees.

Reasons for Leave: To participate in school-related events, including activities sponsored by either a school or an associated organization such as a parent-teacher association. Activities may include meetings with a teacher or counselor as well as student performances and sports activities in which the child is a participant, not merely a spectator. Employer may deny a request for leave only if it would disrupt the employer's business and make the achievement of production or service delivery unusually difficult.

Family Members: Those who may take leave include not only parents, guardians, and stepparents, but also a child's aunts, uncles, and grandparents.

Amount of Leave: Twenty-four hours of unpaid leave in any 12-month period.

Universal Paid Leave

Beginning in July of 2020, the District of Columbia will begin a paid family leave program, funded by payroll taxes. Eligible employees will receive pay from the district for a combined total of eight weeks of leave: two weeks may be used for their own health conditions, six weeks may be used to care for an ailing family member, and eight weeks may be used to bond with a new child. The rules of this program have yet to be finalized; check the District's website, at https://does.dc.gov, for more information.

Florida

Domestic Violence Leave (Fla. Stat. § 741.313)

Covered Employers: Employers with 50 or more employees.

Eligible Employees: Employees who have been employed for at least three months and are victims of domestic or sexual violence, or who have a family or household member who is a victim of domestic or sexual violence.

Reasons for Leave: Leave is allowed to:
- seek an injunction
- get medical care or counseling
- get services from a victims' rights group, shelter, or rape crisis center
- relocate or make the home more secure, or
- seek legal assistance.

Amount of Leave: Up to three days of leave in a 12-month period. Leave may be paid or unpaid, at the employer's discretion.

Hawaii

Family and Medical Leave (Haw. Rev. Stat. §§ 398-1 to 398-11)

Covered Employers: Employers with at least 100 employees.

Eligible Employees: Employees who have worked for at least six consecutive months.

Reasons for Leave: Employee may take leave to care for a family member with a serious health condition or to care for a newly born or adopted child. Leave is not provided for employee's own serious health condition. Leave for a new child must be taken within a year of the child's birth or adoption.

Amount of Leave: Four weeks in any calendar year. Spouses who work for the same employer do not have to combine leave; each is entitled to four weeks.

Family Members: Same family members as FMLA, plus parents-in-law, grandparents, grandparents-in-law, siblings, and reciprocal beneficiaries.

Pregnancy Disability Leave (Haw. Admin. Rules § 12-46-108)

Covered Employers: All employers.

Eligible Employees: All employees.

Reasons for Leave: Employees may take leave while they are disabled due to pregnancy, childbirth, and related conditions.

Amount of Leave: A "reasonable" period of leave, as determined by the employee's physician.

Domestic Violence Leave (Haw. Rev. Stat. §§ 378-71 to 378-74)

Covered Employers: All employers.

Eligible Employees: Any employee who has worked at least six consecutive months and who is—or whose minor child is—a victim of domestic abuse, sexual assault, or stalking.

Reasons for Leave: Leave is allowed to:
- seek medical attention
- obtain victim services
- get counseling
- temporarily or permanently relocate, or
- take legal action.

Amount of Leave: A "reasonable period," up to 30 days in a calendar year if the employer has at least 50 employees, or up to five days for smaller employers.

Temporary Disability Insurance (TDI)

Hawaii has a state temporary disability insurance program. Eligible employees who are unable to work due to a temporary disability (including pregnancy) can receive compensation. Employers may self-insure by adopting a particular type of sick/disability leave program. For detailed information, go to the state's TDI website, www.labor.hawaii.gov/dcd.

Illinois

Military Family Leave (820 Ill. Comp. Stat. §§ 151/1 and following)

Covered Employers: Employers with at least 15 employees.

Eligible Employees: Employees who have worked for the employer for at least 12 months, have worked at least 1,250 hours in the past 12 months, and are the spouse or parent of someone who has been called to military service lasting longer than 30 days with the state or the United States, pursuant to an order of the governor or president.

Reasons for Leave: To spend time with a spouse or child whose federal or state deployment orders are in effect.

Amount of Leave:

- Employers with at least 50 employees must provide up to 30 days of unpaid leave.
- Employers with 15 to 49 employees must provide up to 15 days of unpaid leave.

Small Necessities Law (820 Ill. Comp. Stat. §§ 147/1 and following)

Covered Employers: Employers with at least 50 employees.

Eligible Employees: Employees who have worked for at least six consecutive months immediately preceding the leave request, and for at least as many hours per week, on average, as one-half of a full-time position.

Reasons for Leave: To attend school conferences or classroom activities relating to their children if they cannot be rescheduled during nonwork hours.

Amount of Leave: Eight hours of unpaid leave in any school year, with no more than four hours in one day.

Domestic Violence Leave (820 Ill. Comp. Stat. §§ 180/1 and following)

Covered Employers: All employers.

Eligible Employees: Any full-time or part-time employee who is a victim of domestic or sexual violence or has a family or household member who is a victim of domestic or sexual violence.

Reasons for Leave: Leave is allowed to:

- seek medical treatment
- obtain services from a victim services organization
- get counseling

- engage in safety planning, relocate, or otherwise take steps to increase the victim's safety, or
- seek legal assistance or remedies.

Amount of Leave: Up to 12 weeks of leave in a 12-month period for employers with 50 or more employees; eight weeks for employers with 15 to 49 employees; and four weeks for employers with 14 or fewer employees.

Pregnancy Disability Leave (775 Ill. Comp. Stat. § 5/2-102)

Covered Employers: Employers with at least 15 employees.

Eligible Employees: All employees of covered employers.

Reasons for Leave: As a reasonable accommodation for pregnancy, pregnant employees may be entitled to time off necessitated by pregnancy, childbirth, or medical or common conditions resulting from pregnancy or childbirth.

Child Bereavement Leave (820 Ill. Comp. Stat. § 154/1 and following)

Covered Employers: Employers with at least 50 employees.

Eligible Employees: Employees who have been employed for at least a year, have worked at least 1,250 hours in the previous 12 months for the employer, and who work at a site with 50 or more employees within a 75-mile radius.

Reasons for Leave: To grieve the death of a child, make arrangements necessitated by a child's death, or to attend a funeral or alternative to a funeral for a child.

Amount of Leave: Up to ten working days (two weeks), unpaid.

Family Members: A child is the employee's son or daughter, whether biological, adopted, foster, or stepchild; the employee's legal ward; or someone to whom the employee acts as a parent. The law doesn't specify an age limit.

Indiana

Military Family Leave (Ind. Code §§ 22-2-13-1 and following)

Covered Employers: Employers with at least 50 employees in at least 20 calendar workweeks.

Eligible Employees: Employees who have worked for at least 12 months, have worked at least 1,500 hours during the last 12 months for the employer, and are the spouse, parent, grandparent, or sibling of someone ordered to active duty for 90 days or more.

Reasons for Leave: For military family reasons:
- during the 30 days before the family member's active duty orders are in effect
- while the family member is on leave during active duty, or
- during the 30 days after the family member's active duty orders are terminated.

Amount of Leave: Up to ten days each year.

Iowa

Pregnancy Disability Leave (Iowa Code § 216.6(2))

Covered Employers: Employers with at least four employees.

Eligible Employees: All employees of covered employers.

Reasons for Leave: Disability relating to pregnancy, childbirth, or related conditions.

Amount of Leave: Unless employee is otherwise entitled to time off via sick leave, disability leave, or temporary disability insurance, employer must allow employee to take leave for the period of time she is disabled by the above conditions, or for eight weeks, whichever is shorter.

Kansas

Pregnancy Disability Leave (Kan. Admin. Regs. § 21-32-6)

Covered Employers: Employers with at least four employees.

Eligible Employees: All employees of covered employers.

Reasons for Leave: Disability relating to pregnancy, childbirth, miscarriage, abortion, or recovery from any of these conditions.

Amount of Leave: A "reasonable" period of leave.

Domestic Violence Leave (Kan. Stat. Ann. § 44-1132)

Covered Employers: Employers with at least four employees.

Eligible Employees: Any employee who is a victim of domestic violence or sexual assault.

Reasons for Leave: Leave is allowed to:

- seek a restraining order, injunctive relief, or any other relief to help ensure the health, safety, or welfare of the victim or the victim's children
- seek medical care
- seek services from a domestic violence program or shelter, or from a rape crisis center, or
- make court appearances.

Amount of Leave: Up to eight days per calendar year.

Kentucky

Adoption Leave (Ky. Rev. Stat. § 337.015)

Covered Employers: All employers.

Eligible Employees: All employees.

Reasons for Leave: For placement of an adoptive child under the age of seven.

Amount of Leave: Reasonable personal leave, not to exceed six weeks.

Louisiana

Pregnancy Disability Leave (La. Rev. Stat. §§ 23:341 and 23:342)

Covered Employers: Employers with 26 or more employees.

Eligible Employees: All employees of covered employers.

Reasons for Leave: Disability relating to pregnancy, childbirth, or related conditions.

Amount of Leave: Up to six weeks for normal pregnancy and childbirth; up to four months for more disabling pregnancies.

Small Necessities Law (La. Rev. Stat. §§ 23:1015 and following)

Covered Employers: All employers.

Eligible Employees: All employees.

Reasons for Leave: To attend, observe, or participate in conferences or classroom activities relating to their children (in school or day care) if they cannot be rescheduled during nonwork hours.

Amount of Leave: Sixteen hours of unpaid leave in any 12-month period.

Maine

Family and Medical Leave (Me. Rev. Stat. tit. 26, §§ 843 and following)

Covered Employers: Employers with at least 15 employees.

Eligible Employees: Employee who has worked for at least 12 consecutive months and works at a site with at least 15 employees.

Reasons for Leave: For the birth or adoption of a child; for the employee's own serious health condition; to care for a family member with a serious health condition; to be an organ donor; or for the death or serious health condition of a family member while on active duty.

Amount of Leave: Ten weeks in a two-year period.

Family Members: Same family members as FMLA, plus domestic partners, children of domestic partners, and siblings.

Military Family Leave (Me. Rev. Stat. tit. 26, § 814)

Covered Employers: Employers with 15 or more employees.

Eligible Employees: Employees who have worked for at least 12 months, have worked at least 1,250 hours in the past year, and are a spouse, domestic partner, or parent of a state resident who has been deployed for military service lasting longer than 180 days.

Reasons for Leave: For family military leave:
- during the 15 days prior to the family member's deployment
- during the family member's deployment, if the family member is granted leave, or
- for 15 days following the period of deployment.

Amount of Leave: Up to 15 days of leave per deployment.

Domestic Violence Leave (Me. Rev. Stat. tit. 26, § 850)

Covered Employers: All employers.

Eligible Employees: Any employee who has been a victim of violence, assault, sexual assault, stalking, or domestic violence, or whose parent, spouse, or child has been a victim.

Reasons for Leave: For the employee to:

- prepare for and attend court proceedings
- receive medical treatment or attend to medical treatment for a victim who is the employee's child, spouse, or parent, or
- obtain necessary services to deal with a crisis caused by domestic violence, stalking, or sexual assault.

Amount of Leave: "Reasonable and necessary" leave. Employer does not have to grant leave if: the employee's absence would cause undue hardship; the employee doesn't request leave within a reasonable time under the circumstances; or leave is impractical, unreasonable, or unnecessary under the circumstances.

Maryland

Parental Leave (Md. Code [Lab. & Empl.] § 3-1201 and following)

Covered Employers: Employers with 15 to 49 employees.

Eligible Employees: Employees who have been employed for at least a year, have worked at least 1,250 hours in the previous 12 months for the employer; and who work at a site with 15 or more employees within a 75-mile radius.

Reasons for Leave: For the birth of a child or the placement of an adopted or foster child.

Amount of Leave: Up to six weeks of unpaid leave in a 12-month period. However, employer may deny leave if it would cause substantive and grievous economic injury and notifies employee before leave begins.

Pregnancy Disability Leave (Md. Code [State Gov't] § 20-609)

Covered Employers: Employers with at least 15 employees.

Eligible Employees: All employees of covered employers.

Reasons for Leave: As a reasonable accommodation for pregnancy, pregnant employees may be entitled to time off work, unless it creates undue hardship for the employer.

Adoption Leave (Md. Code [Lab. & Empl.] § 3-801)

Covered Employers: All employers.

Eligible Employees: All employees.

Leave Provided: Employer that provides paid parental leave following the birth of a child must make the same amount of leave available to adoptive parents.

Military Family Leave (Md. Code [Lab. & Empl.] § 3-803

Covered Employers: Employers with at least 50 employees.

Eligible Employees: Employees who have worked for a covered employer for the last 12 months and for at least 1,250 hours in the last 12 months.

Reasons for Leave: Employees may take the day off when an immediate family member leaves for or returns from active military duty outside of the United States.

Amount of Leave: One day.

Massachusetts

Paid Sick Leave (Mass. Gen. Laws ch. 149, § 148C)

Covered Employers: All employers. However, employers with ten or fewer employees must provide only unpaid leave, not paid leave.

Eligible Employees: All employees of covered employers. Leave begins to accrue from the start of employment, but employees may not use leave for the first 90 days of employment.

Reasons for Leave: Employee may take paid sick leave to:

- attend routine medical or dental appointments, for the employee or a family member
- for the employee's or a family member's physical or mental illness, injury, or medical condition that requires home care, professional care for treatment or diagnosis, or preventative medical care, or
- to address the psychological, physical, or legal effects of domestic violence on the employee or the employee's dependent child.

Amount of Leave: Employees must accrue one hour of leave for every 30 hours worked, up to 40 hours of paid sick leave per year.

Family members: Parents, spouses, children, and parents-in-law.

Small Necessities Law (Mass. Gen. Laws ch. 149, § 52D)

Covered Employers: Employers with at least 50 employees.

Eligible Employees: Employees who are eligible under the FMLA.

Reasons for Leave: Employee may take leave to:

- participate in school activities directly related to the educational advancement of the employee's child, such as parent-teacher conferences or interviewing for a new school
- accompany the employee's child to routine medical or dental appointments, and
- accompany an elderly relative (someone who is related to the employee by blood or marriage and is at least 60 years old) to routine medical or dental appointments or appointments for other professional services relating to the relative's care.

Amount of Leave: Twenty-four hours in any 12-month period. This leave is in addition to FMLA leave.

Parental Leave (Mass. Gen. Laws ch. 149, § 105D)

Covered Employers: Employers with at least six employees.

Eligible Employees: Employees who have completed the employer's probationary period, or if there is no probationary period, employees who have worked for the employer for three months.

Reasons for Leave: For birth or adoption of a child.

Amount of Leave: Up to eight weeks of leave. If employer's policies provide for longer leave, the additional period of leave is treated as protected under this law, unless the employer notifies the employee otherwise before leave commences.

Pregnancy Disability Leave (Mass. Gen. Laws ch. 151B, § 4)

Covered Employers: Employers with at least six employees.

Eligible Employees: All employees.

Reasons for Leave: Employers must make reasonable accommodations for pregnant employees, which might include time off to attend to a pregnancy complication or recover from childbirth.

Amount of Leave: None specified.

Domestic Violence Leave (Mass. Gen. Laws ch. 149, § 52E)

Covered Employers: Employers with at least 50 employees.

Eligible Employees: Employees who are victims of abusive behavior (domestic violence, stalking, sexual assault, or kidnapping) or family members of such victims.

Reasons for Leave: Employee may take leave to:
- seek medical care, counseling, victim services or legal assistance
- obtain housing
- get a protective order
- appear in court or before a grand jury
- meet with a district attorney or another law enforcement official
- attend child custody proceedings, or
- deal with other issues directly related to the abusive behavior against the employee or the employee's family member.

Amount of Leave: Up to 15 days in a 12-month period.

Minnesota

Family and Medical Leave (Minn. Stat. §§ 181.940 and following)

Covered Employers: Employers with at least 21 employees.

Eligible Employees: Employees who have worked for at least 12 months for the employer and at least half-time during the 12 months immediately prior to requesting leave.

Reasons for Leave: Leave is available for:
- the birth or adoption of a child, or
- prenatal care or incapacity due to pregnancy, childbirth, or related conditions.

Amount of Leave: Up to 12 weeks. Parental leave must begin within 12 months of the child's arrival; if child has to stay in the hospital longer than the mother, leave may begin within 12 months of the child's discharge.

Military Family Leave (Minn. Stat. §§ 181.947 and 181.948)

Covered Employers: All employers.

Eligible Employees: Employees with a grandparent, parent, legal guardian, sibling, child, grandchild, spouse, or fiancé on active duty.

Reasons for Leave: Leave is available:
- to attend a send-off or homecoming ceremony for the family member, or
- if a family member is injured or killed in active service.

Amount of Leave:
- To attend ceremony, only time necessary may be taken, up to one day per calendar year.
- If a family member is injured or killed, up to ten days of leave.

Small Necessities Law (Minn. Stat. Ann. § 181.9412)

Covered Employers: All employers.

Eligible Employees: Employees who have worked at least half time.

Reasons for Leave: To attend school conferences or other school-related activities for the employee's child, if they cannot be scheduled during nonwork hours.

Amount of Leave: Sixteen hours of unpaid leave in any 12-month period.

Domestic Violence Leave (Minn. Stat. § 518B.01(23))

Covered Employers: All employers.

Eligible Employees: Employees who are victims of domestic abuse.

Reasons for Leave: Leave is available to seek an order for protection from domestic abuse.

Amount of Leave: "Reasonable" time off work.

Montana

Pregnancy Disability Leave (Mont. Code Ann. §§ 49-2-310 and 49-2-311)

Covered Employers: All employers.

Eligible Employees: All employees.

Reasons for Leave: Pregnancy-related disability.

Amount of Leave: "Reasonable" leave of absence for pregnancy.

Reinstatement: Employer must reinstate employee to the same or an equivalent position, unless the employer's circumstances have changed so much that it would be impossible or unreasonable to do so.

Nebraska

Military Family Leave (Neb. Rev. Stat. §§ 55-501 and following)

Covered Employers: Employers with 15 or more employees.

Eligible Employees: Employees who have worked for at least 12 months for the employer, have worked at least 1,250 hours during the past 12 months, and are the spouse or parent of someone called to military service of at least 179 days, for the state or the United States, on orders of the governor or the president.

Reasons for Leave: For family military leave while state or federal deployment orders are in effect.

Amount of Leave:

- Employers with 50 or more employees must provide up to 30 days of leave.
- Employers with 15 to 49 employees must provide up to 15 days of leave.

Adoption Leave (Neb. Rev. Stat. § 48-234)

Covered Employers: All employers.

Eligible Employees: All employees.

Leave Provided: Employer that provides parental leave following the birth of a child must make the same leave available to parents who adopt a child under the age of nine or a special needs child under the age of 19. Employer does not have to provide leave for stepparent or foster parent adoptions.

Nevada

Small Necessities Law (Nev. Rev. Stat. §§ 392.920 and 392.4577)

Covered Employers: Employers with at least 50 employees for time off provision; all employers for nonretaliation provision.

Eligible Employees: All employees.

Reasons for Leave: Employees may take time off to:
- attend parent-teacher conferences
- attend a child's school activities during school hours
- attend a child's school-sponsored events, and
- volunteer or otherwise be involved at the child's school.

Amount of Leave: Four hours per school year.

Nonretaliation: No employer, regardless of size, may fire, or threaten to fire, an employee who appears at a conference requested by an administrator of his or her child's school, or who is notified, during work hours, of an emergency regarding the child.

Domestic Violence Leave (2017 NV S.B. 361)

Covered Employers: All employers.

Eligible Employees: Employees who have worked for the employer for at least 90 days.

Reasons for Leave: Employees who are victims of domestic violence, or whose family members are victims, may take leave:
- for diagnosis, care, or treatment of a health condition related to domestic violence
- to obtain counseling or assistance
- to participate in court proceedings, or
- to engage in safety planning.

Amount of Leave: Up to 160 hours in a 12-month period.

Family members: Spouses, domestic partners, minor children, parents, or other adults who are either related to the employee within the first degree of affinity or blood, or who were actually residing with the employee when the domestic violence took place.

New Hampshire

Pregnancy Disability Leave (N.H. Rev. Stat. § 354-A:7)

Covered Employers: Employers with at least six employees.

Eligible Employees: All employees of covered employers.

Reasons for Leave: Disability relating to pregnancy, childbirth, or related conditions.

Amount of Leave: The period of time during which the employee has a disability relating to the above conditions.

Reinstatement: Employee is entitled to be restored to the same or a comparable position, unless business necessity makes this impossible or unreasonable.

New Jersey

Family and Medical Leave (N.J. Stat. §§ 34:11B-1 and following)

Covered Employers: Employers with at least 50 employees.

Eligible Employees: Employees who have worked for at least one year and at least 1,000 hours in the previous 12 months.

Types of Leave: To care for a family member with a serious health condition, or to care for a newly born or adopted child. Leave for a new child must begin within one year of the child's birth or adoption. Employees are not entitled to leave for their own serious health conditions.

Amount of Leave: Twelve weeks in any 24-month period.

Family Members: Same family members as FMLA, plus parents-in-law and partners in a civil union.

Domestic Violence Leave (N.J. Stat. §§ 34:11C-1 and following)

Covered Employers: Employers with at least 25 employees.

Eligible Employees: Employees who have worked for the employer for at least 12 months, and at least 1,000 hours in the 12 months prior to taking leave.

Types of Leave: Employees who are victims of domestic violence or sexual violence, or whose family members are victims, may take leave to:

- seek medical attention or recover from physical or psychological injuries
- seek help from a victim services organization
- seek counseling
- participate in safety planning, relocate, or take other steps to ensure the future physical safety and economic security of the employee or family member victim
- seek legal assistance or prepare for legal proceedings, or
- attend court proceedings.

Amount of Leave: Up to 20 days in a 12-month period.

Temporary Disability Insurance (TDI)

New Jersey has a state temporary disability insurance program. Eligible employees who are unable to work due to a temporary disability (including pregnancy) can receive up to two-thirds of their wages, up to a maximum amount.

Paid Family Leave

New Jersey's temporary disability insurance program also funds paid family leave. Eligible employees may collect the same benefits available for a temporary disability for up to six weeks to care for a seriously ill family member or bond with a new child. For information on New Jersey's TDI and paid family leave programs, go to the website of the New Jersey Department of Labor and Workforce Development, http://lwd.state.nj.us.

New Mexico

Domestic Violence Leave (N.M. Stat. §§ 50-4A-1 and following)

Covered Employers: All employers.

Eligible Employees: Employees who have been victims of, or whose family members have been victims of, domestic abuse.

Types of Leave: Employees may take leave to:
- seek an order of protection or other judicial relief
- meet with law enforcement officials
- consult with attorneys or victim advocates, or
- attend court proceedings relating to the domestic abuse.

Amount of Leave: Up to 14 days of leave per year. Leave may be taken intermittently or in increments of up to eight hours per day.

New York

Military Family Leave (N.Y. Lab. Law § 202-i)

Covered Employers: Employers with 20 or more employees at one or more sites.

Eligible Employees: Employees who work an average of 20 or more hours per week and are spouses of a member of the National Guard, Reserves, or Armed Forces deployed during a period of military combat to a combat theater or combat zone of operations.

Reasons for Leave: While the spouse is on leave during deployment.

Amount of Leave: Up to ten days.

Adoption Leave (N.Y. Lab. Law § 201-c)

Covered Employers: All employers.

Eligible Employees: All employees.

Leave Provided: Employer that provides parental leave for the birth of a biological child must make the same amount of leave available for adoption of a child who is preschool age or younger, or up to age 18 if the child is disabled.

Temporary Disability Benefits (TDI)

New York has a state temporary disability insurance program. Eligible employees who are unable to work due to a temporary disability (including pregnancy) can receive up to 50% of their wages. For detailed information, go to the state website for workers' compensation, www.wcb.ny.gov. Select "Employers/Businesses," then scroll down to "Disability Benefits."

Paid Family Leave

Beginning on January 1, 2018, virtually all New York employers must carry paid family leave insurance, funded entirely or partly by withholdings from employee pay. Partial wage replacement will be provided to employees who need time off to bond with a new child, care for a family member with a serious health condition, or handle matters relating to a family member's deployment to active military duty. Like other states with similar programs, New York's program pays employees a percentage of their usual wages, set to increase each year from 50% in 2018 to 67% in 2021. Unlike other states, however, New York's program is a true family and medical leave statute, meaning that it also guarantees employees the right to health insurance continuation and reinstatement when their leave is over. Eligible employees are entitled to eight weeks of leave in 2018, ten weeks of leave in 2019 and 2020, and 12 weeks of leave in 2021. Learn more about this new program at www.ny.gov/new-york-state-paid-family-leave/paid-family-leave-information-employers.

North Carolina

Domestic Violence Leave (N.C. Gen. Stat. § 50B-5.5)

Covered Employers: All employers.

Eligible Employees: All employees.

Amount of Leave: Employer may not fire, discipline, demote, or refuse to promote an employee who takes "reasonable time" off work.

Reasons for Leave: To obtain or attempt to obtain an order of protection from domestic violence for the employee or a minor child.

Small Necessities Law (N.C. Gen. Stat. § 95-28.3)

Covered Employers: All employers.

Eligible Employees: All employees.

Reasons for Leave: To attend or otherwise be involved in a child's school.

Amount of Leave: Four hours of unpaid leave per year.

Ohio

Military Family Leave (Ohio Rev. Code § 5906)

Covered Employers: Employers with at least 50 employees.

Eligible Employees: Employees who have worked at least 12 consecutive months, and at least 1,250 hours in the previous 12 months, for the employer.

Reasons for Leave: To care for a parent, spouse, child, or person for whom the employee is a legal guardian, who:

- is called to active military duty to last more than 30 days, or
- is injured, wounded, or hospitalized while on active military duty.

Amount of Leave: Up to ten workdays or 80 hours, whichever is less.

Oregon

Family and Medical Leave (Or. Rev. Stat. §§ 659A.150 and following)

Covered Employers: Employers with at least 25 employees.

Eligible Employees

- **Parental Leave:** Employee must have worked at least 180 days for the employer before leave is scheduled to begin.
- **All Other Types of Leave:** Employee must have worked at least 180 days for the employer and at least 25 hours per week during the 180 days immediately preceding the start of leave.

Reasons for Leave

- **Parental Leave:** For the birth or adoption of a child, or the placement of a foster child.
- **Serious Health Condition Leave:** To care for a family member with a serious health condition or for the employee's own serious health condition.
- **Bereavement:** To deal with the death of a family member.
- **Pregnancy Disability Leave:** For prenatal care or pregnancy disability.
- **Sick Child Leave:** To care for a sick child who does not have a serious health condition but requires home care. Employer does not have to allow employee to take sick child leave if another family member is willing and able to care for the child.

Amount of Leave: Twelve weeks within any one-year period (including up to two weeks of bereavement leave per family member), with the following additional entitlements:

- An employee who takes 12 weeks of any other leave may take an additional 12 weeks of pregnancy disability leave.
- An employee who takes 12 weeks of parental leave may take an additional 12 weeks of sick child leave.
- An employee may combine these entitlements to take up to 36 weeks of leave: 12 for pregnancy disability, 12 for parental leave, and 12 for sick child leave.

Two family members (including spouses) who work for the same employer are each entitled to 12 weeks of leave, but the employer does not have to allow them to take this leave at the same time unless (1) both have serious health conditions; (2) one has a serious health condition and the other needs to care for him or her; or (3) one has a serious health condition and the other needs to care for a child who has a serious health condition.

Family Members: Same family members as FMLA, plus parents-in-law, domestic partners, grandparents, grandchildren, and the parents and children of domestic partners.

Paid Sick Leave (Or. Rev. Stat. § 653.601 and following)

Covered Employers: All employers. Employers with fewer than ten employees (or fewer than six, in Portland) must provide only unpaid leave, not paid leave.

Eligible Employees: All employees of covered employers. Leave begins to accrue from the start of employment, but employees may not use leave for the first 90 days of employment.

Reasons for Leave: Employee may take sick leave:

- for the employee's or a family member's physical or mental illness or health condition (including preventative care, treatment, and recovery)
- to bond with a new child
- to care for a child who has a non-serious health condition or illness
- for bereavement following the death of a family member
- to seek medical attention, legal assistance, counseling, and other services relating to domestic violence, stalking, harassment, or assault against the employee or the employee's minor child or dependent, or
- for certain public health emergencies, including the closure of a child's school.

Amount of Leave: Employees must accrue one hour of leave for every 30 hours worked; alternatively, employers may give employees 40 hours of sick time at the start of the year. Employers may limit employees to using 40 hours of sick time per year and may cap accrual at 80 hours.

Family members: Same family members as FMLA, plus parents-in-law, domestic partners, grandparents, grandchildren, and the parents and children of domestic partners.

Military Family Leave (Or. Rev. Stat. §§ 659A.090 and following)

Covered Employers: Employers with at least 25 employees.

Eligible Employees: Employees who work an average of 20 or more hours per week.

Reasons for Leave: Employee may take military family leave when spouse or same-sex domestic partner is called to active military duty or deployed.

Amount of Leave: Employee may take up to 14 days of leave per deployment:

- after notice of spouse's or same-sex domestic partner's call to active military duty but before spouse or same-sex domestic partner is deployed, and
- while spouse or same-sex domestic partner is on leave from deployment.

This time off counts against the employee's total leave entitlement under the state's family and medical leave law.

Domestic Violence Leave (Or. Rev. Stat. §§ 659A.270 and following)

Covered Employers: Employers with six or more employees.

Eligible Employees: Employees who have worked an average of 25 or more hours per week for 180 days and are the victims of, or the parent or guardian of a minor child who is a victim of, domestic violence, stalking, or sexual assault.

Reasons for Leave: Leave is available to:

- seek legal remedies or the assistance of law enforcement, including a protective order
- seek medical treatment or recuperate from injuries
- attend counseling
- obtain services from a victim services provider, or
- relocate or make the home safe.

Amount of Leave: "Reasonable" leave.

Rhode Island

Family and Medical Leave (R.I. Gen. Laws §§ 28-48-1 and following)

Covered Employers: Employers with at least 50 employees.

Eligible Employees: Full-time employees who average at least 30 hours of work per week and have been employed for at least 12 consecutive months.

Reasons for Leave
- **Family Leave:** For the employee's own serious illness or to care for a family member with a serious illness.
- **Parental Leave:** For the birth or adoption of a child.

Amount of Leave: Thirteen weeks in any two calendar years.

Family Members: Same family members as FMLA, plus parents-in-law.

Paid Sick Leave (R.I. Gen. Laws § 28-57-1 and following)

Note: This law goes into effect on July 1, 2018.

Covered Employers: Employers with 18 or more employees must provide paid leave; employers with 17 or fewer employees must provide unpaid leave.

Eligible Employees: All employees of covered employers. Leave begins to accrue from the start of employment, but employees may not use leave for the first 90 days of employment. (Employers may adopt longer waiting periods for temporary and seasonal employees.)

Reasons for Leave: Employee may take sick leave:
- for the employee's or a family member's physical or mental illness or health condition (including diagnosis, preventative care, treatment, and recovery)
- when needed due to domestic violence, stalking, or sexual assault against the employee or the employee's family member, or
- when the employee's place of business or the employee's child's school has been closed for a public health emergency, or when the employee or the employee's family member has been exposed to a communicable disease such that the person's presence in the community may jeopardize the health of others.

Amount of Leave: Employees must accrue one hour of leave for every 35 hours worked, up to 24 hours of sick leave in 2018, 32 hours in 2019, and 40 hours in 2020. These are the same amounts employees may use in each of these years. This time is paid leave, unless the employer has 17 or fewer employees.

Family Members: Same family members as FMLA, plus parents-in-law, domestic partners, grandparents, grandchildren, siblings, the parents and children of domestic partners, any other person in the employee's household, and any other person for whom the employee is responsible for arranging care relating to safety or health.

Pregnancy Disability Leave (R.I. Gen. Laws § 28-7.4)

Covered Employers: Employers with at least four employees.

Eligible Employees: All employees.

Reasons for Leave: Employers must make reasonable accommodations for pregnant employees, which might include time off to recover from childbirth.

Amount of Leave: None specified.

Military Family Leave (R.I. Gen. Laws § 30-33-1)

Covered Employers: Employers with at least 15 employees.

Eligible Employees: Employees who have worked at least 12 months, have worked at least 1,250 hours in the last 12 months for the employer, and are the spouse or parent of someone who has been called to military service lasting more than 30 days in the state or the United States, by orders of the governor or the president.

Reasons for Leave: For family military leave while federal or state orders are in effect.

Amount of Leave:

- Employers with 50 or more employees must allow employees to take up to 30 days of leave.
- Employers with 15 to 49 employees must allow employees to take up to 15 days of leave.

Small Necessities Law (R.I. Gen. Laws § 28-48-12)

Covered Employers: Employers with at least 50 employees.

Eligible Employees: Full-time employees who average at least 30 hours of work per week and have been employed by the same employer for at least 12 consecutive months.

Reasons for Leave: To attend school conferences or other school-related activities for the employee's child.

Amount of Leave: Ten hours of unpaid leave in any 12-month period.

Procedural Requirements

- **Notice:** Employee must provide at least 24 hours' notice of need for leave and must make a reasonable effort to schedule leave so as not to unduly disrupt employer's operations.
- **Paid Leave:** Employee may substitute accrued paid vacation or other appropriate paid leave.

Temporary Disability Insurance (TDI)

Rhode Island has a state temporary disability insurance program, funded by withholdings from employees' paychecks. Eligible employees who are unable to work due to a temporary disability (including pregnancy) can receive $89 to $831 per week for 30 weeks. Employees may also receive salary, paid sick leave, or vacation time from their employer while receiving temporary disability payments and may receive benefits while working part time due to a temporary disability. For detailed information, go to the state's TDI website, www.dlt.ri.gov/tdi.

Temporary Caregiver Insurance Program (TCI)

Starting in 2014, Rhode Island expanded its temporary disability insurance program to include a small amount of paid family leave. Employees may receive up to four weeks of partial wage replacement when they take time off to bond with a new child or care for a seriously ill child, spouse, parent, grandparent, parent-in-law, or domestic partner.

Tennessee

Family and Medical Leave Law (Tenn. Code § 4-21-408)

Covered Employers: Employers with at least 100 full-time employees at the jobsite or location where the employee works.

Eligible Employees: Employees who have worked full-time for at least 12 consecutive months.

Reasons for Leave: For pregnancy, childbirth, nursing an infant, and adoption.

Amount of Leave: Up to four months.

Texas

Foster Parent Leave (Tex. Labor Code § 21.0595)

Covered Employers: All employers.

Eligible Employees: All employees.

Leave Provided: All employers that provide personal leave for employees to assist or care for a sick child must make the same leave available to assist or care for foster children.

Vermont

Family and Medical Leave Law (21 Vt. Stat. §§ 470 and following)

Covered Employers

- **Parental Leave:** Employers with at least 10 employees.
- **Family Leave:** Employers with at least 15 employees.

Eligible Employees: Employees who have been continuously employed for one year, for an average of at least 30 hours per week.

Reasons for Leave

- **Parental Leave:** (1) During the employee's pregnancy and following the birth of an employee's child, and (2) within a year after the initial placement of an adopted child up to 16 years old.
- **Family Leave:** For the employee's own illness or to care for the employee's family member.

Amount of Leave: Up to 12 weeks in a 12-month period. Spouses working for same employer are entitled to 12 weeks each; they need not combine leave.

Family Members: Includes all family members covered by FMLA plus parents-in-law and employee's civil union partner.

Paid Sick Leave (21 Vt. Stat. § 481 to 486)

Covered Employers: All employers; new employers do not have to comply until one year after they hire their first employee.

Eligible Employees: Most employees of covered employers who work an average of 18 hours or more per week. Leave begins to accrue from the start of employment, but employers may require employees to wait up to one year before using accrued leave.

Reasons for Leave: Employee may take sick leave:

- for the employee's or a family member's illness or injury (including diagnosis, preventative care, therapeutic care, or routine care)
- to accompany a spouse, parent, grandparent, or parent-in-law to appointments regarding long-term care
- to arrange for legal, medical, social, or counseling services for the employee or a family member who has been a victim of domestic violence, stalking, or sexual assault, or
- to care for a family member when the school or business where that person usually spends the day is closed due to public health or safety reasons.

Amount of Leave: Employees must accrue one hour of leave for every 52 hours worked. Employers may limit use of leave to 24 hours in 2018 and 40 hours in subsequent years.

Family Members: Same family members as FMLA, plus parents-in-law, grandparents, grandchildren, and siblings.

Small Necessities Law (21 Vt. Stat. § 472a)

Covered Employers: Employers with at least 15 employees.

Eligible Employees: Employees who have been continuously employed for one year, for an average of at least 30 hours per week.

Amount of Leave: Twenty-four hours in a 12-month period; not more than four hours may be taken in any 30-day period. Employer may require employee to take at least two hours of leave at a time.

Reasons for Leave: For the employee to:

- participate in school activities directly related to the academic educational advancement of the employee's child, stepchild, foster child, or ward
- attend or accompany a family member to routine medical or dental appointments
- accompany the employee's parent, spouse, or parent-in-law to appointments for professional services related to their care and well-being, and
- respond to a medical emergency involving a family member.

Washington

Family and Medical Leave Law (Wash. Rev. Code §§ 49.78.010 and following)

Covered Employers: Employers with at least 50 employees.

Eligible Employees: Employees who have worked for at least a year and at least 1,250 hours during the previous year.

Reasons for Leave: For the birth, adoption, or foster placement of a child; for the employee's own serious health condition; or to care for a family member with a serious health condition. Parental leave must be taken within one year of the child's birth, adoption, or placement.

Amount of Leave: Twelve weeks in a 12-month period. Spouses who work for the same employer may be limited to a combined total of 12 weeks of leave for the birth, adoption, or foster placement of a child and care for a parent with a serious health condition.

Paid Sick Leave (Wash. Rev. Code §49.46.200 and following)

Covered Employers: All employers.

Eligible Employees: All employees of covered employers. Leave begins to accrue from the start of employment, but employees may not use leave for the first 90 days of employment.

Reasons for Leave: Employee may take sick leave:

- for the employee's or a family member's physical or mental illness or health condition (including diagnosis, preventative care, treatment, and recovery)
- when the employee's place of business or the employee's child's school has been closed for a public health emergency, or
- for any reason covered by the state's domestic violence leave law (described below).

Amount of Leave: Employees must accrue one hour of leave for every 40 hours worked.

Family Members: Same family members as FMLA, plus parents-in-law, domestic partners, grandparents, grandchildren, siblings, and the parents of domestic partners.

Military Family Leave (Wash. Rev. Code §§ 49.77.010 and following)

Covered Employers: All employers.

Eligible Employees: Employees who work an average of 20 or more hours per week and are the spouse of a member of the National Guard, Reserves, or Armed Forces deployed or notified of a call to active duty during a period of military conflict.

Reasons for Leave: Employee may take leave only:
- after spouse has been called to active duty and before actual deployment, or
- while spouse is on leave during deployment.

Amount of Leave: Up to 15 days of unpaid leave per deployment.

Pregnancy Disability Leave (Wash. Admin. Code § 162-30-020)

Covered Employers: Employers with at least eight employees.

Eligible Employees: All employees of covered employers.

Reasons for Leave: Disability relating to pregnancy, childbirth, or related conditions.

Amount of Leave: For the period of disability. This time is in addition to the time provided under the FMLA and Washington's family and medical leave law.

Domestic Violence Leave (Wash. Rev. Code §§ 49.76.010 and following)

Covered Employers: All employers.

Eligible Employees: Employees who have been, or whose family members have been, victims of domestic violence, sexual assault, or stalking.

Reasons for Leave: For the employee to:
- seek legal assistance
- seek medical assistance
- get services from a domestic violence shelter, rape crisis center, or other social services program
- get counseling, or
- engage in safety planning or relocate.

Amount of Leave: Reasonable leave.

Family Members: Child, spouse, parent, parent-in-law, grandparent, or person the employee is dating.

Paid Family and Medical Leave

Beginning in 2020, Washington employees will be eligible to collect up to 12 weeks of paid family leave benefits to bond with a new child, to care for a family member with a serious health condition, or for qualifying exigencies arising from a family member's military service. Paid medical leave is also available for up to 12 weeks for the employee's own serious health condition. An employee who takes both paid family and paid medical leave may receive pay for a combined total of 16 or 18 weeks, depending on the circumstances. The program will be funded by contributions from employees and employers, scheduled to begin in 2019. Benefits will be based on the employee's earnings and will range from $100 to $1,000 per week to start.

Wisconsin

Family and Medical Leave Law (Wis. Stat. § 103.10)

Covered Employers: Employers with at least 50 permanent employees.

Eligible Employees: Employees who have worked for more than 52 consecutive weeks and at least 1,000 hours in the preceding 52 weeks.

Types of Leave

- **Family Leave:** For birth, adoption, or to care for a family member with a serious health condition; does not cover foster care placements.
- **Medical Leave:** For the employee's own serious health condition that makes him or her unable to do the job.

Amount of Leave

- **Family Leave:** Up to eight weeks total, consisting of up to:
  - six weeks in a calendar year for birth or adoption (leave must begin within 16 weeks of the child's birth or placement), and
  - two weeks in a calendar year to care for a family member with a serious health condition.
- **Medical Leave:** Two weeks in a calendar year for the employee's serious health condition.

Family Members: Same family members as FMLA, plus parents-in-law and domestic partners.

State Departments of Labor

Alabama
Department of Labor
Montgomery, AL
334-242-8055
www.labor.alabama.gov

Alaska
Department of Labor and
    Workforce Development
Juneau, AK
907-465-2700
www.labor.state.ak.us

Arizona
Industrial Commission
Phoenix, AZ
602-542-4661
www.azica.gov

Arkansas
Department of Labor
Little Rock, AR
501-682-4500
www.labor.arkansas.gov

California
Labor Commissioner's Office
Department of Industrial Relations
Oakland, CA
510-285-2118
www.dir.ca.gov/DLSE/dlse.html

Colorado
Department of Labor and Employment
Denver, CO
303-318-9000
www.colorado.gov/CDLE

Connecticut
Department of Labor
Wethersfield, CT
860-263-6000
www.ctdol.state.ct.us

Delaware
Department of Labor
Wilmington, DE
302-761-8000
http://dol.delaware.gov

District of Columbia
Department of Employment Services
Washington, DC
202-724-7000
www.does.dc.gov

Florida
Department of Economic Opportunity
Tallahassee, FL
850-245-7105
www.floridajobs.org

Georgia
Department of Labor
Atlanta, GA
404-232-7300
http://dol.georgia.gov

Hawaii
Department of Labor and
    Industrial Relations
Honolulu, HI
808-586-8844
http://labor.hawaii.gov

Idaho

Department of Labor
Boise, ID
208-332-3570
http://labor.idaho.gov

Illinois

Department of Labor
Chicago, IL
312-793-2800
www.state.il.us/agency/idol

Indiana

Department of Labor
Indianapolis, IN
317-232-2655
www.in.gov/dol

Iowa

Division of Labor
Des Moines, IA
515-242-5870
www.iowadivisionoflabor.gov

Kansas

Department of Labor
Topeka, KS
785-296-5000
www.dol.ks.gov

Kentucky

Labor Cabinet
Frankfort, KY
502-564-3534
www.labor.ky.gov

Louisiana

Louisiana Workforce Commission
Baton Rouge, LA
225-342-3111
www.ldol.state.la.us

Maine

Department of Labor
Augusta, ME
207-623-7900
www.state.me.us/labor

Maryland

Department of Labor, Licensing,
and Regulation
Baltimore, MD
410-767-2241
www.dllr.state.md.us/labor

Massachusetts

Labor and Workforce Development
Boston, MA
617-626-7122
www.mass.gov/lwd

Michigan

Department of Licensing and
Regulatory Affairs
Lansing, MI
517-373-1820
www.michigan.gov/lara

Minnesota

Department of Labor and Industry
St. Paul, MN
651-284-5005
www.dli.mn.gov

Mississippi

Department of Employment Security
Jackson, MS
601-321-6000
www.mdes.ms.gov

Missouri
Department of Labor and
Industrial Relations
Jefferson City, MO
573-751-9691
www.labor.mo.gov

Montana
Department of Labor and Industry
Helena, MT
406-444-2840
www.dli.mt.gov

Nebraska
Department of Labor
Lincoln, NE
402-471-9000
www.dol.nebraska.gov

Nevada
Office of the Labor Commissioner
Las Vegas, NV
702-486-2650
http://labor.nv.gov

New Hampshire
Department of Labor
Concord, NH
603-271-3176
800-272-4353
www.nh.gov/labor

New Jersey
Department of Labor and
Workforce Development
Trenton, NJ
609-659-9045
http://lwd.state.nj.us/labor

New Mexico
Department of Workforce Solutions
Albuquerque, NM
505-841-8405
www.dws.state.nm.us

New York
Department of Labor
Albany, NY
518-457-9000
888-469-7365
www.labor.ny.gov/home

North Carolina
Department of Labor
Raleigh, NC
800-625-2267
www.nclabor.com

North Dakota
Department of Labor and
Human Rights
Bismarck, ND
701-328-2660
800-582-8032
www.nd.gov/labor

Ohio
Division of Industrial Compliance
Reynoldsburg, OH
614-644-2223
www.com.ohio.gov/dico

Oklahoma
Department of Labor
Oklahoma City, OK
405-521-6100
www.ok.gov/odol

Oregon
Bureau of Labor and Industries
Portland, OR
971-673-0761
www.oregon.gov/boli

Pennsylvania
Department of Labor and Industry
Harrisburg, PA
800-932-0665
www.dli.pa.gov

Rhode Island

Department of Labor and Training
Cranston, RI
401-462-8000
www.dlt.state.ri.us

South Carolina

Department of Labor, Licensing,
and Regulation
Columbia, SC
803-896-4300
www.llr.state.sc.us/labor

South Dakota

Department of Labor and Regulation
Pierre, SD
605-773-3101
www.dlr.sd.gov

Tennessee

Department of Labor and
Workforce Development
Nashville, TN
844-224-5818
www.tn.gov/workforce

Texas

Texas Workforce Commission
Austin, TX
512-463-2222
www.twc.state.tx.us

Utah

Labor Commission
Salt Lake City, UT
801-530-6800
800-530-5090
www.laborcommission.utah.gov

Vermont

Department of Labor
Montpelier, VT
802-828-4000
www.labor.vermont.gov

Virginia

Department of Labor and Industry
Richmond, VA
804-371-2327
www.doli.virginia.gov

Washington

Department of Labor and Industries
Tumwater, WA
360-902-5800
www.lni.wa.gov

West Virginia

Division of Labor
Charleston, WV
304-558-7890
www.wvlabor.com

Wisconsin

Department of Workforce
Development
Madison, WI
608-266-3131
http://dwd.wisconsin.gov

Wyoming

Department of Workforce Services
Cheyenne, WY
307-777-7261
www.wyomingworkforce.org

Company Policies Regarding FMLA Leave

As explained throughout this book, your company's policies can affect its rights and obligations—and the rights and obligations of its employees—regarding FMLA leave. What you say in your FMLA policy and other company policies relating to leave is therefore very important.

This appendix explains how various policy choices affect your responsibilities under the FMLA. Here, we provide:

- A sample FMLA policy. As explained in Chapter 2, covered companies must include accurate, complete information about the FMLA in their employee handbooks, written policies, or other documents describing leave, wages, absences, and similar matters. The policy we provide will help you meet this obligation.

- A guide explaining how your company's FMLA policy affects its rights and obligations. You will have some choices to make when creating your company's policy; this section explains the ramifications of these choices. Use the guide in conjunction with the sample policy.

This material will help you draft a family and medical leave policy that complies with the FMLA, but remember that you may have additional obligations under state laws. Appendix A summarizes each state's family and medical leave laws. If the family or medical leave law of a state in which your company has employees is more generous than the FMLA or your policies, you must comply with the state law.

As a practical matter, if your company has employees in more than one state, it may be simpler to draft your family and medical leave policy to comply with the most generous of the state laws that apply and adopt that as the companywide policy. This way, you won't have to draft separate policies for offices in the different states. You should consult with a lawyer for help devising a family and medical leave policy that meets both the FMLA's requirements and the legal requirements imposed by the state(s) where your company does business.

RESOURCE

Get this policy—and all other forms in this book—online. You can find a digital version of this sample policy, as well as other FMLA forms, blog posts, legal updates, and more on Nolo's website. (See Appendix C for information on accessing this book's companion page.)

Family and Medical Leave Policy

It is our policy to grant family and/or medical leave to employees eligible under the Family and Medical Leave Act of 1993 ("FMLA") or any other applicable law.

Definitions

Alternative Position: A position to which an eligible employee may be temporarily reassigned during a period of intermittent or reduced-schedule leave. The alternative position will have the same pay and benefits as the employee's original position.

Child: For purposes of FMLA leave that is not military family leave, the son or daughter of an eligible employee who is under 18 years of age, or 18 years or older and incapable of self-care as a result of physical or mental disability. For purposes of this policy, "child" includes the eligible employee's biological child, adopted child, foster child, stepchild, or legal ward. It also includes a child for whom the employee assumes or intends to assume the role of parent by providing day-to-day care or financial support. For purposes of military caregiver or qualifying exigency leave, "child" includes children of any age.

Eligible Employee: An employee who has: (1) been employed by the company for at least 12 months as of the start date of the requested leave; (2) worked at least 1,250 hours in the 12 months immediately preceding the start date of requested family or medical leave; and (3) worked at a worksite within a 75-mile radius of 50 or more employees of the company as of the date of the leave request.

Equivalent Position: A position: (1) with pay equivalent to the employee's original job; (2) with benefits equivalent to the employee's original job; (3) with job duties and responsibilities substantially similar to the employee's original job; (4) with a schedule that is the same as or equivalent to that of the employee's original job; and (5) located at the same worksite or one that is geographically proximate to the employee's original worksite.

Family Member: The eligible employee's spouse, child, or parent. For purposes of military caregiver leave, "family member" also includes next of kin.

Health Care Providers: Doctors of osteopathy, podiatrists, dentists, optometrists, chiropractors (only for manual manipulation of the spine to treat a subluxation of the spine—that is, misalignment of vertebrae—identified by X-ray), physician assistants, clinical psychologists, nurse practitioners, nurse midwives, clinical social workers, Christian Science practitioners, and other providers whose documentation is accepted for the purposes of employee health insurance.

Key Employee: A salaried employee in the highest-paid 10% of the company's employees working within 75 miles of the employee's worksite.

Military Caregiver Leave: Leave to care for a family member who suffers or aggravates a serious illness or injury in the line of duty on active duty.

Military Caregiver Leave Year: The 12-month period beginning on the first date an eligible employee takes military caregiver leave.

Next of Kin: For purposes of military caregiver leave, an employee is "next of kin" to a covered servicemember if the employee is a blood relative and the servicemember has designated the employee as next of kin for purposes of military caregiver leave. If the servicemember has not designated a next of kin, the nearest blood relative is next of kin, in the following order or priority:
- blood relatives who have been granted legal custody of the servicemember
- siblings
- grandparents
- aunts and uncles, and
- first cousins.

Parent: The eligible employee's biological, adoptive, or foster parent, or an individual who assumed the role of parent by providing day-to-day care or financial support when the employee was a child.

Parenting Leave: Leave following birth, adoption, or foster placement of an eligible employee's child, including bonding leave.

Qualifying Exigency Leave: Leave taken to handle the following matters when a family member is on active duty or called to active duty in the military:
- short-notice deployment
- military events and related activities
- child care and school activities
- financial and legal arrangements
- counseling
- rest and recuperation
- postdeployment activities, and
- parental care.

Reinstatement: Restoration of employee to his or her original position or an equivalent one when the employee returns from family or medical leave, if the employee is able to perform the essential functions of that position.

Serious Health Condition: Illness, injury, impairment, or physical or mental condition that involves one of the following: (1) inpatient care at a hospital, hospice, or residential medical care facility; (2) incapacity for more than three full days with continuing treatment by a health care provider; (3) incapacity due to pregnancy or prenatal care; (4) incapacity or treatment for a chronic serious health condition; (5) permanent or long-term incapacity for a condition for which treatment may not be effective (such as a terminal illness); or (6) absence for multiple treatments for either restorative surgery following an injury or accident or a condition that would require an absence of more than three days if not treated.

Serious Illness or Injury: For purposes of military caregiver leave, a serious illness or injury is one that renders a current servicemember unfit to perform the duties of his or her office, grade, rank, or rating, and for which the servicemember is undergoing medical treatment, recuperation, or therapy; is otherwise in outpatient status; or is on the temporary disability retired list. For a veteran, a serious illness or injury is (1) a continuation of a serious illness or injury (as defined above) incurred or aggravated when the veteran was in the military, which rendered the veteran unable to perform the duties of his or her office, grade, rank, or rating; (2) a physical or mental condition for which the veteran has received a Veterans Affairs Service Related Disability Rating (VASRD) of 50 percent or greater, at least in part because the condition requires caregiver leave; (3) a physical or mental condition that substantially impairs the veteran's ability to get or maintain a substantially gainful occupation due to a service-related disability (or would create such an impairment without treatment); or (4) an injury (including a psychological injury) for which the veteran has been enrolled in the Department of Veterans Affairs Program of Comprehensive Assistance for Family Caregivers.

Spouse: A person to whom the eligible employee is legally married in any state (or country, if the marriage could have been entered into in at least one state).

Twelve-Month Leave Year: The rolling 12-month period measured backward from the first day that an eligible employee takes family or medical leave.

1. Leave Available

[*Option 1—if company policy provides more than 12 weeks of leave*] An eligible employee may take up to ____ weeks (____ days) of unpaid family or medical leave in the 12-month leave year for any of the following reasons:

- because the employee's own serious health condition makes the employee unable to work
- to care for a spouse, child, or parent who has a serious health condition
- to care for a newborn, newly adopted child, or a recently placed foster child, or
- for a qualifying exigency related to a family member's active duty or call to active duty.

[*Option 2—if company policy does not provide more than 12 weeks of leave*] An eligible employee may take up to 12 weeks (60 workdays) of unpaid family or medical leave in the 12-month leave year for any of the following reasons:

- because the employee's own serious health condition makes the employee unable to work
- to care for a spouse, child, or parent who has a serious health condition
- to care for a newborn, newly adopted child, or a recently placed foster child, or
- for a qualifying exigency related to a family member's active duty or call to active duty.

If you have questions about how much leave time is available to you, please contact

_____ .

An eligible employee may take a one-time leave of up to 26 weeks of unpaid leave in a single 12-month period for military caregiver leave. This is a per-servicemember, per-injury entitlement; it does not renew every year.

2. Serious Health Condition—Examples

Here are some examples of serious health conditions for which an eligible employee may take family or medical leave (Note: this is not an exhaustive list; it is for purposes of illustration only):

- A condition requiring inpatient care, such as medically necessary surgery.
- A condition that results in incapacity for more than three full days and continuing treatment by a health care provider, such as a stroke.

- Incapacity due to pregnancy or prenatal care, such as hypertension requiring bed rest.
- A chronic condition, such as epilepsy.
- A condition for which treatment may not be effective, such as terminal cancer.
- Absence for multiple treatments for restorative surgery, such as skin grafts following a burn.
- A condition that could require an absence of more than three days if not treated, such as kidney disease requiring dialysis.

3. Notice Requirements

To request family or medical leave, you are required to give notice of the need for leave at least 30 days in advance of the start date of the leave if the need for leave is foreseeable. If you fail to do so, we may delay the start of your leave. If the need for leave is unforeseeable, or you are using qualifying exigency leave, you must give as much notice as is practicable under the circumstances, usually the same or the next business day after you learn you will need leave.

To request family or medical leave, inform _____ that you need leave, when the leave will begin, and the reason for the leave (for example, for a serious medical condition or for parenting leave).

[*Option—if the company requires written requests for other types of leave*]
You must submit the reasons (for example, for a serious medical condition or for parenting leave) for the requested leave, the anticipated duration of the leave, and the anticipated start date of the leave in writing within the notice period described above. We will provide a form for this purpose.

4. Certification

You may be required to provide a form from a health care provider certifying the need for leave when you request leave for your own or a family member's serious health condition or for a family member's serious illness or injury for which you need military caregiver leave. We will request certification from you in writing and provide you with a form to be used for this purpose. The company also has the right to seek a second opinion and periodic recertifications if you take leave for a serious health condition.

You may also be required to submit a certification form when you request qualifying exigency leave, along with a copy of your family member's active duty orders or other military documentation. We will provide you with a form to be used for this purpose.

The company may also require that employees provide documentation or certification of parental status when requesting parental leave, qualifying exigency leave, or military caregiver leave. Such documentation includes, for example, birth certificates, adoption decrees, court orders, or a statement signed by the employee.

5. Notice and Designation of Leave

Soon after you request FMLA leave, we will provide you with notification as to your eligibility for leave and a statement of your rights and responsibilities under the FMLA. If we determine that you are eligible for FMLA leave, we will provide you with a designation notice informing you whether or not your leave is approved as FMLA leave and, if so, how much time will be counted against your available FMLA leave time, if known. If the amount of FMLA leave you will need is unknown when we provide the designation notice, we will provide you with an accounting of the time counted against your available FMLA leave time, upon your request, no more often than every 30 days. These notice forms will also provide information about other requirements that may apply to you during or after your leave.

6. [*Option*] Substitution of Paid Leave

FMLA leave is unpaid leave. However, under this policy, if you are an eligible employee who has accrued paid time off, you [*Option 1*] may [*Option 2*] must use these benefits to receive pay for all or a portion of family or medical leave.

If you take paid sick leave, vacation leave, or other leave for a reason that qualifies for family or medical leave under the FMLA, the company will designate that time off as such and will count it against your 12-week leave entitlement.

In order to use accrued paid time off, you must meet all requirements of our paid leave policies. Your reason for leave must be covered by the paid leave program. In addition, you must meet all the usual notice and other requirements in order to use paid leave. If you don't meet these requirements, you may be ineligible to substitute paid leave (but you will still be eligible for unpaid FMLA leave as long as you meet the notice requirements set forth in Section 3, above).

7. Parenting Leave

An eligible employee taking parenting leave must complete this leave within one year of the birth, adoption, or foster placement of the employee's child.

[*Option 1*] Married parents of a new child who are both employed with the company may take a combined 12 weeks of leave in connection with the birth, adoption, or foster placement of their child and for a parent's serious health condition.

[*Option 2*] Parents of a new child who are both employed with the company may each take 12 weeks of leave in connection with the birth, adoption, or foster placement of their child and for other FMLA purposes.

8. Military Caregiver Leave

An eligible employee may take up to 26 weeks of unpaid military caregiver leave in the 12-month period beginning on the first day of leave; this may be different from the usual 12-month leave year. Employees who are eligible for military caregiver leave may take no more than 26 total weeks of FMLA leave for all purposes during the military caregiver leave year, and no more than 12 of those weeks may be used for all other types of FMLA leave in the 12-month leave year. Any unused portion of the 26-week leave is lost; it may not be used for other types of FMLA leave, nor carried over to a new 12-month period.

[*Option 1*] Employees who are married to each other and need military caregiver leave may take a combined total of 26 weeks of leave for military caregiver leave, parental leave, and leave to care for a parent with a serious health condition in the military caregiver leave year.

[*Option 2*] Employees who are married to each other and need military caregiver leave may each take up to 26 weeks of leave in the military caregiver leave year.

9. Intermittent and Reduced-Schedule Leave

An eligible employee may take leave all at one time or intermittently—that is, hours or days at a time—for his or her own serious health condition, to care for a family member with a serious health condition (for example, to attend doctor appointments or chemotherapy), or for military caregiver leave, if it is medically necessary to do so. An eligible employee may also take leave in the form of reduced hours for his or her own serious health condition, or to care for a family member with a serious health condition, if it is medically necessary to do so (for example, to recover from an illness or medical treatment), or for military caregiver leave.

An eligible employee may take intermittent or reduced-schedule leave for a qualifying exigency related to a family member's active military duty or call to active duty.

If you need intermittent or reduced-schedule leave for planned medical treatment, we may temporarily reassign you to an alternative position that is better able to accommodate your need for intermittent or reduced-schedule leave. You must make a reasonable effort to schedule your intermittent or reduced-schedule leave so it doesn't unduly disrupt the company's operations.

[*Option 1*] Intermittent and reduced-schedule leaves are not available to employees seeking parental leave.

[*Option 2*] The company will consider requests for intermittent or reduced-schedule parenting leave on a case-by-case basis and will grant such requested leave if the leave does not create an undue hardship to the operations and work schedules of the company.

You may take intermittent leave in increments of [*Option 1*] one hour [*Option 2*]. [*If your company allows employees to use leave in less than one-hour increments for other types of leave, include that time frame here (for example, 30-minute increments).*]

10. Employees Who Work Part-Time or Irregular Hours

An eligible part-time employee or an employee who works variable or irregular hours may take intermittent or reduced-schedule leave in proportion to the amount of time he or she normally works. For example, if you usually work 20 hours per week and need a work schedule reduction to ten hours per week due to a serious health condition, that amounts to one-half of your normal working hours. You would use up your 12-week leave entitlement in 24 weeks under that reduced-schedule leave.

If your schedule varies from week to week, the leave workweek is measured by calculating the weekly average hours worked in the 12 months prior to the start of the leave. We will calculate this average and put it in writing for your review and signature.

11. Health Insurance

During an approved family or medical leave, the company will continue your health care benefits. You must continue to pay any share of the premium for which you are currently responsible by the usual due date of payment. If your premium payments are more than 30 days late, we may discontinue your coverage for the rest of your leave. If you choose not to return to work at the end of your leave, you will be required to reimburse the company for its share of the premiums paid during your leave.

12. Other Benefits

[*Option 1—if the company does not allow employee benefits to continue or accrue during other types of leave, including paid leave*] With the exception of health care benefits, discussed above, employee benefits will not continue or accrue during the period of your family or medical leave. These benefits will be restored when you return from leave at the same level as before the leave.

[*Option 2—if the company allows employee benefits to continue and/or accrue, but only during paid leave*] If your family or medical leave is paid leave, discussed above, all employee benefits will continue and accrue during the period of the paid family or medical leave.

[*Option 3—if the company allows employee benefits to continue and/or accrue during all types of leave*] In addition to the health care benefits discussed above, employee benefits continue and accrue during the family or medical leave period. You will be required to reimburse the company for the portion of the benefits premiums for which you are usually responsible for but which the company paid during the leave.

13. Premium Payments

Any premium payments for which you are responsible during the leave period must be paid on or before your regular payday. If you fail to make timely payment of the premiums, your benefit coverage, including insurance coverage, may be discontinued.

14. [*Option*] Status Reports

You must periodically contact the human resources manager during your leave and inform the manager of your status and intent to return to work.

15. [*Option*] Moonlighting

You may not work for another employer while on family or medical leave. Such outside employment is grounds for immediate termination.

16. Reinstatement

When you return from family or medical leave, you have the right to return to your former position or an equivalent position, except:

- You have no greater right to reinstatement than you would have had if you had not been on leave. If your position is restructured for reasons unrelated to your leave, for example, you have no right to reinstatement to the exact same position you held before leave.
- The company is not obligated to reinstate you if you are a key employee—that is, if you are among the highest-paid 10% of our workforce—and reinstating you after your leave would cause the company substantial economic harm. If the company classifies you as a key employee under this definition, you will be notified soon after you request leave.
- You might not be entitled to reinstatement to your original or an equivalent position if you are unable to perform the essential functions of that job. See the company's policy on reasonable accommodation for a disability to learn more.

Two weeks prior to your intended return date, you should notify the human resources manager of your intent to return to work. And, if anything has changed concerning your return to work while you have been on leave, you should notify human resources of the change.

If you are returning from leave for your own serious health condition, the company may ask you to provide a fitness-for-duty report from your health care provider before you return to work. We will provide a form to be used for this purpose.

How Your FMLA Policy Affects Company Obligations

As we've explained, if your company's leave policy is less generous than the FMLA, you must follow the FMLA with respect to FMLA-eligible employees or FMLA-qualified leaves. Here are a few areas of particular importance; review them while using the sample policy above to create your own policy.

Definitions

Your company may define terms more broadly than the FMLA. If it does, it may extend the FMLA's protections to employees who would not otherwise be eligible. Here are some things to consider:

- **Eligible employee.** Your company can offer family and medical leave to employees who don't meet the FMLA's eligibility requirements (12 months' employment/1,250 hours in 12 months preceding leave). However, such a decision has ramifications. For example, you can deduct reduced-schedule FMLA leave time (less than a full week of leave) from an eligible, exempt employee's pay without affecting the employee's exempt status. But, if you grant reduced-schedule leave to an exempt employee who is not eligible under the FMLA and deduct his or her pay, you risk eliminating the employee's exempt status and violating the Fair Labor Standards Act.
- **Family member.** Your company can also elect to include in its family and medical leave policy family members not included under the FMLA, such as domestic partners. But, you cannot deduct the leave granted for such individuals' care from the employee's available FMLA leave time.
- **Twelve-month leave year.** The rolling leave year method is the most advantageous to employers because it limits employees' ability to be out of work for more than 12 weeks in any 12-month period. However, you are free to calculate the leave year using one of the alternative methods. In fact, some state laws may mandate a different calculation.

Clause 1: Leave Available

Your company can offer more leave than the FMLA's 12 weeks (or 26 weeks, for military caregiver leave). You may want to consider this option if your company has employees in more than one state, including a state that requires you to provide more leave time. By offering the leave time required under the state law to all employees in all states, you can adopt a single, uniform leave policy for all company locations.

Clause 3: Notice Requirements

Your company can require employees seeking family and medical leave to comply with the usual and customary notice requirements and procedures (for example, requiring that the employee notify you of the need for leave in writing) that it imposes for other types of leave requests.

However, you cannot require more notice (in other words, more than 30 days for foreseeable leave) or more information (in other words, more than leave dates and general statement of reason for leave) than the FMLA requires. And, you cannot impose stricter requirements on employees seeking family or medical leave than you impose on employees seeking other types of leave.

If an employee doesn't give the required leave notice, you can delay the start of an employee's leave, but only if you have informed the employee of the duty to provide notice.

Clause 6: Substitution of Paid Leave

If your company has a paid leave policy, an employee's use of it during family or medical leave is subject to the policy's terms. For example, if your company offers paid sick leave for the employee's own illness, you must allow an employee taking FMLA leave for his or her own serious health condition to use the paid sick leave available. However, you do not have to let the employee use that paid sick leave policy to care for family members, since the sick leave policy does not provide for that.

Remember, it's not really a substitution, but an overlap. The employee isn't using paid leave instead of FMLA leave but is using the two types of leave at the same time. So, don't forget to deduct the paid leave taken from the employee's available FMLA leave time.

Clause 7: Parenting Leave

Even though the FMLA requires you to offer only 12 weeks of combined parenting leave to married employees when both are employed by the company, your company can offer 12 full weeks of leave to each parent.

Clause 8: Military Caregiver Leave

As is true of parenting leave, the FMLA allows you to limit married employees who are both employed by your company to a combined total of 26 weeks of leave for military caregiving, parenting, and caring for a parent with a serious health condition. However, you may choose to offer each parent the full 26-week entitlement.

Clause 9: Intermittent or Reduced-Schedule Leave

Your company can allow employees to take intermittent or reduced-schedule parenting leave, but the FMLA doesn't require it. On the other hand, you can impose restrictions on the leave that you usually can't impose on intermittent FMLA leave, such as requiring the employee to take the leave in larger increments than those used by your company for payroll.

Clause 11: Health Insurance

You can terminate an employee's health coverage if the employee is required to pay a portion of the premium and fails to do so within 30 days (after being given notice). However, the date that an employee's coverage officially terminates depends, in part, on your policies for other types of paid leave. If your company has an established policy that allows it to terminate coverage retroactively to the date of the missed payment, it may do so. If it doesn't have this type of policy, it may terminate coverage effective 30 days after the missed payment. And remember, you may need to continue health coverage even if the employee fails to make payments, to ensure that the employee's benefits are restored upon reinstatement.

Clause 12: Other Benefits

If your company usually allows employee benefits to continue and accrue during other types of leave, you have to follow that practice when an employee takes FMLA leave. If your company usually does not continue employee benefits during leave, you do not have to continue benefits (other than health benefits) during FMLA leave. However, regardless of company policy, you must restore all employee benefits to the employee upon return from leave. The benefits must be restored to the same level as before leave and without any requalification. For this reason, it may be easier and less costly to simply continue the benefits during leave, regardless of company policy on other types of leave.

You have to follow your company's policy regarding the continuation and accrual of benefits during paid leave for employees who substitute paid leave for FMLA leave. So, if your company's employee benefits continue to accrue during paid leave, they must also continue to accrue during an FMLA leave that is taken as paid leave.

Clause 13: Premium Payments

You can require employees to pay premiums for benefits during FMLA leave, but you must inform them of this requirement in your policies and you must also inform them when premium payments are due and the possible consequences of failing to pay.

Clause 14: Status Reports

You can request periodic status reports during an employee's FMLA leave, asking whether the employee intends to return and, if so, when. Just make sure you are reasonable: Don't ask too often, and don't ask for more information than is allowed. Avoid the appearance of bullying the employee to return from leave earlier than the employee is ready to. Don't try to get additional medical information via the status reports.

Clause 15: Moonlighting

You can prohibit an employee from working for another employer during FMLA leave, as long as your company has a uniform policy against moonlighting that applies to all employees. However, some states—such as California—limit an employer's ability to restrict an employee's lawful conduct during nonwork hours.

How to Use the Downloadable Forms on the Nolo Website

This book comes with interactive files that you can access online at: **www.nolo.com/back-of-book/FMLA.html**

To use the files, your computer must have specific software programs installed. Here is a list of types of files provided by this book, as well as the software programs you'll need to access them:

- **RTF.** You can open, edit, print, and save these form files with most word processing programs such as Microsoft *Word*, Windows *WordPad*, and recent versions of *WordPerfect*.
- **PDF.** You can view these files with *Adobe Reader*, free software from www.adobe.com. Government PDFs are sometimes fillable using your computer, but most PDFs are designed to be printed out and completed by hand.
- **XLS.** You can use this spreadsheet with Microsoft *Excel* and other spreadsheet programs that read XLS files.
- **MP3.** You can listen to these audio files using your computer's sound system. Most computers come with a media player that plays MP3 files, or you may have installed one on your own.

Editing RTFs

Here are some general instructions about editing RTF forms in your word processing program. Refer to the book's instructions and sample agreements for help about what should go in each blank.

- **Underlines.** Underlines indicate where to enter information. After filling in the needed text, delete the underline. In most word processing programs you can do this by highlighting the underlined portion and typing CTRL-U.
- **Bracketed and italicized text.** Bracketed and italicized text indicates instructions. Be sure to remove all instructional text before you finalize your document.
- **Alternative text.** Alternative text gives you the choice between two or more text options. Delete those options you don't want to use. Renumber numbered items, if necessary.
- **Signature lines.** Signature lines should appear on a page with at least some text from the document itself.

Every word processing program uses different commands to open, format, save, and print documents, so refer to your software's help documents for help using your program. Nolo cannot provide technical support for questions about how to use your computer or your software.

CAUTION

In accordance with U.S. copyright laws, the forms and audio files provided by this book are for your personal use only.

List of Forms and Podcasts

To download any of the files listed here, go to: **www.nolo.com/back-of-book/FMLA.html**

The following files are in rich text format (RTF):

Title	File Name
FMLA Policy	Policy.rtf
FMLA Leave to Care for a Family Member	LeaveForm.rtf
FMLA Hours Worked	WorkHours.rtf
FMLA Leave Tracking	Tracking.rtf
Request for Medical Certification	MedCertifRequest.rtf
Notice to Key Employee of Substantial and Grievous Economic Injury	NoticeEconInjury.rtf
Notice of Termination of Group Health Coverage	CoverageTerm.rtf

The following files are in portable document format (PDF):

Title	File Name
Family and Medical Leave Act Poster (English)	Fmlaen.pdf
Family and Medical Leave Act Poster (Spanish)	Fmlasp.pdf
Notice of Eligibility and Rights & Responsibilities (Family and Medical Leave Act)	WH-381.pdf
Designation Notice (Family and Medical Leave Act)	WH-382.pdf
Certification of Health Care Provider for Employee's Serious Health Condition	WH-380-E.pdf
Certification of Health Care Provider for Family Member's Serious Health Condition	WH-380-F.pdf
Certification of Qualifying Exigency for Military Family Leave	WH-384.pdf
Certification of Serious Injury or Illness of Covered Servicemember for Military Family Leave	WH-385.pdf
Certification for Serious Illness or Injury of a Veteran for Military Caregiver Leave	WH-385-V.pdf
Does the FMLA Apply to My Company?	Apply.pdf
Is the Employee Eligible for FMLA Leave?	Eligible.pdf
Leave for a New Child	ChildLeave.pdf
Military Family Leave	MilitaryLeave.pdf
Duration of Leave	LeaveDuration.pdf
Giving Notice and Designating Leave	LeaveNotice.pdf
Medical Certifications	Certifications.pdf
Managing FMLA Leave	ManagingLeave.pdf
Reinstating an Employee	Reinstatement.pdf
If an Employee Doesn't Return From Leave	EmployeeDeparture.pdf
Record Keeping	RecordKeeping.pdf

The following spreadsheet is in Microsoft *Excel* Format (XLS):

Title	File Name
Calculating Intermittent/Reduced-Schedule Leave	CalculateLeave.xls

The following files are Audio (MP3):

Title	File Name
FMLA: Policy and Enforcement	PolicyandEnforcement.mp3
FMLA: Management and Requirements	ManagementandReqs.mp3
The Essential Guide to Family and Medical Leave: Scenario 1	Scenario1.mp3
The Essential Guide to Family and Medical Leave: Scenario 2	Scenario2.mp3

Index

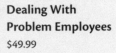

⚖ NOLO *Online Legal Forms*

Nolo offers a large library of legal solutions and forms, created by Nolo's in-house legal staff. These reliable documents can be prepared in minutes.

Create a Document

- **Incorporation.** Incorporate your business in any state.
- **LLC Formations.** Gain asset protection and pass-through tax status in any state.
- **Wills.** Nolo has helped people make over 2 million wills. Is it time to make or revise yours?
- **Living Trust (avoid probate).** Plan now to save your family the cost, delays, and hassle of probate.
- **Trademark.** Protect the name of your business or product.
- **Provisional Patent.** Preserve your rights under patent law and claim "patent pending" status.

Download a Legal Form

Nolo.com has hundreds of top quality legal forms available for download—bills of sale, promissory notes, nondisclosure agreements, LLC operating agreements, corporate minutes, commercial lease and sublease, motor vehicle bill of sale, consignment agreements and many, many more.

Review Your Documents

Many lawyers in Nolo's consumer-friendly lawyer directory will review Nolo documents for a very reasonable fee. Check their detailed profiles at **www.nolo.com/lawyers/index.html**.

Nolo's Bestselling Books

Dealing With Problem Employees
$49.99

Smart Policies for Workplace Technologies
Email, Social Media, Cell Phones & More
$34.99

Essential Guide to Federal Employment Laws
$49.99

The Manager's Legal Handbook
$49.99

The Employer's Legal Handbook
$49.99

Every Nolo title is available in print and for download at Nolo.com.

⚖ NOLO   *Save 15%* _{off your next order}

Register your Nolo purchase, and we'll send you a **coupon for 15% off** your next Nolo.com order!

Nolo.com/customer-support/productregistration

On Nolo.com you'll also find:

Books & Software

Nolo publishes hundreds of great books and software programs for consumers and business owners. Order a copy, or download an ebook version instantly, at Nolo.com.

Online Legal Documents

You can quickly and easily make a will or living trust, form an LLC or corporation, apply for a trademark or provisional patent, or make hundreds of other forms—online.

Free Legal Information

Thousands of articles answer common questions about everyday legal issues including wills, bankruptcy, small business formation, divorce, patents, employment, and much more.

Plain-English Legal Dictionary

Stumped by jargon? Look it up in America's most up-to-date source for definitions of legal terms, free at nolo.com.

Lawyer Directory

Nolo's consumer-friendly lawyer directory provides in-depth profiles of lawyers all over America. You'll find all the information you need to choose the right lawyer.

FMLA5